TRAINING FOR
CYCLING

TRAINING FOR
CYCLING

The Ultimate Guide to Improved Performance

Davis Phinney
and
Connie Carpenter

written with Peter Nye

A PERIGEE BOOK

Not all exercises are suitable for everyone, and this or any other exercise program may result in injury. To reduce the risk of injury in your case, consult your doctor before beginning any exercise program, especially if you have any serious medical condition or if you are taking medication. Responsibility for any adverse effects or unforeseen consequences resulting from the use of any information contained herein is expressly disclaimed.

Perigee Books
are published by
The Berkley Publishing Group
200 Madison Avenue
New York, NY 10016

Library of Congress Cataloging-in-Publication Data

Phinney, Davis.
Training for cycling : the ultimate guide to improved performance
/ Davis Phinney and Connie Carpenter ; written with Peter Nye
p.   cm.
"A Perigee book."
Includes bibliographical references and index.
ISBN 0-399-51731-6 (alk. paper)
1. Cycling—Training.   I. Carpenter, Connie.
II. Nye, Peter, date.   III. Title.
GV1048.P48   1992   91-42348 CIP
796.6—dc20

Cover design by Richard Rossiter
Front cover photo © by John Kelly
Back cover photo courtesy of Raleigh Bicycles
Illustrations © by Cecily Currier

Printed in the United States of America
8   9   10   11   12   13   14   15

This book is printed on acid-free paper.

This book is dedicated to the memory of Darcy Carpenter,
an exceptional woman and mother. We miss you.

CONTENTS

ACKNOWLEDGMENTS

Our athletic careers were touched by countless people, from supportive spectators, course marshals, race promoters, and journalists, whom we never knew, to a very close circle of very special people without whom we couldn't have accomplished much of what we have. That circle starts with both of our parents, Damon and Thea Phinney; and Darcy and Charlie Carpenter. You believed in us, and even though you might have had some doubts, you let us find our own way. To our brothers and sister—Chuck, Bob, Jim and Alice—who gave us great latitude because we were driven by something that wasn't always easy to explain or understand.

Special thanks to Jim Ochowicz, who took the 7-Eleven team from a collection of guys to a team of professionals. To all the many players and support personnel on the 7-Eleven team over the years. Thanks to all of you for the teamwork, but especially to my lead-out men, Ron Kiefel, Jock Boyer, and Sean Yates, and to Andy Hampsten for the big wins. My everlasting gratitude to Alex Stieda, and to Mike Neel for his solid direction and belief. Thanks to Len Pettyjohn and my current Coors Light teammates.

Special thanks to Monica McWhirter Van Haute for her steadfast loyalty and support of Connie's teams, and to Sue Novara-Reber, who was that special combination of both inspiration and friend.

Thanks to our creative friend and Coors Classic race promoter, Mike Aisner. To Dr. Andy Pruitt, Dr. Jim Holmes, and Dr. Massimo Testa, who play such vital roles in keeping us on the road.

Thanks to Laura Shepherd, for her interest in cycling and in us.

Finally, we would like to pay tribute to the memory of a very special person who had a strong influence on us, as a cyclist and a friend—Bob Cook.

INTRODUCTION: PERFORMING ON THE WORLD'S STAGE

This is a book about performance. Our performance has been measured by winning bike races but it isn't limited to statistics. Performance is about being your best, and learning to do something better. Excellence does not come easily, nor is it automatic for even the most talented, highly-motivated individuals. Rather, it stems from the desire to be really good at something and the discipline to make a lasting commitment. Improved cycling performance involves harnessing your talent through a systematic approach to training. We have designed this book to give you the information you need to help you pave the way to developing your technique, tactics, and training methods.

We have spent the last fifteen years studying and performing in the theater of cycling. The world has been our stage, from Paris to Tokyo, Moscow to Caracas, Los Angeles to Boston, from Oshkosh to Palmdale, and many wonderful—and not so wonderful—places in between. Through a process of experimentation, careful thought and continuous study, we have developed a philosophy of training that has enabled us to perform at the highest level. This system works for us as well as for many of the people we have had the opportunity to work with over the years. We know it will work for you.

The idea for this book comes from our Carpenter/Phinney Bike Camps, which are now in the sixth season. It wasn't until we first started to teach and coach in 1985,

Paving the way to your potential.

that we realized how much we know about cycling. It was overwhelming, and learning how to teach took some experimentation, innovation, and thought. We are grateful to our friends who gather each summer to comprise our elite Camp staff for their valuable contributions to the Camps and to this book. We feel satisfied with this format, because it is designed for cyclists of all abilities, for anyone who takes their cycling seriously.

This is not a book limited by scientific fact, but is based instead on the laboratory of daily life, on intuition and insight culled from our combined experience from three decades of racing, training, coaching, and studying. We teach you to think for yourself, to coach yourself. We do not tell you where to go and what to do, as much as give you a good road map. You must find your own way, based on your own needs, talent, and objectives.

Why Read This Book?

You want to improve your cycling and that requires more than just going out and riding. We provide you with direction in this book, and a method for putting your time on the bike to better use which will help you achieve your goals. Whether you are a weekend warrior who loves to ride "centuries" at your own personal-best speed or a triathlete seeking the cycling advantage, this book will help you to ride better. If you are a racing cyclist who has just started, this book will save you years of experimentation because we've already done that for you. If you have ridden for years and hit a plateau or simply not realized your dreams, we have presented some ideas to spark your program and improve your performance. This book doesn't contain shortcuts, although the knowledge gained from this book will surely speed your progress. Read this book because you want to improve your cycling on *all* levels—including technique, training, and tactics.

Give yourself time to develop as a cyclist. Set reasonable goals for yourself and let the confidence you get from reaching these goals spill over into other areas of your life. Cycling adds punch and spark to your life because it is challenging and exciting. We know you will never regret the time you spend on your bike. It is time that is well-invested.

To help keep the reading more intimate and share our varied experiences, we are writing this book in the first person. As we do in the Camps, we prefer to give you individual attention. Writing in the first person helps us to give more personalized information, as well as to share some of our own stories. Since there are two of us talking, you will have to take note of who is speaking. We hope this won't be confusing.

We look forward to seeing you on the road,

CONNIE AND DAVIS 1991

PROLOGUE

CONNIE CARPENTER—A PROMISE TO FULFILL

As a fourteen-year-old, I made the 1972 U.S. Winter Olympic speed-skating team and competed in Sapporo, Japan. Suddenly, this tomboy from Sherman Junior High School who hadn't even learned to slow-dance was thrown into the world of talented adults who took their sport—and themselves—quite seriously. It was scary and wonderful.

International competition helped prepare me for the Sapporo Olympics, where I competed in the 1,500-meter event. My mother, Darcy, filmed the event until the middle of the race, when she became so excited that she tossed the camera to my dad, Charlie, because at the halfway point I was on medal-winning time. At the finish, my time was just short of breaking the Olympic record, but the first six finishers broke the record. I finished seventh.

Being part of the Olympic Games was a heady feeling, especially at fourteen. I felt that I would fulfill my promise and win an Olympic gold medal someday soon. There was no way of knowing that twelve years would pass, involving several career-threatening injuries and many discouraging moments, before I would win an Olympic gold medal in another sport altogether.

Speed skating requires systematic year-round training, which gave my life focus and great intensity. Moreover, I was doing something I loved. I grew up in Madison, which schoolchildren know as the capital of Wisconsin, college students identify with the University of Wisconsin, and athletes the world over know as the home of speed skater Eric Heiden, who swept all five gold medals at the 1980 Lake Placid Winter Olympics. I was the only daughter in a family of four children. Growing up with three brothers tells you something about the development of my competitive instincts.

15

Flowers for Connie and the 1991 U.S. Professional Championship jersey for Davis after the Corestates Championship in Philadelphia.

PHOTO CREDIT:
KAREN SCHULENBURG

Soon after I learned to walk, I started to skate. Wisconsin winters are notoriously long and cold, and an almost unlimited number of frozen ponds, lakes, and flooded schoolyards offered plenty of places to skate. We lived across the street from Lakewood School, where I followed in my father's footsteps and went to elementary school. More important, it boasted a large field that in the winter was the center of my life. Late in the fall hockey boards went up, and a large field adjacent to the hockey rink was flooded for open skating. There was a little aluminum-sided shelter that sat quiet all summer but came to life in the winter. Lights were mounted high above the hockey and open skating rinks. Sometime before Christmas, when the ice was ready, the lights would come on and we skated our evenings away.

As long as there was ice, we were constantly skating. We played skating games all the time. One was "pom-pom," where everyone lines up and whoever is "it" has to tag others, who then also become it, and in the end it's all of them against you. Often I was one of the few left standing. Another popular game that involves eluding chasers was "capture the flag." We played hard. I was always fast, wily, and intense during these games. My competitive instincts are rooted in those early games— they were important, and doing well was important to me.

My parents were the antithesis of competitive. My mother wore a large smile and had a calm and understanding demeanor, which drew the neighborhood children like a magnet. She made everyone feel comfortable. At our house, the living was not too regimented and there was just the right pitch of chaos. To Mother's dismay, people would describe our house as "lived-in." It was certainly that. My father, an only child, used his children as a vehicle to relive his own childhood. He endeavored to make up for the lonely existence he had known as a child: growing up with a nanny, summer camp, and boarding school, but no siblings. One year he caught rheumatic fever and was confined in a hospital room alone for two months. He was only thirteen years old, and the illness set him back in school. The darkness of his childhood contrasted sharply with the lightness of the family he created.

Mom was the youngest of four children and remembered happy times as a child growing up in New Jersey. Her hard times hit at age thirty when, just after the birth of my brother Jim, she was diagnosed with multiple sclerosis, a debilitating disease of the central nervous system. It is to her credit that I rarely felt the disease affect my life, though it greatly affected hers. There were things she could not do, but she fought the disease head-on with laughter, not tears.

Every year I competed in the city-sponsored skating championships, and from kindergarten on won my age group. By the sixth grade, I had accumulated an impressive streak—until the Lunda girls came to race. They were Kathy and Kay, twins who were fast and competed for the local speed-skating club. After Kathy beat me, I decided it was time to join the club, too. My parents had been reticent over the years about encouraging me to join because it would mean more of their time and substantial commitment from me. But I was determined. So in seventh grade, I got serious—as serious as a twelve-year-old can be.

That was 1970, before the running boom made exercise chic. I would not have been caught dead running in broad daylight in my own neighborhood. No way! But running was a good way to stay in shape during the warm summer months, so I rode my bike four to five miles across town to run in the sanctity of anonymity, or I waited to train after dark. This troubled my mother, but gave me peace of mind.

I was a fast speed skater and finished second in my first national championships, behind Kay Lunda. Mother was impressed that Nancy Heiden, Eric's mother, told her that my thighs were developing nicely. That may not be the kind of observation that a mother normally would take kindly to, but in this case it was a compliment; Mother beamed.

In 1971, Norwegian speed-skating coach Finn Halvorsen came to the United States at the invitation of the U.S. International Skating Association, the sport's governing body. Halvorsen was a graduate of the prestigious Norges Idrettshogskole (Norwegian Sports School) and earned an advanced degree that has no comparison in the United States. Norges Idrettshogskole produces elite coaches and physical educators.

Speed skating's competitive season is a relatively short period of ten to twelve weeks, but the training season lasts eight months. The sport requires not only considerable physical fitness but also a high degree of technical expertise; good coaching is imperative. In the fall of 1972, I went to Norway for training, once again under Finn Halvorsen's gentle guidance.

In Norway, I trained almost daily at the sports school. The school is nestled on the outskirts of Oslo, where there are plenty of woods and fields for running and exercising, and hills for sprinting or low-walking (simulated skating exercises). The school also has a weight room and physiotherapists. They tried to keep my adolescent body on track with vitamin and iron therapy to treat the anemia I had developed, and ultrasound therapy for my sore and overtrained lower back.

Training for speed skating was detailed and well planned. Every day was accounted for and mapped out. Finn took the time to educate his pupils. He introduced me to Per-Olaf Astrands's *Textbook of Work Physiology,* considered the bible of exercise scientists in the 1970s and now regarded as a classic. Finn was a fan of Arthur Lydiard, the New Zealander who advocated long slow distance (LSD) training to promote circulatory adaptations without the expense of fatigue. Finn introduced me to the biochemistry of the body, trying to translate the nuances of the cell—words like mitochondria, lactic acid, and aerobic became part of my vocabulary. He also tried to teach me to listen to myself, which I now know is the hardest thing to ask of any athlete.

I loved to skate fast from my early childhood. Eventually I found my way to the Madison speed-skating club and quietly earned a spot on the 1972 Olympic team.

PHOTO CREDIT:
PERSONAL ARCHIVES

I listened and learned a lot from Finn Halvorsen, but in the end I did not do a very good job of listening to myself. The prevailing ethic was "more is better," and ego prevents athletes from giving in and admitting to being fatigued. Speed skaters by nature are fiercely competitive. In my first year of competition after the Olympics, I suffered from anemia and developed a back problem. Then I developed a stress fracture in my foot from running, but I preferred to think that the pain was mental rather than physical. I waited until the stress fracture had begun to heal itself before I went to see a doctor. The next year, I developed peroneal tendonitis (an inflammation of the tendon that controls lateral movement of the ankle), which eventually led to the end of my speed-skating career.

I never developed my potential as a speed skater—partly because I was too young, partly because my body was still developing, but mostly because I lacked a basic ingredient: confidence. I found myself constantly fighting self-doubt and mood swings—typical for teenagers, no matter how successful. I was a child in an adult world; the pressure was sometimes impossible to bear.

Just five days before the 1976 Olympic speed-skating trials, I shot out of a turn, doing one of my last race-pace intervals, when I felt my left ankle give out. It wouldn't support me any more, and it hurt when I tried to stand on it. I had to be helped off the ice and was taken to a hospital for X rays. I had torn my peroneal tendon, and although I managed to skate in the trials with a heavily taped ankle, it was extremely painful and my results were below my ability. I came close to making the team, finishing fourth when the top three made the cut. I was devastated.

Moving On

In the spring I started cycling for fun, with an eye toward bicycle racing. My ankle didn't work well from side to side, but the up–down motion that cycling required for pedaling was no problem. My brother Chuck had raced as a national-class Category I-2 rider, as had many of my skating friends, so it seemed natural that I would try cycling, too.

The cycling bug bit me, and I started with regional races. When the Summer Olympics were held in Montreal, I took off to watch them with my friend Sheila Young. She was a remarkably versatile athlete and a very good friend. As a speed skater, Sheila had won a gold, a silver, and a bronze medal earlier in the year at the Winter Olympics in Innsbruck, Austria, and was training to win her second world cycling sprint championship. (Women didn't have an Olympic cycling sprint event until the 1988 Seoul Olympics.) Her fiancé Jim Ochowicz, had made the Olympic cycling team in the four-rider 4,000-meter (2.5-mile) team pursuit. Because of Sheila's fame, she received an infield pass, and I tagged along.

Watching the Olympic Games psyched me up. I had missed a great opportunity over the winter, but I was still fit enough to qualify for the national championships in track and road racing. At the national track championships in Northbrook, Illinois, I won the 3,000-meter (1.9-mile) individual pursuit in gale-force winds by defeating Miji Reoch of Philadelphia by two-tenths of a second. Miji had won a silver medal in the event at the 1975 world championships in Rocourt, Belgium, and was highly respected. Soon after the national track championships were the national road championships in Louisville, Kentucky, where we dueled again in the thirty-eight-mile race. I sprinted up the final hill leading to the finish and nipped her to become national road champion. Clearly, I had found a new sport.

The Early Years

Everyone always asks why speed skaters excel at cycling. Speed skaters rely on the same upper-leg muscle groups as cyclists and are very well-trained. Skaters look like cyclists without a bike to support them. Because speed skaters must carry the weight themselves, the activity itself is more intense, and less sustainable, than cycling. But the strength built up from skating transfers nicely to cycling.

My cycling career got off to a fast start that continued in high gear into 1977. At the national championships I successfully defended my titles in the 3,000-meter individual pursuit and the road race. That led to the cycling world championships—in San Cristóbal, Venezuela. I won a silver medal in the thirty-one-mile road race. Soon I was invited to the Mediterranean island of Majorca, off the coast of Spain, where I won an exhibition match against world pursuit champion Anna Riemersma of Holland. Then I went up to Holland, where I won three more races, demonstrating my emerging presence in the cycling world.

But in 1978, I got derailed. To live in a climate and terrain more favorable for cycling, I moved to northern California and rode all winter. In an early-season international race in Arizona, I sprinted out of a turn for the finish and crashed, taking a hard fall on my head, which resulted in a concussion, whiplash, and multiple contusions. My chief rival in the race was Keetie Van Oosten-Hage of Holland, the toughest competitor I ever raced against. Van Oosten-Hage was aggressive, unrelenting, and good in everything—from time trialing and pursuiting to climbing and sprinting. Keetie would destroy me later that summer in the Red Zinger Bicycle Classic stage race in Colorado, the only major stage race for women in North America.

For the rest of the season, nothing came together. I rode poorly in the nationals as well as in the Red Zinger, which was gaining international stature. My year concluded with a trip to the world road championship in Cologne, Germany. The women's road race was thirty-two miles over a flat course. It finished just a few blocks from the home of Beate Habetz, the seventeen-year-old German wunderkind. She won, making the race a fairy tale story for her but one of great disappointment for me.

I was disillusioned with cycling. What could I do with it? Where could I go? There was no cycling in the Olympics for women. I had gone as far in the sport as I

I couldn't believe it when I won the 1976 U.S. National Championships in Louisville, Kentucky, in my first competitive season at the age of nineteen. I was barefoot because my cycling shoes bothered the injured ankle that ended my skating career but obviously had no impact on my cycling.

PHOTO CREDIT:
MICHAEL CHRITTON

could. So I went back to school. In the winter of 1979, I enrolled at the University of California in Berkeley to continue my college education, which had begun in 1975 at the University of Wisconsin. I had an eye on trying a new sport—rowing— which, once again, I had been introduced to by my brother Chuck, who had rowed at Yale.

A lot changed for me when I went to Berkeley. At the University of Wisconsin, I had been a German major, primarily due to the influence of my travels as a speed skater to German-speaking countries. Then I took a course that had a big impact on me: human anatomy. I learned a new language, the language of the human body, and I was fascinated. When I transferred to Berkeley, I changed my major to physical education and studied exercise physiology in the Physical Education Department under one of the country's preeminent physiologists, George Brooks. I rowed on the crew team and rode my bike only infrequently. I was very happy.

After six months of rowing, I made the varsity-eight shell, mostly on the strength of my endurance, which compensated for my lack of rowing technique and size.

Most of my crewmates were taller and bigger. At almost five foot eleven inches tall and less than 140 pounds, I was considered—for the first time in my life—"petite." We took second place in the 1979 Collegiate Nationals, held near Detroit. In 1980, I rowed in and stroked the varsity four. We won the National Collegiate Championships held in Oakridge, Tennessee. What I remember most about that event were the nights when we lay in bed telling stories and laughing until our bellies ached so much we wondered if we would be able to row the next day.

After my fling with crew and graduation in 1981 with a bachelor of arts degree in physical education, I was faced with a decision: get a job, or go back and race bikes. Then came the timely announcement that the women's individual road race was introduced to the 1984 Los Angeles Summer Olympic Games. This was the first cycling event open to women in the Olympics. My decision was an easy one.

Davis

I had discovered a great guy named Davis Phinney. We met in 1978, on a training ride in Tucson. He was soft-spoken, funny, and, of course, very handsome. When I went to his hometown of Boulder, Colorado, to train for the Red Zinger, I looked forward to mountain rides with Davis.

What Davis brought to my cycling was the notion that I had not begun to live up to my potential. He trained with me and knew how strong I was, but he felt that my results were short of my ability. I knew that Davis was a good cyclist, but when we started heading off to races together in 1981, I was amazed to see just how good he was.

Part of the fun was winning races together. We raised each other's level of expectation while also offering each other objective advice on training and race tactics. It was a support system that worked for me. My teammates did not always like waiting for the men's race to finish, but being part of his racing was part of the deal.

Davis had studied the sport much more thoroughly than I had, and his perspective was invaluable. My college education made me well-versed in the physiological mechanisms that I applied to training and racing, but the more subtle and complex art of cycling was lacking. With Davis, my education continued.

The four-year stretch leading to the Los Angeles Olympics was a whirlwind. It started with a struggle to regain my form after having taken a season off from cycling, but my confidence returned quickly in 1981. I won the Red Zinger, which had changed its name under a new sponsor to the Coors International Bicycle Classic, won three more national titles, and took a bronze medal in the thirty-four-mile world championships road race in Prague, Czechoslovakia. Four of us crossed the finish line with no more than the width of the finishing tape between us at the world championships. I took it as a crushing defeat. I also realized that I needed to learn a technique that would give me the extra edge in such close finishes—throwing my bike to the finish. That technique would make the difference in 1984.

Once again, the world championship distances were short and the racing seemed so negative—where attacks were countered and the racing lacked boldness. But a young Frenchwoman named Jeannie Longo finished second in that race. In 1982, a supremely fit Italian named Maria Canins would make her way into cycling, along with Marianne Berglund of Sweden and Americans Cindy Olavarri and Rebecca Twigg. It was the beginning of an era of competitiveness rooted in very strong rivalries.

A career highlight was winning the 1983 world pursuit championship in Zurich, Switzerland, less than two months after breaking my arm in the Coors Classic. U.S. national team coach Eddie Borysewicz (pronounced *bori-say-vitch*) decided that Rebecca should focus on the road, since that was all that was offered in 1984 at the Olympics. Eddie thought I should ride the pursuit and road, with emphasis on pursuit since I had broken my arm and was still weak climbing, although my all-around fitness was good. I met Eddie three times at the 7-Eleven velodrome prior to the worlds. I learned more in those three sessions than in my seven years of pursuiting.

In Zurich I qualified first. In the semifinal ride I rode a world-best time of 3 minutes 49.53 seconds to beat Jeannie Longo of France. Remember that this was before disc wheels, which have less wind resistance, were introduced. Yet that time is still competitive today. In the final ride, less than two hours after my ride against Jeannie, I began slowly. But in traditional pursuit style, I came from behind to defeat teammate Cindy Olavarri by two-tenths of a second in the final half lap. We made it a one-two finish for the United States. Becoming world champion was a long time in the making, but the feeling of ecstasy and accomplishment made it worthwhile. That night, my mind was still racing and I couldn't sleep at all.

The following week I made the break of seven riders on a tough world championship road course in Altenrhein on the shores of Lake Constanz in Switzerland. On the second of four laps, Maria Canins skidded on the wet pavement, which had an 18 percent downhill grade, and I braked to avoid her, sending me into a skid.

Sparks flew from my pedals as I hit the slippery pavement. I got up and caught the leaders, but the chase had wasted me and soon I was dropped. My teammates, Cindy and Rebecca, were also in the lead group and did nothing to help me. This was fairly typical at that time. My teammate and friend, Marianne Berglund of Sweden, was also in the lead group. On the final lap, I listened as I rode to the finish to hear who would become world champion. Of the four contesting the sprint, Rebecca was the strongest, but not the smartest. She sprinted strongly and looked to her left to see if anyone was coming. At that moment, Marianne surged around to the right. Rebecca never saw her and had to settle for the silver medal. I rode in well ahead of the pack for seventh place, and spotted Marianne. She was radiant. Rebecca was in tears. She had missed a very big opportunity.

The next day, Greg LeMond set the world on its ear with a solo victory in the 169-mile professional race. We watched the race in its entirety on television from our hotel in Zurich. It was awe-inspiring.

But that was all prologue for the Los Angeles Olympics. After suffering through knee surgery and a broken arm in 1983, I knew anything could happen in 1984. I had learned what every athlete comes to know eventually: I could not take anything for granted.

1984

In January 1984, Davis and I were in Long Beach, California, for the annual bicycle-industry trade show, where we represented our sponsors (mine was Raleigh bicycles), signed autographs, and met bicycle dealers. Afterward, we visited my team manager, Monica McWhirter, in San Diego, where we trained a few days and got our first look at the Olympic road course. It was in Mission Viejo, about a forty-five-minute car drive south of Long Beach. One of the Olympic Committee organizers volunteered to show us the course, which had been described as un-challenging. I was almost afraid to see it.

We met in the start/finish area and pedaled through the suburb of neatly built California-style homes, around a few turns, and up the first hill, on a road called Vista del Lago. The hill was steep and nearly a mile long. We descended quickly down the other side and took a sharp right turn onto the flat and fast Marguerite Parkway, which led us to a left turn up a long, gradually steeper climb on La Paz. It was a hard course, and I was euphoric.

With about 200 days to go before the Olympics, I had a rejuvenated mission. Davis and I talked about what likely would happen in my race. A group of six to eight of the fittest women would break away, and that group would sprint for the medals. I knew that I could be in the lead group—barring unforeseen circumstances. I would have to be fresh, powerful for the climbs, and fast for the finish. No excuses. Davis had a foreshadowing: He was confident that I was the best rider, but he felt that my competition, especially my American teammates, would resort to anything to beat me. What he was talking about was taking drugs to enhance performance—cheating to win.

I didn't want to hear or believe any of it. So I scoffed and said, "No one can take anything that will enable them to be better than me." I did not know if that was true. But I wasn't going to lie awake nights in fear of what others might do.

So much was happening. We trained consistently and used minor races as stepping-stones for preparation. In April, Davis left for two months in Europe with the U.S. national team; I opted to stay and race in America. I had decided on six

Through thick and thin. Davis and I were a matching pair during the 1983 Coors Classic where I broke my left arm. We were married later that fall.

PHOTO CREDIT:
COURTESY MICHAEL AISNER

weeks of men's races, mostly in California, as my means of best preparation. It was a gamble, but I was confident that it was the right move. I had become tired of racing in women's fields, where the racing was predictable and lacked challenge, and looked forward to racing with the men. I felt that the races in Europe would be difficult, but they did not suit my game plan, which was for my Olympic competitors overseas to forget about me. I had seen them in March at the Tour of Texas and then not again until July at the Coors Classic in my backyard, as a tune-up for the Olympics. That would be enough.

Sue Novara-Reber, my teammate and good friend, would also follow this plan with me. Monica filled the manager role, as she had done so well since 1981. She became so adept that I rarely had to ask her to do something, because invariably she had already done it. Both Sue and Monica were a source of great comfort. We were more than a team that won bike races; we were family—through thick and thin—and they played a big role in my success.

Before I flew to California I got the good news that Davis had won in France. I was really excited. Things were clicking.

My racing went well in California until Easter Sunday, when I was riding in a men's Olympic trials qualifying race north of Los Angeles called the Tour of Santa Clarita. I had ridden strongly on the first long climb. A strong side wind had split the field. I sat on the back of a fast-moving chase group. We had a great tail wind and were flying back up to the main group just before the climb called Spunky, when suddenly the rider in front of me went down. With no time to react, I hit him squarely, catapulted straight up, and landed on the back of my head. I sat with my head in my hands trying to collect myself, then saw that my hands were bright red and felt that my neck was wet. The force of the impact had cut a small artery in the back of my head, just below my leather strap helmet (hardshells were not required then). Blood was squirting all over. Team manager Monica took me to the hospital. Six stitches were required.

(Months later in Los Angeles, the memory of that day would make it easy for me to announce my retirement from competition. I did not have the heart or head to continue to take these chances anymore. And no matter how strong or fit I was to become, the human body is very frail. And nobody is invincible.)

I took the next weekend off from racing and recovered more quickly than I thought I would. I flew to Atlanta for some weekend men's races in the college town of Athens before riding in a four-day men's stage race in North Carolina. I was a little skittish in the Athens race from my crash in California, but the pace was so high that I had no time to think about it. I had to keep the momentum; every day counted.

Less than 100 days now and many obstacles, like the Olympic trials, to overcome.

The Final March

The Olympic trials were held in Spokane, a beautiful city in the middle of Washington. Wildflowers bloomed and caught my eye even during the races—beautiful fields full of color, like Claude Monet paintings. The courses were challenging. They suited the demands that the Olympic course would make of us in the race for the medals. Davis won the individual time trial on the opening day of competition, June 18, to secure a berth in the 100-kilometer (62.5 miles) four-rider team time trial (TTT). Soon after came the road trials to determine who the five riders would be to make the men's team for the 119-mile race. Davis made the long team for the road, too. That made things easier in our camp.

Rebecca Twigg beat me in the first trials race. Winning the trials was not a priority, but I wanted to win and always disliked being beaten, especially by Rebecca. In the next race, she beat me again. The worst thing about it was that I did not care. I had lost my intensity. I should have felt angry, but I only felt mildly irritated. But that set a warning light off: I was physically tired and mentally stale. In the third race, I snapped around and won in a photo finish. I qualified second in the trials behind Rebecca, which guaranteed me a ride in Los Angeles.

On July 1, I took a killer four-hour ride that turned my form around. I started out with Davis, several of his Olympic teammates, and Canadian Olympian Steve Bauer on a long ride that went out to Golden. My intention was to stop and double back before the long, arduous climb out of Golden, but I kept going with them and did the whole climb up Golden Gate Canyon. When we got to the summit and turned onto the Peak to Peak Highway, I was exhausted. But after eating a big piece of cherry pie with the guys at a roadside café, I felt myself come back to life. I had turned a corner in my training. I felt good again.

We flew late on July 9 to Los Angeles. We went to ride the Olympic course and make ourselves familiar with the private housing where each of us would stay and to have one last hard training on the course. It was Monday, and we were scheduled to start the Coors Classic Friday. Were we doing too much? For some of us, riding on the course was for training, and for others it was the final team selection to determine who would compete and who would be alternates for the Olympic race—the coaches had the sole authority to make the decision. The stakes were high. Riders were tense.

Cindy Olavarri and I trained together on the course. We rode behind a motorcycle to help us get familiar with the course at race speed. But something weird happened. On the first lap, Cindy was flying up the hills; I couldn't believe how strong she looked. Then, on the next lap, she died and was holding on to the back of the motorcycle to get over the rest of the hills. I did not think much about it, except to note how careful a rider had to be with efforts on this course. It was deceptively difficult. I stuck to my own business and did several motorpaced sprints through the finish area to learn what to do and what not to do. On one practice sprint, I went too soon and died before the line. The road leading to the finish line made it a tough sprint—slightly uphill but fast and very long. You could see that finish line from a mile away. The practicing I did for the finish line later proved immensely beneficial. I learned not to start my sprint too soon. I did not think about the consequences of going too late.

The guys were racing around the course in the 100-degree heat, but the rest of the women's team had yet to appear. The final competition between Inga Thompson, Peggy Maas, and Janelle Parks would determine who would be the fourth rider on our team—the U.S. Olympic women's cycling team. Rebecca Twigg's bike had not come in yet, so the women waited and ended up staying another night.

Davis and I flew home right after the training session. It was his twenty-fifth birthday, and we planned a quiet dinner to celebrate. I felt good about the course. Davis had ridden well, *almost* ensuring that he, too, would ride the road race in addition to the TTT. I say *almost* because Eddie had a knack for keeping everyone on edge, thinking that it would keep everyone sharp until the last minute. In many cases it worked, but not always.

On the flight home, I sat by the window and Davis sat on the aisle seat opposite

Eddie. I remember a conversation that he and Eddie had regarding "strong brothers or sisters" that Davis might have, and if they had the same blood type. Davis told Eddie that he was not interested in what Eddie had in mind: *blood doping*.

This is a process in which an athlete donates a substantial quantity of blood that is then spun in a laboratory to separate the red blood cells from the plasma, the liquid part of blood. The red blood cells, which carry oxygen, are stored. The athlete's body regenerates blood supply naturally over a period of weeks, and then, prior to a major event, he reinjects his stored blood. This makes the blood thicker and capable of carrying more oxygen to enhance performance. Blood doping was not new. It was not on the International Olympic Committee's list of banned substances, because it is undetectable (there is no known test for it). Blood doping is, however, unethical and potentially dangerous.

(After the Olympics, news of cyclists using blood doping caused a worldwide scandal and resulted in Eddie's suspension without pay from the USCF. The method used by the cyclists in question—guesstimated at seven of the twenty-four-member U.S. team—was barbaric because it was done outside of a hospital setting, and, since the idea came up late, relatives donated blood. The blood was not properly handled or screened. With grave consequences like AIDS and hepatitis, it was a risky venture. It was also cheating. The IOC declared blood doping illegal because of this episode.)

On the airplane, Davis told Eddie, "Leave us out of this, because we are definitely not interested." For my part, I buried my head in my book and tried not to listen. But I could not believe my ears. What was happening?

USCF coaches also had been encouraging riders to experiment with high dosages of caffeine, which Davis and I also refused to try. Caffeine was placed on the banned-substance list—not to catch coffee and cola drinkers, but to stem what appeared to be a dangerous trend toward extremely high dosages of caffeine in athletes' systems, far exceeding what was possible to drink. Such high dosages are dangerous because of the stress they impose on the body, especially the heart, thereby increasing the risk of heart attack.

(We thought nothing more of all this until months later when the scandal unfolded. I remember being in a hotel swimming pool with Eddie after Davis and his teammates won the bronze medal in the TTT. Eddie contended that if they had taken the caffeine that he wanted them to—which was in a dose considered to be illegal— it's possible they would have got the silver medal. I felt disgusted and disturbed to think that this was the prevailing attitude of our coaching staff. At the time, I just felt relieved that the Games were over.)

Back in Colorado two days after the Mission Viejo training session, Cindy Olavarri dropped off the Olympic cycling team with the excuse that she had mononucleosis. At first I thought it preposterous. Then I thought about her training, and how badly she had ridden on the Olympic course the day we rode together. Maybe she did have mono, I told myself. I wanted to believe it.

Cindy's departure created an opening for Inga Thompson to race in the Olympics, a remarkable development for Inga. She was a former cross-country runner who had become serious about cycling only three months earlier. Jannelle Parks had the fourth spot, but now both would get the chance to ride in Los Angeles. None of us had much time to think about Cindy, who had left town faster than the news traveled. While there was some speculation about the real reason for Cindy's departure, it was only rumor as far as I was concerned.

(Not until several years after the Olympics was it disclosed that Cindy voluntarily withdrew from the Olympic team because she tested positive for steroids. Had she not withdrawn, she would have been removed. Cindy subsequently had serious health problems, including tumors and weak tendons. She became so weak, in fact, she could barely walk. For several years she lived in the hell that was her secret world. When she decided to come public, she reached out to high-school kids with a very strong, very personal message: "Don't do it, it's not worth it. Look at me.")

We also were preoccupied with the Coors Classic, which would start the next day. Only seventeen days were left until the Olympics. Things were definitely heating up.

The Coors Classic was a lark for me. My form was good, and so was Davis's. Tensions were eased with the realization that we were this close to the Games and we had the form we had hoped for. I won the first three Coors races in an almost effortless way; at the end of the week I won the Morgul-Bismark race for the fourth time in my career. Davis won in Estes Park and in Denver's Washington Park criterium, and even wore the leader's jersey. We both quit the race with two days remaining, because we needed that extra edge of freshness. Even though I was leading the race and perhaps could easily have won, it would have cost me energy that I needed to get through just one more week. It was a tough decision, but I knew that for the Olympics, I had to be fresh. I also knew that the Coors Classic was getting too easy for me. At the bottom of The Wall, the long steep hill where the Morgul-Bismark course finishes, I was so distracted that I could hardly focus on the racing. I won the race too easily and knew I had to quit if I wanted to stay sharp.

I had won the Coors Classic before, but the Olympics, especially the inaugural women's cycling event, was another story.

Only nine days remained until the Los Angeles Olympics. It was a time to rest and avoid the maelstrom of press that swirled around us. These were the first Summer Olympics in the United States since the 1932 Los Angeles Olympics. We were competing on home ground, and the pressure was intense. Davis and I were picked by *Sports Illustrated* to win the Olympic road races. The scenario that *SI* set for Davis was of a nine-rider breakaway in which Davis would take the sprint. It was plausible. We knew that his chances were much slimmer than mine. But there was that chance, and it made a great story.

We flew to Los Angeles on Wednesday, July 25, and spent the entire day in processing, which meant obtaining credentials and clothing. Women also were required to take a gender test: The inside of the cheek is scraped for cells that are

I was flying during the 1984 Coors Classic, winning here in Vail, with Jeannie Longo in a familiar spot—second.   PHOTO CREDIT: MICHAEL CHRITTON

analyzed to determine genetic gender identification. Despite all the pressure, we were having a good time. In fact, there was a lot of levity as we wended through the maze of accreditation and team outfitting. The women had to visit the Olympic Village for the gender test. There, in front of the "Gender Verification" sign, I took a photo of my teammates Inga Thompson and Janelle Parks. On impulse, they laughed and lifted up their shirts to show their breasts and verify their gender.

The Olympic Village was colorful and exciting to visit. A total of 7,078 athletes (5,458 men and 1,620 women) from 141 countries competed and were housed primarily in two villages, which were the transformed campuses of the University of California—Los Angeles and the University of Southern California. Eastern-bloc countries had boycotted Los Angeles in retaliation for the U.S. boycott of the 1980 Moscow Summer Olympics, but their absence wouldn't have been felt in the women's cycling event because they weren't influential in international road racing.

All the athletes gathered in the Olympic Village had to deal as best they could with many of the same demons of fear, anxiety, anticipation, and destiny. The air was thick with it.

The village was a compelling place to visit. It also was a good reminder of the huge event we were participating in, but we would not be staying there and I was glad to leave it behind. It was too distracting, too far from any decent terrain for cycling, and fifty-five miles from the road-racing course in Mission Viejo. On Thursday we trained on the course. It was a hard training day for me, and it felt good after a day off. On Friday, we rode away from the course. But we came back to ride the course once more on Saturday.

Thousands of spectators watched us practice. The closed-in suburb of Mission Viejo had been completely transformed. Colorful flags of the Los Angeles Games lined the ten-mile course. The five interlocking Olympic rings represent the five continents and are colored black, yellow, blue, green, and red, on a white background. At least one of those colors appears in the national flag of every country. But the flags of the Los Angeles Olympics were different. They were muted yellow, mint green, and coral pink—colors of the sea and sunsets, not of nations and their politics. The atmosphere was beautiful, inviting, and festive.

As I returned home Saturday, at the end of my last training before race day, I took time to ride around the neighborhood and practice throwing my bike, a technique that Davis and I had worked on extensively. Throwing a bicycle is tantamount to a runner's leaning at the finishing tape. I practiced the motion of easing up off my saddle and straightening my arms in front to throw the bike forward several inches. We worked on perfecting the move. Technique was critical and timing was everything. I had lost the 1981 worlds in Prague, Czechslovakia, by the tiniest margin, and I had resolved never to lose by so little again.

I also was testing out my race wheels. They were specially built with twenty-eight spokes (eight fewer than what was standard), had slightly narrower rims, and 185-gram (six-ounce) narrow-profile Vittoria Corsas tires. The wheels felt very responsive and fast. Tim Zasadny, my Raleigh team mechanic, had camped in my driveway working on my bike, and his diligence at keeping my bike tuned and ready showed. Everything was working beautifully. My gearing for the race was a seven-speed cluster, with a thirteen-to-twenty-one range on the back; chainrings of fifty-three and forty were on the front. My red-and-black Raleigh frame was custom built in Montreal. My backup bike was a Serotta, also painted in the Raleigh colors.

Race Day—Sunday, July 29, 1984

On race day morning, I was up at six o'clock for a light breakfast of a bagel and fruit before our 9:30 A.M. start. I was so excited that I did not sleep well, but I was fairly well rested. We drove to the course early, because we expected that traffic would choke the roads later. Surprisingly, traffic was remarkably light for most of the first week of the Games. Many of the local residents had left town, and many businesses had changed their hours to ease congestion. That not only succeeded in reducing traffic, but it also reduced smog. The air was remarkably clear—especially for Los Angeles.

As we drove to the course in our USA team van, we were amazed to see all the people already queued up for the race. As they do in Europe, many people appeared to have slept out overnight on the course to make sure they had a spot with a good view during the race. The entire Mission Viejo race course was going to be a huge, joyous tailgate party. American flags were flying everywhere.

Janelle was sitting in the front seat going absolutely crazy. She was so excited that she could hardly contain herself, even though it was a great waste of energy. Rebecca and Inga were quietly observing. Eddie B. had packed Rebecca's bag because she was well-known for forgetting crucial items, like her riding shoes or shorts. On the drive, we were awestruck by the frenzied intensity of the crowd. It was scary. The pressure was on. I told my teammates, "Geez, we better win, or we'll have to crawl out of here."

Yet it was also race day, a day we had devoted ourselves to preparing for. This was where years of races and more than 100,000 training miles led. For me, it was also where I had been heading since the 1972 Sapporo Winter Olympics. We were ready for the race, which helped keep us from being overwhelmed. Our relative calm in the tumultuous atmosphere added another amazing dimension to a potentially intoxicating experience. Everything was amazing.

I had prepared for races a thousand times before. It was, after all, just another bike race. But this also was a historic event. Although cycling had always been part of the program when the Olympic Games were revived in Athens in 1896, when five cycling events were held, Olympic cycling had been exclusively a men's sport. Recognition of international women's cycling came slowly. World cycling championships started including women in 1958, and over the years there was increasing pressure to include cycling for women in the Olympics. The Los Angeles Olympics introduced the first-ever women's Olympics cycling event, and the organizers lobbied to have the road races on the first day instead of the team time trial, which was traditionally the opening event for cycling. This schedule change really showcased the women; it was the opening day, and the eyes of the world watched.

After we lined up and the starter's pistol got us rolling, the five-lap, forty-nine-mile race itself shaped up just as I imagined so many months before when Davis and I had previewed the course. Italian Maria Canins had set a fierce pace early. The fast speed and high temperature, which was near 100 degrees, split up the field.

At the race's midpoint, six of us emerged as leaders in a breakaway: Canins, Jeannie Longo of France, Sandra Schumacher of West Germany, Unni Larsen of Norway, teammate Rebecca, and me. Longo was suffering from an off day. She and Rebecca seemed to struggle on the climbs. Yet Longo was a threat in any sprint, and my tactic was to key off of her. Canins lacked sharp speed to attack successfully, but she always chased strongly. A break from this group seemed pointless, and I had been sprinting well. I stayed in close contact with my breakaway companions and gambled on being ready for the burst over the final 200 meters.

One scary moment occurred when Canins ran into the back of Longo's bicycle just before the finish stretch with two laps to go. Canins fell down. She quickly got back up and promptly caught us. But Longo suffered a mechanical problem with her rear derailleur that she later blamed on that incident.

It was hellishly hot. The tail wind up the long climb on La Paz Road was like breathing in an inferno. Spectators were spraying us on the climbs, but the heat and the crowd noise had turned oppressive. Despite all the distractions and physical discomfort, however, I remained completely focused. I was battling the elements, my rivals, and myself. When Canins chased after Rebecca, pulling the rest of the breakaway up with her, I thought of counterattacking. It was a temptation. But we were still too far from the finish for a lone attack, and it seemed unnecessary. If I went solo, then Canins, Longo, Schumacher, and Larsen would work together to chase me down. This would of course be an advantage for Rebecca, who would be obligated to sit back rather than work against her teammate, and she would be fresh for the end. But that did not cross my mind. What did was the likelihood that they would catch me too close to the finish for me to recover and sprint well. So I waited.

Fortunately, on the next lap around I was able to take two bottles—one of water, one of both Coca-Cola and water—which I really needed. On the final climb up Vista del Lago, I felt some tiredness in my legs, a warning sign to take it easy so as not to jeopardize my chances in the sprint.

On the final straight, with the finish banner in sight, I lined up behind Longo, but suddenly she stopped pedaling and dropped behind me. I thought she was playing a strategic game. It distracted me. What was Longo doing behind us? At the 1981 world championships, she had edged me for the silver medal and I had to settle for the bronze. Since then, she had rarely beat me. Here in the Los Angeles Olympics, I didn't want her to pass me. I had no way of knowing that her rear derailleur was broken and that her chain was coming off.

But I had to direct my attention to action going on at the front. Canins went early, nearly a half-mile from the finish. The sprint for the medals was on. I sat back, collected myself, controlled my breathing, and shifted in the right gear.

With 200 meters left, Rebecca made a hard jump to the left with everything she had and zoomed to the lead. Afraid of going too soon, I went too late. I was quickly building speed, flying ahead of everyone else, but the finish line was coming up too fast and Rebecca had opened a good lead on me. I rode a straight line to the finish. Rebecca veered toward me. The distance between us was shortening. At fifty meters to go, Rebecca led by a bike length. But the road went uphill, and I was closing fast. In the final yards, I started to draw even. Then, just before the line, I threw my bike in a well-timed move that sent my front wheel across the finish just inches ahead of Rebecca.

I threw my bike to the finish, overtaking Rebecca Twigg (right) just at the line to win by inches.
PHOTO CREDIT: PRESSE SPORTS, PARIS

In most photo finishes, rival riders usually know who has won. I knew I had won, but I couldn't believe it. When I crossed the line, the crowd lining the road and thousands more spectators spread out on the hillsides surrounding the finish all were going nuts. They yelled their lungs out, jumped up and down, and waved the Stars and Stripes. Eddie and other cycling coaches were leaping in the air. As I rounded the turn to the team area, I spotted Davis, whose race start was less than an hour away.

"Who won?" he asked.

"I did."

Moments later, when the official announcement boomed over the public-address system, we fell to the ground laughing. It was most definitely the moment of my dreams.

Schumacher came in third for the bronze medal. As the rest of the thirty-eight finishers completed the race, I changed into a dry red-white-and-blue cycling suit and climbed up into the ABC Television viewing area to telephone home. The phone rang forever, nine or ten times, when finally my mother, breathless, answered.

"Mom—"

"Oh, Connie!" she gasped. "We were already out back shooting off fireworks." It was truly a moment for all of us who had persevered and believed.

The race, which took two hours, eleven minutes, and fourteen seconds, was over. The promise that I had showed as a speed skater in the 1972 Sapporo Winter Olympics had finally been fulfilled on home ground in the 1984 Olympics. It had been a long road. I felt emotionally and physically drained.

The medal ceremony was anticlimactic only in that we were on the podium in front of the VIP viewing area, which was far from the noisy and enthusiastic crowds.

Making Olympic history on July 29, 1984—from the left, Rebecca Twigg, myself, and Sandra Schumacher of West Germany become the first women to earn Olympic medals in cycling.

PHOTO CREDIT:
PRESSE SPORTS, PARIS

The Olympic gold medal was heavy to wear and beautiful to look at. I was still thinking that Davis's race was yet to come. It would be several hours before I could truly relax.

Not until the next day when I saw a tape of the finish of my race on television did I really know how close the finish was. Only inches. All those years and all that hard work for a few inches.

DAVIS PHINNEY—A PASSION TO RACE

My Tour de France stage victories, the more than 300 races I've won, and my 1991 national professional road-racing championship title in Philadelphia all contribute to my enjoyment of bicycle racing, but don't ever think any of those victories came easily. Each success came after considerable hard work and dedication, and without any sort of guarantee.

You would not have noticed me as a junior rider at sixteen and seventeen. In fact, in the junior world trials my best finish was an invisible tenth in one race, putting me far out of contention. In my era, riders like Andy Weaver, Ian Jones, and Doug Shapiro made the team. Fifteen-year-old Greg LeMond won the trials but was too young to make the team. The next generation—LeMond, Ron Kiefel, Jeff Bradley, and Greg Demgen—went to the junior world championships and brought back medals. I wasn't in their league—not yet.

I grew up skiing and playing normal childhood games. At school I tried baseball, football, track and field, and soccer. I was always pretty good in those sports because I had a certain amount of natural talent, but I didn't understand the value of hard work. I didn't want to practice. I just wanted to play with my friends and mess around. Then I would show up out of shape at a game or a meet and just die.

In June 1975, the month before I turned sixteen, I saw a stage of the Red Zinger Bicycle Classic, then in its first year and one of the few multiday bicycle races in the United States. The stage took place in North Boulder Park, in my hometown of Boulder, Colorado. The race was so fast, exciting, and colorful, it inspired me. I wanted to race.

Cycling was the perfect sport for me. I was disenchanted with high school. I didn't run with a very big crowd and did little to distinguish myself. Cycling became a statement of my individuality—something that I could call my own. I wasn't doing it because my parents or friends were telling me to do it. That alone inspired me.

Boulder is now the home of many professional and top international-level amateur cyclists, but when I got involved, cycling was still an underground sport in America. I wasn't really sure about what I was doing. I just wanted to do it. I tried to get information, but it was difficult to find. I am also stubborn by nature: once I get an idea, I hold on to it. In the end, my perseverance merged with my talent and I started to get results.

Even though my father, Damon, had competed in twelve-hour American Youth Hostel bike races in Pittsburgh in the early 1950s, I didn't associate cycling with him. My dad and a friend would work all week, and on the weekend go out and ride 150 miles. Records show that in the third annual Pittsburgh Council AYH twelve-hour race in October 1953, my dad, then twenty-five, went 227.8 miles for fourth place. Riders rode a flat circuit that was three-quarters of a mile around in downtown Pittsburgh, near where Three Rivers Stadium is today.

That was when my dad was living in Lima, Ohio. Soon after, he married my mom, Thea Welsh, and they moved to Boulder, where I was born. My parents enjoyed climbing and hiking in the mountains, which is part of the reason they wanted to be near the Rocky Mountains. They weren't involved in cycling. My only sister, Alice, was a good student and a good athlete. I was a lazy student, but I loved athletics. This made my parents a little anxious about me, but they let me find my own way.

In the fall of 1975, after seeing the Red Zinger, my best friend, Peter Thron, said he would be my trainer, but neither of us knew much about training. After school, we would play intramural soccer for a few hours. Then we would meet after dinner at the pinball machines, because Peter was a master of pinball. After a few games, he would announce that we should go for a ride.

It didn't matter that it was dark outside and we had no lights on our bikes. We didn't even bother changing clothes. Just strapped a little light around our jeans and off we went, for twenty-mile rides on country roads around Boulder County. Sometimes before going to school I would ride twenty miles and think that was a big deal. I didn't know any better, so I rode my biggest gear all the time—who would tell me any differently?

In rides out in the country, I would visualize a rider like Dale Stetina of Indianapolis up ahead of me and I would catch him—no matter what. Dale was eighteen when I saw him competing so well in the Red Zinger. He was an early idol. I would imagine myself racing against him. I took it a step further and I beat him.

My first race was a team time trial. I was frustrated with my teammates, because they couldn't go fast enough. I rode off alone to the finish. I had no idea that the time was taken on the third rider, not the leader. I wondered why the officials were laughing at me at the finish. This was only one of many lessons I would learn.

One of my first road races was three laps around the thirteen-mile Morgul-Bismark course south of Boulder. At that time, my racing wardrobe consisted of black wool shorts and cleated shoes, a jersey that was simply a wool long-sleeved T-shirt, and a helmet designed for rock-climbing. But that was standard. Lycra was for swimming suits back then, and one-piece riding suits were still on the drawing table. Wool jerseys were imported from Italy, and expensive.

I was racing against other juniors (ages sixteen to eighteen) and Category IV seniors (entry-level riders nineteen and up). I towed the lead group in for the last few miles and was outsprinted. Joe Leiper, who would later become my first coach, told me after the race, "We've got to teach you how to sprint." But I had finished in second place and I was excited. This was great.

Cycling was the first thing that I really stuck with. What cycling showed me, especially as a teenager, was that dedication, commitment, and focus will get you somewhere. Even though being a cyclist didn't help my school grades or popularity, what it did help was my self-esteem. Cycling gave my life excitement. I was crazy about it.

My parents took more interest in my new pursuit when I won the district time trial and finished second in the 1976 state championship to qualify for the junior boys' national championship road race in Louisville, Kentucky. Dad drove me to my first nationals. In the race, I went 500 yards and got a flat tire. Dad was waiting on the sidelines down the road and saw the pack go past. He looked closely and thought he missed me, until about three minutes later I went by, chasing alone after a wheel change. I kept going on my own until a short distance later, when I got a second flat that forced me out. It was my first big race, and I did poorly. When I saw my father, I was so frustrated that I burst into tears.

We looked at my tires and saw that they were just plain worn out. I had been training and racing on the same tires.

One thing that stands out from my first nationals experience was seeing a red-haired woman named Connie Carpenter racing in the women's event. She was competing in her first national road-racing championships, but she did a whole lot better than I did. She won.

Locally, I started getting good results, but national-caliber races were a struggle. I was outclassed and, often, underprepared. But I was determined to get better. In 1977, I went to Acton, California, for a junior worlds qualifying road race. During the event I was feeling good, and attacked with a kid named Greg LeMond from Reno, Nevada. We were away for several miles before the pack chased and caught us. Greg attacked again and won the race, but I finished out of the top ten.

In another qualifier race, I was riding well when we went around a turn and my wheel fell apart. As the pack went on, I looked up and saw a van loaded with spare wheels that was following close behind. The driver stopped just long enough to ask, "Well, did you bring any spare wheels?" I told him, "No." He drove away. Talk about bad luck—but I learned a lot from these experiences.

Those junior years were a struggle. Back home in Boulder, I did a little better in local races and developed more confidence. Late in the summer of 1977, I drove to Superweek in Milwaukee with my friends Tony Comforte and Alexi Grewal. We were pulled over in Nebraska by the State Highway Patrol at midnight when Alexi was driving. I was sleeping in the back seat when Alexi shouted, "Hey, I'm not old enough to drive!" I quickly jumped in the front seat and exchanged places with him, since I had a license. The policeman shined the flashlight on my face and then in the back seat, where Alexi was now pretending to be asleep. "Nope, you weren't the guy driving," he said to me as he looked at Alexi. "So what's going on?" After I promised to drive the rest of the way on my own, he let us go.

We were teenagers and didn't have any idea what we were doing. I remember doing poorly in the first race and making a lot of excuses afterwards. That made me feel kind of stupid, and I resolved to do better. The next day, I sat directly behind junior national champion Larry Shields for the whole race. I would have followed Larry into Lake Michigan if he went that way. Fortunately, he stayed on course and I followed him to the finish and took third. No more excuses for me. That small success helped me to develop more confidence.

I started to come around at the 1977 Tour de l'Abitibi, a prestigious stage race in eastern Canada for junior riders. At the nationals, I met Tom Chew of Pittsburgh, who invited me to race with him in Canada. I had a good race, winning the points jersey and finishing second overall.

After the race, I drove back to Pittsburgh with Tom and his dad. I spent the fall racing with Tom on the East Coast. This cemented a friendship that set me up to race on the newly forming McDonald's team for 1978, my first year as a senior rider.

In early spring 1978, I moved to Pittsburgh to compete for the McDonald's racing team. I shared an apartment above a garage with team manager Bob Firth. My bed was a small mattress on the floor. Rather spartan, but it was a start. I was now a full-time bicycle racer.

Riding with Tom Chew was important for my early development. He was a good rider who approached the sport analytically. I was lazy and just went out and rode my bike. He couldn't understand how I could achieve the results I got on such monotonous training. Tom showed me that I needed to practice different things to get better—such as climbing techniques and sprinting. He was my first teammate, and I respected him. We balanced each other: he was strong and I was fast. We were a good team.

We went to Colorado for the Red Zinger, the race that inspired me to get into the sport, and I took third in the Vail stage. That did a lot for my self-confidence. The Red Zinger drew racers from Europe, and I was nervous about competing against them. But I did well. That taught me a valuable lesson—that it was all right to put myself in over my head, because I could rise up to the competition.

I finally made my first big impression in Milwaukee during Superweek. Superweek's events culminated in the downtown PAC criterium. It was a big race and many of the big guns were there, including riders like Jim Ochowicz, Wayne and Dale Stetina, and Danny Van Haute. The criterium was a points race; every five laps there was a sprint for points.

Tom was my pilot. I sat on his rear wheel as he led me through the pack to set me up for every sprint lap. Every time we sprinted for the line, I was first. Everybody

I was a first-year senior racing for McDonald's when I won the McDonald's Cup in Pittsburgh,
Pennsylvania, by beating a surprised Kent Bostick right at the line.
                              PHOTO CREDIT: PERSONAL ARCHIVES

started wondering who I was. By the time we finished, I had won and they knew. I
was greasing the big guns.

Tom and I earned a couple hundred dollars. We thought we were rich. My father's
twin brother, Warren, lives in Milwaukee, and we stayed at his home. Tom and I
drove a van around the country to races, especially in the Northeast, Midwest, and

Middle Atlantic. It was common practice to stay in the homes of relatives—or friends, or friends of friends. We rarely slept in a hotel. When we did, we drove around to shop for the cheapest one, and ordinarily shared a room with three or four other riders, which usually meant someone slept on the floor. Saving five or ten dollars was a big deal.

Many people began assuming that I was from Pittsburgh. There are still people who think my hometown is Pittsburgh, because I lived there when I first started to get national-level results.

It was a summer of great times and escalating expectations.

Living Day to Day

Both my parents are college graduates, and when I completed high school in 1978 the expectation was that I would attend college, too. But college was their idea. I wanted to become a bicycle racer. One of my high-school teachers had warned me that I couldn't make a living racing bicycles. I guess I knew he was right at the time, but that had no impact on what I wanted to do. At eighteen, I was living day to day— just doing what I wanted. My ideal was to go to the Olympics, realistic or not. But that was my ideal, and I adjusted my goals step by step and went up the ladder that way.

I had a chance to go to college on scholarship, but not for cycling. I had grown up skiing and had developed into a fairly good cross-country skiier, despite the limited time I had put into it. I had scholarship offers to small schools in Wyoming and Colorado that had strong ski programs. But skiing offered me a short season—only three months long. Cycling was far more appealing, with a season extending eight months and money to be won.

My approach to the sport has been consistent. It's good to try new things, but not all the time. Athletes are classic reachers. They always reach for something that is going to make them better, make the difference in competition. In doing the right things, you have to be aware of the effect that training has on you, be aware of your technique on the bike, and what you're trying to do.

When I want to do something, I focus on it. For instance, when I was nineteen and had started to enjoy some success, my hero was Freddy Maertens of Belgium. He was the best professional rider in Europe. Freddy won fifty-plus races a year, including two world road championships. That was when we didn't have much information on Europeans in the United States. But I got all the old *International Cycle Sport* magazines, which arrived weeks late from England, and really studied the sport. The magazines told the history of professional cycling, at least from the 1960s, and gave me insight into current racing and Freddy's career.

I would take a mental picture of Freddy Maertens to work. In the winter after I came back from Pittsburgh in 1978, I had a dull job at Celestial Seasonings packing tea—assembly-line stuff. I worked the shift from four o'clock to midnight so that I could train in the day. But I got the job because Mo Siegel, who founded Celestial Seasonings and started the Red Zinger, had a soft spot in his heart for cyclists. I would sit there working with this picture in my mind of Freddy Maertens. I would daydream all the details: the way he sat on the bike, how he pedaled, what his legs looked like, how he held his arms and his head. I never tired of that image, but I did tire of the job.

In 1979, I got my first salary as a bike racer—$100 a month riding for the AMF team. It was a good team that included top U.S. road rider George Mount, Jim Ochowicz, Thomas Prehn, Tom Schuler, and the following year, Eric Heiden. We got some additional expense money and a bicycle, but it was the day-to-day prizes that kept me on the circuit. I earned the nickname "Cash Register" for my penchant of ringing up the cash during the prime (short for premium) sprints, which are races within the races for "easy money." Nick Wolf, an importer from New Jersey, put the team together and arranged for the sponsorship. Nick was an eccentric guy who always wore white clothes to the races, but he supported cycling and my team.

Early in the year, I earned a berth on the U.S. national squad that went to Europe for spring races against other national teams. Riding in Europe was eye-opening. I was racing on the roads that the legends had raced on; I was breathing their air and eating their food. I had been on a healthy vegetarian diet before going to Europe. Once in Europe, my diet changed radically to white bread and heavy meat. Further, I went from spinning a small gear to hammering a big gear, even in training. It was intoxicating to see legendary names like Felice Gimondi, Eddy Merckx, and Francesco Moser, still printed across the road on the famous climbs. But the racing brought me to reality. It was very hard.

That summer I proved that I was a national-class rider. I had moved back to Boulder and entered the Red Zinger. The Vail stage was a miss-and-out race, in which the last rider across the line at the end of each lap drops out until only two riders remain to fight it out in a match race. It came down to Australian Phil Anderson and me, and I beat him in the final sprint to win the stage. It was my first stage win in the Red Zinger, and I felt as if I had made it to the big leagues.

By the end of the summer of 1980, Connie and I had become serious about each other. Our biggest problem was geography: She lived in California and I lived in Colorado. At the end of 1980, I sold all the merchandise I had won in races and raised a total of $400. After the first of the year, I got in my Volkswagen Rabbit and drove to Berkeley to join Connie, who was there attending the University of California. Making the trip took all my money, but it was worth it. We stayed together from then on.

I would sit there working with this picture of Freddy Maertens, daydreaming all the details.

Connie changed my life. She made me appreciate other things besides cycling, thereby expanding my personal growth and forcing me to be less self-centered. I had been like a racehorse with blinders on; when I took them off, I saw a whole world out there. Becoming more diverse indirectly helped my own cycling. At the same time, I was able to help Connie to focus on her cycling. We balanced each other despite each possessing strong individualistic personalities. We would stay up occasionally and party all night with friends, but more often we were hunkered in our cozy house reading, writing, or talking. When it rained in Berkeley, we put on our rain gear and took long walks through the neighborhoods all the way to the top of the hills, a thousand feet above the campus, or we would drive to a redwood forest and wander through the hushed shelter of those immense trees. We shared our thoughts and our time. We were comfortable with each other. After she finished school in Berkeley we headed back to Boulder, which suited us better. It was a small, quiet town, and it was my home.

The Dawn of a New Decade

In 1981, Southland Corporation funded the 7-Eleven team, with Jim Ochowicz, who retired from competition to become the team's manager. Jim had competed on Olympic cycling teams in 1972 and 1976, when cycling was still in its counterculture underground days. He helped manage the world and Olympic speed-skating teams in the late 1970s and 1980, when Eric Heiden was at his peak. Jim knew how to take care of athletes, because he had been one. He saw the level of greatness Eric achieved and wanted to bring it to cycling. Eric would be a cornerstone rider on the team. His name carried instant worldwide recognition, and he was a promising cyclist.

The Southland Corporation was a publicly held firm headed by John and Jere Thompson, brothers who took a personal interest in cycling and the team. Doug Thompson, Jere's son, traveled to several races with the team, which was a good experience for him and offered an invaluable education on cycling. Doug acted as a liaison, and that helped keep the team in a favorable position with the company.

7-Eleven got into cycling because they wanted to be a venue sponsor of the 1984 Olympic Games in Los Angeles. They had wanted to sponsor swimming, but it was already spoken for. Cycling was one of the few sports left that needed major corporate support. The Southland Corporation not only built the 333-meter velodrome at Dominguez Hills for the Olympic Games, but also built a training facility in Colorado Springs, Colorado. Each velodrome cost in excess of three million dollars. Over the ten years that they sponsored the team, they spent more than fifteen million dollars. It was an unprecedented commitment in the United States and would probably have continued but for the financial troubles within the company that ultimately forced them to cease sponsorships after 1990.

I was offered a contract for $8,000 to ride with their new team, but it meant signing a three-year commitment with agent George Taylor, whom I hardly knew. Three years sounded like a long time, and I declined. What a big mistake that turned out to be.

In early 1981, I was training in San Diego with a friend and ran into the 7-Eleven team out on the road. I took note of their top-quality clothing and bikes. Their uniformity and professionalism impressed me. That night I had dinner with them, and Jim Ochowicz made a point of showing me their customized team van and introducing me to their full-time mechanic. These were clear signs that I had missed the boat. I felt like groveling right there. I knew I had to get on that team.

Just before I went to San Diego, a promising team offer fell through. That left me in the undesirable position of having to get a temporary job working construction—digging ditches. The manual labor did nothing to help my cycling form. I had left the U.S. Cycling Federation National Team that winter in an argument with the coach, Eddie Borysewicz. I was starting to question the folly of my ways, but I kept riding and doing well, which got me on Connie's women's team as the token male. In 1981, sponsorships and race prizes were nothing like they are today. Connie and I drove our Volkswagen Rabbit to races and slept on the floors of friends' houses.

Connie and I enjoyed considerable success in the Coors Classic. She and her teammates dominated the event in 1981. Because of their success and the attention they received, 7-Eleven decided to start a women's team in 1982. But it was centered around Rebecca Twigg, so Connie maintained her own team identity. I raced well in the Coors Classic in 1981, winning the prestigious Vail stage in a three-up breakaway that included 7-Eleven's Greg Demgen and 1980 Olympic road champion Sergei Sukhoruchenkov of the former Soviet Union.

Jim Ochowicz offered me a contract of $10,000 to ride for them in 1982. This time I didn't have to sign a contract with agent Taylor, and the two-year obligation sounded much better. I accepted. My performance level made a big jump when I got on the 7-Eleven team. It sparked something in me. There was a spark to the team and the dynamics of the individuals.

My first nickname came from the 1980 Olympic trials in Lima, Ohio, when Greg Demgen pegged me as "Thor," after some Canadian bodybuilding rock and roller he had seen on an album cover in a music store. Demgen said, "He looks just like you, Thor." Alan McCormack later set it in stone with his Irish pronunciation, "Tor."

We all had nicknames. They were part of the fun. We raced hard, but we had great camaraderie. Demgen was Doughboy. Danny Van Haute was Beast. Tom Schuler was Plowboy. Jeff Bradley was Brad Dog. Alex Steida was Link, as in missing link. Ron Hayman was Skin. Ron Kiefel was Wookie. Chris Carmichael was the Kid. Eric Heiden was Gomer. I don't remember the origin of all the names, but they have endured. Those were great days, but some of those stories are definitely for another book.

I always had great intensity when I raced. It would just come out, like a rage. In the early 1980s, I was winning thirty races a year. I would get in races and just go wild. When I came on the team in 1982, Ron Hayman was the team leader. He possessed awesome ability and won numerous races. He was solid, smooth, and savvy. I loved to race with him. He accepted me immediately onto the team, but I think I must have frustrated him often with my impatience. In those days, I just couldn't hold myself back.

What I love about bicycle racing is that it's an individual sport as well as a team sport. When I was younger, I didn't get to appreciate the team aspect. Once I joined 7-Eleven, I slowly learned to understand the value of a team. As our friendships evolved, and as the racing evolved, we protected and supported each other. Taken a step further, it became less significant whether *I* won, but that *we* won. And believe me, winning was the priority. Winning was the standard, the expectation. This and the infrastructure of our friendships set us apart.

Getting on the 7-Eleven team also helped make life smoother for Connie and me.

She was riding for Michael Fatka's team, which was Raleigh sponsored and gave her good support. We were struggling to achieve, but not to pay the bills. We lived a schizophrenic existence—nomadic during the season and firmly rooted during the off-season. It suited us.

On October 8, 1983, we were married in her parents' backyard in Madison, Wisconsin.

Trophies

Cycling is a sport that pushes athletes to expand their competition range. You sit in your little pond and you get pretty big. Then you go into a big pond and you flounder. After I became a national-class rider I started racing in Europe, and at first I floundered. But, as always, the confidence and the stepping-stones of goals, or just the expectations, were more important to me. What kept me in the sport was the desire to race, but more than that, I wanted to have an impact.

I am competitive. I needed the constant feedback each weekend race offered— getting nervous, having to prepare, then getting in the race. If you finish well, you feel really good about yourself. It's that constant feedback of racing that really kept me involved. Gradually, I really learned to appreciate and enjoy the training. But initially it was the competition and the feeling of both the fear and the excitement. I was addicted.

While we were riding for trade teams as amateurs, the Olympic program continued through the U.S. national team. I competed as a member of the national team in Europe every season after 1981. We had many coaches and team leaders on those trips, but Tim Kelly was my biggest ally and Eddie B.'s number-one road coach. He saw the stubborn streak I had, and my absolute determination to improve impressed him.

At first we floundered in Europe, like fish out of water. But we learned, and soon got faster and stronger. When we raced in Italy, we used to stay upstairs over a famous cycling bar, the Bar Augusto, which has a shrine to cyclists hung with jerseys of all the famous cyclists of the past half-century. In 1982, the Czech team completely waxed us—just kicked our butts. We thought they were gods. They had their trophies stacked up on a table at the bar. We had one. It was puny.

Alternating with campaigns in Europe and races in America helped raise the level of competition in the United States. The trade teams contributed to making American racing faster and more demanding. More people were devoting themselves full-time to the sport, and improvements became evident in international competition. For several decades, talented Americans, who had won national titles and competed in the Olympics, went to Europe and came home disillusioned. They were rugged individuals (like George Mount and Mike Neel) who were on their own for equipment and lived hand to mouth. We went as a supported team and kept coming back year after year, each time with more speed and a greater arsenal of skills. Each year

Eddie B. and the coaching staff expected more out of us, and we expected more out of ourselves.

We started to score victories against the Europeans on their home ground. In 1983, I won the third stage of the Tour des Ardennes in France. That was my first European victory.

Later in the summer, I won the amateur U.S. national criterium championship, followed a week later by an upset win in the U.S. professional criterium championships. As an invited amateur, I could not claim the title and the twenty-five-thousand-dollar first place prize would have jeopardized my amateur standing. Therefore, the money stayed in a trust fund until 1985, when I turned professional and got the money.

I won a second national championship title as part of the 7-Eleven team in the 100-kilometer (62.5 miles) four-rider team time trial, then went on to win the Pan American Games gold medal in the TTT in Caracas, Venezuela. The momentum was going strong; everything was falling into place.

By the spring of 1984, we were considered one of the dominant amateur national teams. During our trip to France and Italy, victories were common. I was racing with the so-called A team of Ron Kiefel, Doug Shapiro, Thurlow Rodgers, Roy Knickman, and Alexi Grewal. Everyone was flying. We were pushing ourselves and the competition.

I was battling Olaf Ludwig of East Germany in the field sprints. (Ludwig went on to win the 1988 Olympic road race, and in 1989 became the first East German to win a stage in the Tour de France.) Ludwig was fast, and so was I. I was constantly putting my bike in a 53-12—a very big gear—and just pounding to the finish in a duel with Ludwig and the Soviets. Eddie B. just hated the Soviets and one day made a bet with the other coaches that I was going to win. He got the team primed for the finishing sprint. I had to be the first guy through the turn to win the race. The leadout went perfectly and my teammate Doug Shapiro was at the front. All he had to do was take a few more pedal strokes and let me fly through the turn, but sensing a good result for himself, he eased up. The pack swarmed around me, and the best I could do was third. Eddie was so mad at Doug that from then on he didn't trust Doug. It was a move that would come back to haunt Doug later that summer.

Naturally, when we went to Italy we stayed at the Bar Augusto. This time, we had stacks of booty, including a table full of trophies. The Czechs finished behind us in race after race and managed only one trophy. They were asking, "What are these guys doing?"

We were doing things American-style. We ate a lot of salads and whole-wheat bread. We were stretching. One evening after about two weeks at the Bar Augusto, a Czech cyclist came over to our dining table, grabbed a whole-wheat roll, and took it away to sample it. A couple days later we were upstairs in the laundry room, when we heard weird noises. We followed the noises and came upon a room where the whole Czech team was lying on the floor, everyone trying to stretch.

We had done a full turnaround. We showed them we can do things our way and still have success in the cycling world.

Trials

From the end of that European trip to the Olympic Games road race, I faced an escalating series of trials to make the team. The formal trials were in June in Spokane, where I clearly made the time-trial team. The road trials ended with Ron Kiefel in first place trials and Alexi Grewal in second to assure them spots on the four-man road team. I finished third and was at the mercy of the coach's decision. The other riders in question were Thurlow Rodgers, Jeff Pierce, Chris Carmichael, and Doug Shapiro. We all had good form, and we all had to perform.

A "ride-off" in Los Angeles on July 10—my twenty-fifth birthday—and the Coors Classic would lead to the final choice. In Los Angeles, Doug, Thurlow, and I were followed by Tim Kelly in this training "race." We rode conservatively because we were afraid of blowing up, and even though Doug and I felt we could have dropped Thurlow, we never did. The other group was vying for the alternate position, followed by Eddie. Chris Carmichael had a very strong day, locking up the alternate spot.

We were still getting strung along as to who would actually get to ride the race. The final decision would come after the Coors Classic. Eddie B. was tied up with the track riders in Colorado Springs and did not follow the race. Tim Kelly was Eddie's eyes and ears. I rode well in Colorado and I quit the race with two days remaining, at Eddie's request. Thurlow also quit, but Doug, sensing his own victory there, refused. Doug did not realize it, but he was cutting himself out of the Olympic team selection.

Ultimately, my Olympic experience left me with mixed emotions. It started with the final selection procedure, which left my friend Doug out in the cold just one night before the race. Our friendship still suffers from that night in Mission Viejo when Eddie announced the team and Doug was not on the list. At that point, we were all fighting for ourselves and no one questioned Eddie's decision. I did not stand up for Doug that night; I was grateful that I was "in." I had no energy to waste on who was "out," even if it was my best friend, the best man at my wedding. The way that Eddie played the game, you had to look out for yourself. When Doug walked out of the meeting and into the night, he had lost a very big opportunity. And I had temporarily lost a friend.

The strength of our team as a whole and the politics of the team time trial resulted in Eddie B.'s decision to put Thurlow Rodgers in the road race and take Doug out. I know Eddie labored over the decision, and the fact that Doug won the Coors Classic just a week before did little to sway his thinking. It might have even worked against Doug, because Eddie thought that maybe Doug would be satisfied with that. How could he have been? The Olympic race was the showcase, the focus of the entire year and, for some, the focus of an entire career. Thurlow was deserving in many respects—he had had a terrific year—but in the end he made it because he was one of Eddie's favorite riders and Doug wasn't.

Who could argue? Thurlow finished sixth. All four of us on the team finished in the top ten, with Alexi Grewal taking the gold medal. I finished fifth and Kiefel was ninth. It was an unprecedented performance. Alexi had pulled off an upset victory over Steve Bauer to win the 119-mile road race. In third was Dag-Otto Lauritzen of Norway, who would later be my teammate on 7-Eleven for many years. My fifth place was nothing short of devastating. I was crushed.

The women's event was the first on the opening day of the L.A. Games. Our road race started only a couple hours after I watched Connie win the race on a little black-and-white television that was set up in our team pit area about 200 meters past the finish line. I was screaming at the TV—"Go now! Go now!"—because it seemed as if Connie had waited too long to start her sprint. She almost did, because it was a photo finish with Rebecca Twigg. Connie brought her gold medal to the start line after her press conference. "Here it is, you guys," she said, holding her medal out to us. "Go out there and get one, too."

It took me years to overcome the disappointment I felt at not winning the Olympic road race. While I had ridden a good race, I had gone out too hard and given too much early on. I had nothing left in the last lap when it counted. Had the eastern Europeans been at the race instead of boycotting it, I feel that maybe I would have been more conservative and actually had a better chance. I couldn't accept the fact that I had ridden the best race I could ride. It just didn't sink in. Winning was everything.

Everywhere I went with Connie after that race, people would say to her, "Why, aren't you the one who won that bike race?" Then they'd look at me, making the connection that I was her husband, and say, "Oh, you must be her husband—what happened to you?" It seemed as though I couldn't get away from it. It had been hyped in the papers and the television, and I had come away from it a loser.

The week after the road race I had no time to recover for the 100-kilometer four-man team time trial. We spent the week testing equipment that continually malfunctioned. It was arduous and offered me little chance to overcome my disappointment. The night before the race I spent hours standing in the parking lot, arguing with Eddie over the best equipment choices. His choices were too risky. On race day, Kiefel and Knickman were the strong men. We lost Andy Weaver (only three riders need finish) after the three-quarter point to a blown wheel and exhaustion. I was dying, too. As the third rider, I had to stay with Knickman and Kiefel. I was barely able to hang on—dehydrated and physically spent—but I crossed the line with Knickman and Kiefel. Happily, we won the bronze medal.

At the conclusion of the games, we were invited to fly across the country in a post-Olympic victory tour. The Southland Corporation (parent company of 7-Eleven, my sponsor) sponsored it. All the 1984 Olympic medalists were invited to attend and bring a guest. Connie invited her manager, Monica McWhirter, and I invited Danny Van Haute, because he was a good friend, a teammate, and he was engaged to Monica. Three planes were chartered for the tour, with stopovers scheduled in Washington, D.C., New York City, Orlando, and finishing in Dallas, home of the Southland Corporation. It was a continuous party, except that Ron Kiefel and I brought our bikes because we planned on going directly to the amateur Tour of Switzerland, called the William Tell. We were preoccupied with the upcoming race and didn't get to enjoy the party—and it was some party.

The trip started off with a breakfast in Los Angeles with President Ronald Reagan and First Lady Nancy. Olympic medalists had photos taken individually with the President and First Lady. President Reagan recognized that we were a married couple and cheerfully said, "Aw, well, let's make it a foursome." I felt as though we were posing next to cardboard cutouts, not the real thing.

Going Pro

After the Olympics, Connie retired from racing and our lives changed radically. No longer were we on the same schedule. No longer did we ride out the door together. Connie was in demand, and we finally signed on with a top sports agency, ProServ, which was based in Washington, D.C. Steve Disson became the architect of our financial future and did an incredible job, lining up major contracts for Connie, who

Connie retired from competition but not from cycling. Shown here interviewing me for NBC after my victory in the Old Sacramento Stage of the 1985 Coors International Bicycle Classic.

PHOTO CREDIT:
TERRY WING

was going to New York or Washington monthly for meetings and television work—
she was incredibly busy. My focus was on racing in Europe and making the jump to
the professional ranks. My childhood dreams were being realized one after the
other.

The Southland Corporation had committed one million dollars to fund a full
professional 7-Eleven squad with an ambitious program in Europe. This was a
momentous shift in American cycling. Our salaries made substantial jumps, and so
did our expectations. We put the Olympics behind us and launched full force into the
European professional peloton—it was the top of the sport—the place I had
dreamed about. Our goal that year was to ride the three-week Tour of Italy, the
second most important stage race in Europe. The following year, we were going to
do the sport's premier event, the Tour de France. Few in Europe—or the United
States, for that matter—took us seriously, but we were brash. They called us the new
cowboys.

Eurotrash

We started out with the spring season in Europe. It was harsh, but I raced well,
placing often. Ron Kiefel won our first pro race in the Italian season opener, the
Trophe Laiguelia. We raced in Italy primarily, and my best finish was a second in the
final stage of the Tirreno-Adriatico (a race from the Mediterranean Sea, or western
coast of Italy, to the Adriatic sea, or eastern coast). We raced in freezing rain and
snow. After that race, the Italian sports daily *Gazzetta Della Sport* listed me as an
outside favorite for the next race, the infamous Milan–San Remo road race, a 180-
mile Classic race in northern Italy from the industrial center of Milan to the seaside
city of San Remo. I was amped—overamped—to do well and got in a crash that
resulteu in a painfully dislocated finger and forced me to quit the race.

When Richard DeJonckeere, our team director, drove past, he said the car was full
and threw me my bag. He said, "Take the bus that is following." I rode my bike for
miles and I was caught only by three other racers who were also looking for the
promised bus. We rode through the feed zone, but no one was there. They had all
gone ahead. We rode for hours—I with my dislocated finger and big clumsy bag
hanging around my neck. It was a nightmare.

Finally, I turned up onto the main highway—the autostrada from Milan to Nice—
with one other rider (the others continued to San Remo), where we saw a tollbooth
and thought we would hitchhike to San Remo. No luck. After a while, I started to see
team cars heading back to Milan out on the highway. As I scrambled up to the road,
a 7-Eleven team car rocketed by at more than 100 miles per hour. Whoa! We were in
big trouble. I had to get back to Milan, because we were scheduled to leave the next
day. I shared my food with my colleagues, and we kept trying to get a ride.
Fortunately, the tollbooth attendant called the police in San Remo to report us. We
must have looked pitiful. Somehow the police found Richard, who managed to

rescue us—well after dark. You never saw two happier guys than when Richard showed up. We were saved!

After six weeks, we returned to the United States to compete in the more comfortable and familiar Tour of Texas, primarily because the Southland Corporation's corporate headquarters is in Dallas. Our team made a strong showing—I won the overall for the third time and Ron Kiefel finished second.

We knew that for the Tour of Italy in May we needed a strong climber. Andy Hampsten was the rider we needed, but he was still an amateur, riding for the Levi's team. We asked him to join our 7-Eleven team going to the Tour of Italy, which the Italians call the Giro d'Italia. It didn't take long to think it over, and he said, "Why not?"

Another rider we picked up at the last moment was Bob Roll, who was racing as an amateur in Europe. We had met Bob the previous year in Switzerland, and he told us how he had lived in a tent for the entire previous summer just to get by. When Ron Hayman got sick just before the Giro, Mike Neel tracked down Bob and asked him if he would turn pro and ride the Giro. He had three days to prepare. "No sweat," Bob said.

Bob Roll and Davis at the start of Milan–San Remo. Right away I liked this guy. He said, "We are all captains." He was right.   PHOTO CREDIT: BETH SCHNEIDER

Prior to the Giro when we stopped on a training ride to get a drink in a café, someone asked us—in Italian—who was our capitain, *capitano* in Italian. Bob, in fluent Italian, answered, "We are all captains." Right away I liked this guy.

1985 Giro d'Italia

Pro racing in Italy then was like an exclusive men's club. I felt like a caddy in a major golf tournament. I halfway expected Italian superstar Francesco Moser to ask me to go fetch his bike for him. But I got down to business pretty fast.

On the very first stage, I worked with teammate Jock Boyer of Carmel, California, who had been racing in Europe for ten years. He was my pilot. I found Jock in the peloton about thirty miles from the finish, when the pace began accelerating. He guided me through the peloton with great skill. Jock found holes between riders and rode through them with me on his rear wheel. He kept me fresh to prepare for the final sprint as we moved forward. The stage was 137 miles over flat terrain, which kept the peloton of 210 riders together for a mass-pack sprint, spread out curb to curb, with all the riders elbow to elbow.

With one kilometer left (about a thousand yards), I was still up at the front, following Jock's wheel, banging elbows with some big Belgians who wanted to take my place. I didn't flinch and stayed right up there. Then the serious sprint started at 400 meters. I caught Italian sprinter Guido Bontempi's rear wheel. Drafting behind Bontempi in the sprint is something that few riders can do. One hundred meters later, I shot past him and was actually leading. Then one rider sneaked by here and another sneaked by there, followed by another one as we galloped to the finish. At the line, I threw my bike—*wham!*—and was fourth.

Andy was shocked. "You got fourth!" he exclaimed. He realized that we were there not just to fill out the peloton but that the team could do really well. The next day, we had another mass pack sprint. With one kilometer to go, I was up at the front, again in good position. With 200 meters left, Dutchman Johan Van Der Velde was leading, followed closely by Giuseppe Saronni of Italy and me. We started an all-out sprint close to the side of the road, within inches of the fence that lined the course to keep spectators off the road. Van Der Velde is a big man, and when he stands out of his saddle to accelerate he looks like the ultimate Spider Man. With each pedal stroke, his body swayed from side to side. In his shadow were Saronni and I—swaying with him at the front of the mass peloton that was surging at high speed.

Right when I moved in unison with Saronni and Van Der Velde, I felt someone try to go past. His handlebars hit my butt and I heard him career into the fence next to us and then slingshot back across my rear wheel. All this at hair-raising speed. I had to exert all my strength to keep from falling while going all out for the line. I finished seventh. Saronni won. For a moment, my only thought was that maybe I could have beat him if that rider hadn't fallen across my back wheel.

Meanwhile, the television broadcast made it look as if I had deliberately hooked the rider and knocked him down. They kept replaying the incident and "tried" me over and over. Italian spectators, *tifosi*, were outraged. The team director of the fallen rider pointed at me and furiously shouted, "There he is! There he is!" Police had to restrain him to keep him from running over and decking me. The only thing that saved me was that Saronni, 1982 world professional road champion, went on television and said, "It wasn't the American's fault. It was a clean sprint." I was vindicated.

Saronni spoke out in my behalf at a crucial point. In a modest way, I had earned my place at the head of the peloton.

The Italians continued to routinely blame the woes of the peloton on us. At one point when Italian sensation Roberto Vissentini was railing on Andy, Eric Heiden rode up, shook his finger at him, and said in loud, authoritative English, "Shut up man, or *you* are going *home*." We weren't bothered again by Vissentini.

Before the race was over, Andy and Ron Kiefel each took a stage, becoming the first U.S. riders to ever do so. Mike Neel came on board as our manager just prior to the Giro and had a big impact on us. Our team took shape with the additions of Jock Boyer, Bob Roll, and, of course, Andy Hampsten. Neel spoke the language, understood the sport, and understood us. He was the right guy at the right time, and we truly flourished under his tutelage.

1986—Doing It Our Way

In 1986 we entered phase two of the plan, and made preparations for racing the prestigious Tour de France. While Americans like LeMond and Boyer had ridden the Tour, no *American team* had ever been entered. We were making history as we went along. One of the biggest obstacles that we had to overcome was constant criticism from our peers. Despite our obvious commitment and our modest results, we were the brunt of many jokes. We did things our way, in our style, and we had a long row to hoe to gain the respect of the cycling community.

European teams are somber. Americans are more lively. We had to hold on to that. Americans have career options and choose to be bike racers out of passion for the sport. Europeans like to race bicycles, but the sport tends to be just a job, one that keeps them out of menial factory jobs or farm labor. In Europe, cycling is mostly a blue-collar sport. Their worldview is totally different from ours.

Our attitude set us apart, and we became known as a rider's team. European teams are dictatorial and hierarchical. The team director is, by tradition, the boss. He tells everybody what to do, and they do it. The team works for the team leader, and nobody else is expected to get results. This was especially true in Italy. Francesco Moser and Giuseppe Saronni were star riders, but they were completely supported by a cast of really good riders who were never given recognition when they won races because they devoted their careers to Francesco and Giuseppe. This is changing now.

Our team rarely had a designated captain. We rode for the one who had the best chance to win that day. Over the season, everybody had the opportunity to do well. Therefore, we all had a chance for success, which is what had drawn us to the sport years ago. We succeeded individually and we succeeded as a team. No longer was it just a matter of getting paid to do a job, the way the European riders looked upon it; it was more. It had always been more.

One guy that made us the talk of the pack was Bob Roll. I know a few special individuals whom I consider true "one-of-a-kinds." Mike Aisner and Eric Heiden are in that category, but Bob stands at the head of it. He is Bob—the one and only.

Bob comes from Pleasant Hill, California. The first time I went riding with him, he had Spokey Dokes in his wheels—those plastic round pieces that come in bright colors, fasten to the spokes, and slide out to the rim when you ride. Spokey Dokes make clacking sounds as the wheels roll. Usually you see these on the wheels of children, but never on the wheels of a seasoned professional in Europe. But here was Bob Roll with his Spokey Dokes, having a good time checking everyone's reaction to him and to his wheels.

The European way of traveling to a race involves uniformity. Everyone dresses the same, wearing identical team warm-up suits. When we traveled to the 1989 Tour of Sicily, teams flew into the Palermo airport, with every team decked out in their team uniforms.

Bob walked off the plane wearing black cowboy boots, black leather motorcycle pants, a big brown leather jacket with full fringes up and down the sleeves, and a black ten-gallon cowboy hat. He was an eyeful. The European riders couldn't stop staring at him. Italian, Belgian, French, and Swiss riders all were murmuring to themselves in every European language, but you'd keep hearing his name over and over, "Bob" this and "Bob" that.

He had recently discovered roller blades. Upon leaving the plane, he pulled his roller blades out of the backpack he was wearing, strapped his roller blades on, and roller-skated around the Palermo airport. This rather excited the local militia. The Carabiniere, seriously on the alert for terrorists, tote automatic rifles that are locked and loaded. A platoon of Carabiniere suddenly ran from every direction to chase after Bob as he glided around. Bob had made another typical Bob entrance.

Bob became famous in Europe during the 1989 Tour of Italy. He rode to the start of a stage to warm up when the rest of us took the team car. For some reason, Bob had been misinformed about the time of the start and arrived early. He sat around the piazza long before any of the riders got there. But the sign-in table was set up, and reporters were milling around. They wondered what this 7-Eleven rider in the snakeskin warm-up tights was doing. So they went over and started talking to him. He had the stage all to himself and gave them Bob Roll industrial strength. Wow.

He told them that he is part Indian, lives in a tepee, and hunts deer in the winter. There he sat, this outlandish individual with a giant feather for an earring, spewing this incredible story, and the jaded cycling press just lapped it up. Feature stories about "Bob Roll, who lives in a TePee . . ." went all over Europe. I don't think he told a single truth, but it didn't even matter. His fame was set. That's Bob Roll. He can tell any story so well that whether it's true or not is beside the point.

In every sport there is usually someone who is considered an enforcer. You see this in hockey or basketball, where one guy might be responsible for making sure that the star players don't get worked over. Well, Bob Roll makes an intimidating enforcer. During the 1990 Tour de France, when Steve Bauer of our team got into a breakaway on the first day and took the race leader's yellow jersey, Bob filled the role as enforcer. When Steve had the yellow jersey, Bob would sit up at the front of the peloton and glare at the riders in the most intimidating way to discourage anyone from going off the front.

Bob was part of the American character in the European peloton. Maybe he was too much for some guys. But Kiefel and I loved him. Having someone like Bob on the team helped keep us lively, keep us American. He made light of all the silly traditions that Europeans have—the uniformity, and the seriousness that hangs over the sport if you let it. Because the sport is so hard and demanding, the humor tends to be drained from most riders. That's where Bob fit in. He could cut through the tension with his wit. We needed that to survive.

1986 Tour de France

On this, our inaugural Tour de France, in a short morning stage, we did more than make a little history. We turned the cycling world upside down. And before we could blink, we were right side up again. It was a crazy day.

Canadian Alex Stieda of our 7-Eleven team had broken away and collected all the time bonuses, all the hill-climb points, and all the intermediate sprint points. He wound up with every jersey in the whole race, including the prized yellow jersey for being the overall leader of the 210 starters from more than fifteen countries. Here was the 7-Eleven team, the first American team *ever* in the Tour de France, and the French and everybody else were shaking their heads, saying, "I don't believe this American luck! This is ridiculous!"

That afternoon was the team time trial, and we fell completely apart. Alex was shattered. He was so tired from the morning effort and ensuing excitement that he could barely hang on. Then we went around a turn that had a traffic island and our last three riders hit it and crashed. It was just a disaster. Alex got dropped. We had to send two riders back to help tow him. He barely made the time limit—by thirty

The first American team to ride the Tour de France. From the top left: Chris "Kid" Carmichael, Ron "Wookie" Kiefel, Raul Alcala, Eric "Gomer" Heiden, Bob "Bobke" Roll. Bottom row from left to right: Doug "Bullet" Shapiro, Alex "Link" Stieda, and me, Thor. Our team was truly American, including Raul from Mexico and Alex from Canada. We turned the cycling world upside down on the first day. (Not in photo: Jeff "Pepe" Pierce.)

PHOTO CREDIT: KAREN SCHULENBURG

seconds. In one day, he went from being the first non-European ever to wear the yellow jersey to nearly dropping out of the race.

It was like the biggest high and the lowest low you could get in one day. Samuel Abt, an editor for the *International Herald Tribune* in Paris who was covering the Tour for *The New York Times,* asked if we had ever even ridden a team time trial. His question made me so mad, I couldn't talk to him for two years. I was in such a mood to be so offended, but now I can laugh and think, "Yeah, we must have looked like total dorks."

The next day, I ended up making the right move at the right time and I got into a breakaway that went off the front. There were a dozen of us, including Dag-Otto Lauritzen of Norway, Charley Mottet of France, and Federicho Echevez of Spain. Everybody was working efficiently in a wheel-to-wheel paceline, except for a Dutch rider and a Swiss rider, who stayed at the back to draft and save their energy. The rest of us alternated taking fast pulls at the front to keep the pace high. We had about fifty miles left and worked hard. Our lead grew to two minutes.

Lauritzen turned to me and said, "This is the chance of a lifetime." That is how much it means to win a stage of the Tour de France.

With twelve miles left, Echevez took off. Nobody went after him. He went up the road and disappeared. That made me feel disappointed, but relaxed, because I thought we were racing for second place. When I saw the sign beside the road that said we had five kilometers (3.1 miles) to go, I looked back and saw the peloton thirty seconds behind us. With four kilometers to go, they were twenty seconds behind. With three kilometers left, they were at ten seconds.

But the road leading to the finish had a lot of turns. When we rounded a corner where the road sign read one kilometer to go, I was riding in the last position in the break. I looked back and saw they weren't going to catch us. I planned my sprint perfectly. It was an uphill finish. *Boom!* I took off, hit stride, and the two riders who hadn't worked at all during the breakaway were battling me for the stage.

I passed everybody. Coming to the line, I eased off and made a little token push— or *throw,* as it is called—across the line. I thought I was sprinting for second place. John Wilcockson, the English journalist, was right at the line and told me I had won the stage.

"What are you talking about?" I asked him. "What about Echevez?"

Wilcockson told me he had a flat miles from the finish. Nobody in our break had seen him, but we had passed him beside the road with his crippled bicycle.

My big statement was "I can't believe it! I can't believe it!" And I really couldn't, because I didn't know that I had won. I won by only two inches. People told me it seemed I eased off at the end of the race, which is true. I was thinking, "It's only second." It turns out that I almost blew winning a stage of the Tour de France.

I just backed into my first Tour de France stage victory. Then, of course, everybody was saying, "I don't believe these Americans! This is impossible! How could they have a stage win, and the yellow jersey?"

But as the three-week Tour went on, I remember struggling desperately. It was so hard and so fast on the flats, and so hilly and hot in the mountains. You never got a break. There were times toward the end of each day's stage when I would be fighting to hold position—around every turn, up every hill, down every descent, along all the straights. The riding was so fast. I'd look back under my arm and see only bikes that matched mine—my teammates—and I'd know I was in trouble: Most of our ten-rider team was at the back. I'd think, "Oh, man! This is desperate!"

I broke my hand in a crash after seventeen days. I was exhausted, and the crash was partly because of my fatigue. Right after that, Eric Heiden crashed badly in a mountain descent and was airlifted out. Only five of our 7-Eleven riders survived, but that was a triumph in itself. We were struggling for respect, and slowly gaining it. Nineteen eighty-six was the year of LeMond's first victory. His teammate Andy Hampsten—who had gotten a contract based on his 1985 results with us in Italy—finished a remarkable fourth in his first Tour. The American presence was emerging. We were no fluke.

1987 Tour de France

The next year I went in with a whole different perspective. I was confident. Our preparation included the ten-day Tour of Switzerland. My teammate, Andy Hampsten, won it for the second time, the first U.S. rider to win what is arguably the fourth most prestigious stage race in Europe.

In the 1987 Tour de France, I was getting consistently good placings—fourths and fifths—in every stage. But in the last fifty meters, riders like Sean Kelly of Ireland and Eric Vanderaerden of Belgium would pass me. Then I had an auspicious feeling that I was going to win Stage 12, to Bordeaux. I was feeling really good, getting stronger and more confident. Two days before the Bordeaux stage, I told our team director Mike Neel, "I'm going to win the Bordeaux stage." He said, "Sure, sure," but he didn't sound convinced.

That day turned out to be a really long stage—142 miles from Brive-la-Maillarde to Bordeaux. It was hilly and hot. A break went away with about thirty miles to go. I was worried that I had missed a great opportunity, but the Italian squad, Super-Confex, went to the front of the peloton and started working. We went faster and faster, and the break came back.

I was so relaxed and calm, I knew I was going to do the right thing. I always stayed out of the wind to protect all my energy exclusively for that burst to the finish. I knew Bordeaux's finishing circuit—two laps around a three-kilometer course. It was as if someone were telling me I would be in the right place, be on the right wheel. And I just seemed to do it.

Racing the last part of each stage is always intense, especially when there is a field sprint. We're talking about 210 professional cyclists at the top of their game, and the speed is as high as they can make it. You try to maintain your position in the peloton.

At that speed—in excess of thirty-five miles an hour—every time you go into the wind, you lose a little off your top speed. You have to be as fresh as possible when you give everything for the final 200-meter burst.

When we hit Bordeaux's finishing circuit, I was the fifth rider in the line, feeling comfortable with the speed. Around the course, I held my position. With about 400 meters left, two sprinters—Dutchmen Teun Van Vliet and Jean-Paul Van Poppel—started battling elbows for the lead. That was when I took off. I felt powerful. Previously, I had sprinted and led but got passed. This time, I felt I was going to make it alone. It was a glorious feeling to rocket to the finish, knowing nobody could beat me.

That year we earned a new Peugeot car for each stage win, and our team racked up three wins when Dag-Otto took Stage 14, from Luz to Ardiden, and Jeff Pierce won in Paris on the final day. But the trophy that I got to keep was the traditional silver statue of France that stands five inches tall and has the Tour route etched in it.

1987 Tour de France. Twelfth stage, 142 miles (from Brive-la-Maillarde to Bordeaux). My team manager didn't really pay attention when I told him that I would win, but I knew that I would. I just knew it.

PHOTO CREDIT:
PRESSE SPORTS, PARIS

Signifying the stage victory are two diamonds, one at the start point and one at the finish point of the stage, with the route between paved in gold.

1988: The Crash, The Giro D'Italia, The Coors

My season was almost over before it began in 1988. I had my head down chasing the peloton after getting tangled up behind a huge group crash in the 169-mile Belgian Classic, Liege–Bastogne–Liege. Crashes are common on the narrow, cobbled roads of the great European hinterland. We ride so far above our physical capacity at times, in such atrocious weather, that even the best cyclists in the world cannot avoid accidents. Pulling myself out of that tangled web of wheels and Lycra, I chased like a madman. I had been fourth in a semi-Classic only a few days before, and so wanted to use my early-season form to gain a good result on that April day.

When you fight to regain the peloton in such a race, you see nothing but the road beneath your wheels and the promise of rest and security in the brightly colored jerseys ahead. You are conscious of your breathing, of the searing pain in your legs and lungs, of your pounding heart, but there is no time to recognize the pain. You take for granted everything and nothing, and it was the vast nothingness that found me halfway through the rear windshield of the Isoglass team car before I could think or react. And even before I could feel, there was the fountain of blood spilling from . . . where—my face? my arm? My blood was everywhere.

The driver had stopped suddenly, pulling not to the side but letting his car stand across the middle of the narrow road. One of his team had been involved in another mishap in the group ahead. He had eyes only forward and violated a cardinal rule of follow-car etiquette by not pulling off to the side, for not signaling his intention. Would I have avoided him if he had acted differently? I don't know. In my own way, I, too, had violated an unwritten rule that says a rider should keep his head up. But I was chasing the good feelings from the days before. The knowledge that I was having a good day overshadowed any common sense. The race, of course, went on without me. Ironically, Isoglass, the race-team sponsor, manufactures safety glass, but the car I struck did not have Isoglass in the rear window.

I was badly cut up and would need more than 150 stitches to the left side of my face and in my left arm. Alex Steida stopped when he saw me lying in a pool of blood and was with me in the ambulance going to the hospital. He kept telling me jokes, even though he was looking at the gaping lacerations in my face. He never let me know how bad it was. Alex and I had had our differences in the past, but at that moment he was the best friend I ever had. And remains so. I would never put a value on friendship with my teammates. The sport is small and extremely personal. I know that I couldn't stay with the sport without that camaraderie. Cycling has truly been my fraternity.

Our team had its ups and downs in Europe, but in 1988 we scored the biggest coup when Andy won the Giro. Two weeks into the 2,256-mile race, he took over the lead high up in the Italian Alps during a fierce snowstorm in the Gavia Pass, at 8,600 feet altitude. The stage began in relatively mild conditions, but deteriorated rapidly. Fortunately, Jim Ochowicz knew that the weather was bad ahead of time and waited on top with extra clothing. Without warm, rainproof clothing and foot coverings, we never could have finished. We rode through a blizzard with six inches of snow and very limited visibility. Andy pressed on, undaunted by the extreme conditions. Eric Breukink of Holland caught Andy to win the stage, but Andy took the overall race lead.

Only 124 of the 199 starters reached the finish that day. Bob Roll finished with a core temperature in the danger zone for hypothermia. It was scary, but we had no time to fret over the cold—we had a job to do.

Andy was "on," and he rode beautifully. He absolutely rose to the occasion, winning two stages and never wavering as the leader. He was clearly the dominant rider. Over the final week, we had to beat back daily challenges to keep Andy in the race leader's pink jersey. In that final week, the race was basically our 7-Eleven team defending Andy's lead against the powerful Dutch Panasonic team, trying to get Eric Breukink into the lead, and the Italian Carrera team, working for the Swiss Urs Zimmerman.

It was a great feeling, helping Andy win the Tour of Italy in 1988. The feeling of camaraderie generated from that experience is long-lasting and supersedes my two stage wins in the Tour de France. We relied on each other, and it was part of what kept us going and kept us from quitting. We were cogs in the machine, each helping to drive the motor that was 7-Eleven. So much of what we did was against the odds, and we could not have done it without each other. Many of us were the class of 1984. We had done so much together, pioneered a whole new frontier. Race wins were few and far between—we savored each of them to the very maximum.

Back Home

Over the years, the Coors Classic race was very good to me. The race gave me the unique opportunity to compete in my home state against top international stars, including five-time Tour de France champion Bernard Hinault of France. Because I had done well over the years, racking up an all-time record of twenty-two stage wins, I drew considerable press attention, which helped foster my career and bolstered sponsor interest.

The 1988 Coors Classic started with a 3.1-mile prologue time trial in San Francisco, wending through city streets that led up a steep climb to Coit Tower, which overlooks the bay. Much to the surprise of many and to my own personal delight, I won the prologue. My teammates Pierce, Hampsten, and Stieda all took the lead during parts of the race. Ultimately everything fell into my lap in the final days and I took the lead after a strong ride in a mountainous stage leading into Copper Mountain Resort, Colorado. By the time we got to Boulder, Ron Kiefel threw up his hands as the winner of the last stage and I savored the overall victory.

But my best memory was in having the opportunity to give the overall prize—a red BMW 320i convertible—to our team manager, Jim Ochowicz. We called Och up to the podium when we took the team prize and I presented him with the keys to the car—his new car. He was floored.

Over the previous eight years, Och had sacrificed a lot to be with us, to support us, and to nurture us. None of us could have done it without his vision and his confidence. In turn, he earned our respect and trust. He knew, too, that at times we responded to his tough direction and at other times we needed to blow off steam. We thrived under his direction. Over the years, he had earned the nickname of "Rock," because he was rock steady and his support was unwavering. But up there on the victory stand on the final day of the 1988 Coors Classic, with the keys to his new car in his hand and that childish grin on his face, well . . . I thought I actually saw him waver a bit. Yes, I did.

By 1990, when I had accomplished much of what I set out to do in cycling, both my personal and professional lives were changing. Cycling had become a business for me—aside from my racing, I had contracts with many of my sponsors. Our Carpenter/Phinney Bike Camps were moving to Beaver Creek Resort, I had formed a partnership with Ron Kiefel and opened a Boulder bike shop named the Morgul-Bismark, and Connie and I had invested in Pearl Izumi, which is a Boulder-based leading manufacturer of clothing for cycling, running, and skiing. I had signed a long-term contract with Ben Serrotta to help him design and promote Serotta bicycles.

But what really started the change in my life was when Connie gave birth to our first child on June 27, 1990. We named him Taylor. A few hours after he was born, I got on a plane and flew to France for the start of the 1990 Tour.

On the opening day, my Canadian teammate Steve Bauer broke away and donned the yellow jersey. We helped keep him in the jersey for ten days. But I will remember that Tour for what I didn't do—I didn't quit. I suffered in the Alps, finishing just under the time limit. Then, with just four days left until the finish, I suffered heatstroke and again wondered if I would be another Tour casualty. I did not win a stage in 1988, but I finished strongly. In 1989, I did not start the Tour due to injury. It is said that the measure of your professional career is in how many Tours you finish. You can understand my intensity and determination to "just finish." And I did. So I had batted .500 in Tour performances, won two stages, and suffered through more than 7,000 career miles of rough Tour riding.

But at the end of the year, the 7-Eleven team was taken over by a new sponsor, Motorola. I wanted to devote more time to racing in the United States to be closer to my family. It was time for a change, and I accepted a contract to race for the Coors Light Racing Team.

Surprising everyone—Coors Light took the team title at the Tour Du Pont in 1991. From left: Greg Oravetz, Alexi Grewal, me, Scott Moninger, Steve Swart, Roy Knickman, and Michael Engleman.   PHOTO CREDIT: BETH SCHNEIDER

Any doubts I might have had about my decision went away in the opening stage of the Tour Du Pont in May 1991. I won the pack sprint to take the 106-mile stage in Wilmington, Delaware. The Tour Du Pont has become America's premier stage race, picking up where the Coors Classic left off in 1988. It is a professional race that offered $350,000 in cash prizes and drew riders from fifteen countries competing in fourteen seven-rider teams. Ten days later, I finished the 1,100-mile event wearing the salmon-colored points-leader jersey. My Coors Light team beat some of the best squads in the world for the $10,000 team prize.

Three weeks later, I took the U.S. national professional road championship in Philadelphia at the 156-mile CoreStates road race. Sometimes it seems like enough. I've exceeded any expectation I ever had. But when you ask me how long will I race, Connie knows. "Two more years," she says. But then, she's been saying that since 1984.

Well, my old high-school teacher warned me that there was no way to make a living from cycling. Boy, was he wrong.

SECTION 1

THE BASICS — GET STARTED RIGHT (Connie)

The Process of Equipment Selection and Setup

GOING SHOPPING

It's been a long time since I had to go into a bicycle shop to buy a bike, but I know it can be an intimidating and overwhelming experience. The information most bike shops give is inconsistent and leads to confusion. There are myriad bicycle choices that extend well beyond the color choice. Because bicycles are an expensive investment, you want to be sure to select the bike that is best for you.

Shop for a shop first. Ask your friends or other cyclists where they shop—and why. When you go into a shop, find out if the employees enjoy riding their bikes— and ask them what kind of riding they do. If they don't ride, do you feel you can trust their recommendations? Is there a good mix of employees? By that I mean a good ratio of men and women, and a good mix of bike specialists—off-road riders, road cyclists, racers, and tourists. It is critical that the employee listen to your needs, respect your interests, and be courteous. A friendly and courteous staff is essential, but they must also be knowledgeable and consistent. Beware of the shop with heavy-handed tactics. What you need is a well-balanced shop, both in the quality of employees and the quality of the merchandise; in short, a shop that you can trust.

Finally, trust your own impression. If you feel ill at ease, go elsewhere. If you feel good in the shop, stay with it.

Every store should make it a policy to service your newly purchased bike at least once and preferably two or three times for *free*. This ensures that your bike will run smoothly during the normal break-in period, when cables may loosen and need minor adjustments. If you get a "great deal" but don't feel comfortable enough to want to go back for the all-important maintenance visits, your "great deal" might end up costing you in the long run.

One of the reasons that we opened Morgul-Bismark Bicycles in Boulder in 1989 was to provide a place for people to get solid, consistent advice on bicycles, componentry, and clothing. We have had many bad experiences in bike shops across the country and wanted to create a place where we could help people enjoy the sport, not be turned off by it. The store's success hinges on the positive feelings people have when they leave the store; otherwise, they won't come back and neither will their friends. Again, if you feel uncomfortable in a store, find another one. Hopefully, you will have some choice (in Boulder there are over a dozen specialty bike shops, which makes for healthy competitiveness in pricing, service, and products).

What are you in the market for? First, decide what price range you can handle. Bikes range in price from $300 to more than $3,000, depending on the quality of the frame and the components. Custom-built frames are more expensive, because they are labor-intensive to build, due to the great care and quality of material that goes into each one. Quality frame building is an art that a factory cannot match. Factory-built frames are less expensive but have less quality control; one frame might be perfect, another out of alignment. When it comes to evaluating your investment, try to envision where you plan to be in a year with your riding. Will you ride daily? Will you ride only on weekend tours? Will you race?

Most people tend to underbuy, then have to spend considerably more to buy a new frame or bike the next season to meet their performance demands. This is especially true of people who buy a mountain bike for road riding. Mountain bikes are slow on the road compared with road bikes. People often buy mountain bikes and then realize they should have purchased the road bike in the first place. You need not buy the most expensive bike on the market just to beat your training partners. What you want is a reliable, relatively light bike that is *your size.*

The Serotta-built Coors Light Team bikes are each valued at $3,000—and worth every penny. This price is a reflection of the bike's labor-intensive custom-built frame and its high-end state-of-the-art componentry. The Shimano STI handlebar gear-shifting system *alone* retailed for over $600 in 1991, but it is a performance system that Davis would gladly pay for—because of its effectiveness. (As the handlebar shifting is duplicated by other companies, the price will inevitably come down.)

You can find great values for under $1,000, but they are getting harder to find. If you are on a low budget, you might try to buy a *used* racing bike. Davis bought his first two racing bikes from a friend. The second bike was a silver Italian Masi frame that lasted through almost five seasons of racing. I bought my first racing bike from Olympian Jim Ochowicz in 1977 for $500. I rode that bike—a relatively heavy but reliable Belgian factory frame—for several years, including during two world championship medal-winning rides. Frames are built to last, but Davis gets at least one new bike every season because he rides them harder than average. A few months for Davis may be a lifetime of riding for someone else.

Buying a used bike presents complications similar to those involved in buying a used car—you don't want to get someone else's lemon. A used racing bike can be a real value, but as with buying a used car you have to be careful. Check whether the bike has crashed severely enough to throw it out of alignment. This will primarily affect your steering, bike control, and overall comfort.

A simple ride around the block and a no-hands test—in which you take your hands off the bars to see how the bike wants to ride, not how you are steering it—will tell you what shape the bike is in. If the bike veers to the right or left, it is out of alignment and you might want to reconsider. If you have a good rapport with a bike shop, they may take a look at it to see if it is in alignment, using tools for this purpose. Also, look the frame over carefully for dents. Used racing bikes hold their value primarily because the frame and the componentry are built to last.

PHILOSOPHY OF A GOOD BIKE FIT: A PERSONALIZED PROCESS

A good bike fit is imperative not only for comfort but also for minimizing potential for injury.

Dr. Andy Pruitt, director of the Western Orthopedic Sports Medicine group in Denver, Colorado, has treated most of our injuries for the past decade. Andy is a world-class cyclist himself and has made the science of cycling his business, treating more than five hundred cyclists who have had injuries that stem from improper fit on the bicycle. As he says, "Cycling is a marriage between the human body, which is somewhat *adaptable*, and a machine that is somewhat *adjustable*." He finds that the ultimate riding position for maximum speed is secondary to the higher priority: an injury-free, pain-free fit. Andy finds that the fixed connecting point—the shoes and the pedals—are the root of most problems. The floating-pedal systems, like the Time System, are ideal because there is no loss of power and they allow for some movement. The natural rotation of the tibial bone (your large shinbone) is to move *in* as you push down in your pedal stroke. If your foot is fixed, your knee must absorb this rotation, which is where most physical problems begin. By having some float in your shoe, the extraneous motion of the knee is minimized, alleviating potentially chronic knee ailments.

Chronic injuries occur over time. If your foot is improperly set on the pedal, and you pedal at a cadence of 90 RPMs, then you will take 5,400 pedal strokes per hour, per leg. Riding ten hours per week works out to roughly 54,000 pedal strokes per week. Added up week after week, it's easy to understand why injury occurs.

Performance on the bike depends on the ability of the muscles to transmit energy—power—through the pedals. A poorly fitted bike will impair your ability to transmit power and inhibit your breathing. Improper fit puts you at risk for injury, especially to the knee and back. You may notice that your feet or hands fall asleep, and your shoulders and seat get stiff and sore, all of which are symptomatic of a poor fit.

We have been fitting people to their bikes for more than six years at the Carpenter/ Phinney Bike Camps. Our approach is personal, so we look at each rider on his or her bicycle when it is mounted on a stationary home trainer. We work with our experienced staff to critically assess each person's riding style first, then try to find a fit that works for each person, working within the constraints of the person's anatomy, physiology, and bicycle. Sometimes simple adjustments to the angle of the handlebar or the seat make the biggest differences. Other times, major alterations are required. This person-by-person approach is the only one that makes sense, because we are each very similar yet very different. None of us is truly *normal*.

We have noticed a positive trend in the last few years. Our campers seem to be better positioned on their bikes than they were five or six years ago, when almost 90 percent of our riders needed some major fit adjustment. Now we tend to make more minor adjustments, because people seem to be better set-up on their bicycles. That means someone (coaches, bike shops, etc.) out there is doing a better job. Bravo.

Bike fit is a personal matter. Even though you may *want* to develop a position that mirrors Greg LeMond's or Miguel Indurain's, you must let your own anatomy dictate your position. Be careful with formulas and systems that are designed for "normal" body types, because who's to say what is normal? Formulas give you a starting point but from there bike fit becomes highly personalized. A little science and a lot of fiddling will yield a good fit. Take the time to get it right. Sometimes even the most minor changes make the biggest differences.

Davis and his former 7-Eleven teammate Jeff Pierce have identical inseams. Current formulas might indicate that their bike frames would be identical—which they are. But Jeff's saddle is two centimeters (three-quarters of an inch) lower than Davis's. Davis found this out the hard way when he had to use Jeff's bike after a mishap during a stage in the Coors Classic. The primary reason for the discrepancy is that Davis has a pointy-toe pedaling style; Jeff has a more flat-footed style. Their individual musculatures dictate their pedaling styles, which in turn accounts for the seat-height difference.

Frame size is static—you can't change what you have, but you can make adjustments by changing the handlebar-stem length and height, the seat height, and saddle position. So if your frame size is approximately correct, you can make it work with a few adjustments. Generally, it is easier to work with a frame that's too small than a frame that is too large.

FRAME SELECTION

There are three points of contact that the cyclist makes with the bicycle—the buttocks on the saddle, feet on the pedals, and hands on the handlebars. The relationship of these three points relative to the bottom bracket (where the axle for the pedals goes through the frame) is what establishes the criteria for determining a frame that fits you.

Historically, frame size was derived from the book *Cycling*, published by CONI (Italian Central Sports School) in 1972, which was the Italian cycling bible. Several formulas are presented, all of them based on *averages*. These formulas are the basis for what is used today to generate a best-guess frame size, and other formulas have been derived more recently. Is this accurate enough? Does it take into account variables like different riding styles, asymmetrical limbs, and differing anatomical postures? Of course not, but these measurements can be used as a starting point, with an accuracy of plus or minus two centimeters, which is significant.

Ben Serotta, a master frame builder from upstate New York, has built Davis's frames for most of the past decade. Because of the demand for foolproof sizing, Serotta has developed a tool for his consumers. Available through Serotta dealers, it is called the SizeCycle. The rider sits on this stationary bicycle that allows for total adjustment of positioning. It is adaptable for alternative saddles and different handlebar sizes and styles (which can affect size). The SizeCycle enables the cyclist to pedal with resistance to find the natural riding posture. After finding the correct posture, the cyclist then has three different positions for comfort—hands on the tops of the bars, on the brake hoods, and in the drops. This setup enables the rider to determine the following: ideal frame size and frame geometry; stem length and height; saddle style, saddle position, and height; and bar style, width, and height.

If you do not have access to a SizeCycle, you might find a bike-shop technician who is well versed in this area. Many shops recommend other systems, like the Fit Kit, which are formula systems based on averages.

Inseam formula. Randy Gaffney, manager of Morgul-Bismark Bicycles, likes to get a customer started by measuring his or her inseam first. Take this measurement by standing on the floor in your stocking feet, and measure from the floor to your pubic bone. By taking two-thirds of this number (multiply the inseam by 0.65), you can determine an approximate estimate of your seat-tube length. Seat tubes are traditionally measured from the center of the bottom bracket to the center of the lug at the top of the seat tube. The lug is the piece of tubing that the tubes fit into at the joints. Most steel bikes have lugs. Note that some manufacturers measure to the top of the lug (which is the center top of the seat tube). Establishing the top tube length is a little more complicated, and it makes more sense to evaluate this length on a fully set-up bike. We will discuss this later.

Demystifying Frame Geometry

Frame angles refer to the angles at which the seat tube and head tube are joined. These generally have a range from seventy-two to seventy-five degrees. (See diagram.)

The function of the seat angle is to enable the rider to place the saddle in the proper position relative to the bottom bracket, fore and aft. Cyclists with proportionately longer upper legs (femur) will ideally have frames with a shallower seat-tube angle. Cyclists with shorter upper legs will have a steeper seat-tube angle. Generally, seat-tube angles go from steeper to shallower as they get larger. However, the characteristics of both frame angles also determine the responsiveness and comfort of the ride.

Steering geometry refers to the combined effect of the fork rake, or fork offset, and the head-tube angle. If you want a bike to turn quickly, the head-tube angle should be steeper, and to maintain stability, the fork offset should be reduced (which

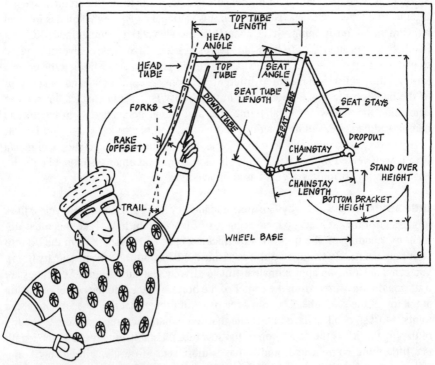

The vocabulary of frame building—part science and part art.

means the fork will be shorter and have less bend in it). The trade-off in quicker handling is less shock absorbency. When comfort and more shock absorbency are desired, the fork offset should be lengthened for a concomitant slackening of the head-tube angle.

The seventy-five-degree angle is the *steepest* seat-tube angle readily available for road riding. The result of the steeper angle is to tighten up—or shorten—the wheelbase (measured from rear hub to front hub). A steeper head-tube angle gives the bike quicker steering capability. This type of frame gives you a position that is farther forward over the pedals. A steeper-angled bike is typically more rigid, or stiff, which means that the bike does not absorb the road shock, *you will*. This will be noticeably less comfortable on longer (over two-hour) rides. This type of frame is also dubbed a "criterium" frame because of its wide use in the shorter, tighter turning races indigenous to America. If you have shorter thigh (femur) length, this type of design will enable you to find the correct fore-aft bike fit more easily.

Alexi Grewal, 1984 Olympic champion, has developed an extreme bike position that works for him. He has a recurring hip problem that has led him to sit very far forward, rotating his hips in a way that enables him to ride pain-free. His severely angled (seventy-eight-degree) seat tube and fully forward saddle put him directly over the pedals. The disadvantage of this position for Alexi is that he sits higher and puts more weight on his arms, but it is effective for him.

The other extreme of frame design is the *relaxed* frame, which has a seventy-two-degree angle. This type of frame is also called *laid back*. When you compare this type of frame to a steep one, you can see the difference that a few degrees makes. The steep bike appears very upright, whereas the relaxed frame appears to lay back toward the rear wheel. The relaxed frame gives you a more comfortable ride, but may be less quick-handling due to the longer wheelbase and steering geometry. The more relaxed frame puts the rider farther back behind the bottom bracket. Long-distance road specialists and tourists favor this type of frame geometry.

Frames with an angle of seventy-three or seventy-four degrees represent the middle of the road and are multipurpose. Davis prefers a seventy-four-degree angle because it gives him responsiveness and comfort, but, more important, because it gives him a good fit.

If you need a frame smaller than 50 centimeters (19.5 inches), you will find that your comfort may be compromised. The top tube may be too long for you because the frame must accommodate the standard twenty-seven-inch wheels, forcing you to have a shorter stem than desirable. The short stem, then, puts your weight far behind the steering center (your head tube and fork) and diminishes your ability to control the bike. This is a compromise that works well.

Some manufacturers are designing these smaller frames with smaller wheels. One option is to use a 24-inch front wheel, which helps to shorten the wheelbase but has two distinct disadvantages: you have to carry two different-size spare tires, and at higher speeds, the different-size wheels handle differently. The other, more

*1984 Olympic gold medalist Alexi Grewal (left) has an extremely steep seventy-eight-degree
seat tube which puts him up and over the pedals. Notice how far forward his hips are in
contrast to Dave Farmer (right), who has a more conventional road position.*

PHOTO CREDIT: JOHN KELLY

common, option is two 26-inch wheels. Practically speaking, your choices are
narrowed with a smaller frame, but you are advised to shop for a frame builder or
manufacturer that specializes in smaller frames.

EVOLUTION OF THOUGHT ON BIKE FIT

Davis's case study of one: himself

My ideas about frame design and performance have changed over time, as
has my riding position. Until I turned professional in 1985, my seat-tube
angle was a steep seventy-five degrees, and the seat position, measured with
a dropped plumb line from the tip of the seat to the ground, was about three
centimeters behind the center of the bottom bracket.

As I started riding more as a professional in Europe, however, my position
slowly changed. During the longer races, my neck and shoulder muscles
often became very tense and sore. I began to realize that my position was
not very aerodynamic. When you ride in such a compact style, your arms

are so close to your legs that when you are tired you tend to sit upright. I must have looked like a reverse wedge going into the wind. With the intensity and difficulty of European professional racing, I needed to reevaluate my position and adapt it to the long hours I was spending in the saddle—typically, five to seven hours every day.

I worked with frame-builder Ben Serotta to come up with a frame design that met my demands. The bicycles I requested had longer top tubes, enabling me to stretch out more. In 1984, my top tube measured 55.5 centimeters. By 1990, it had increased to 57.5 centimeters. In addition to elongating my reach (saddle nose to handlebar stem) by using a longer top tube, I was also lengthening this measurement by pushing my saddle back while keeping the same 12.5- to 13-centimeter handlebar stem length. This gave me a better all-around position for climbing and riding long distances. Since I was spending a lot of time racing in a big gear, this lower, less upright position also enabled me to roll along more comfortably. My seat-tube angle also decreased to a more relaxed seventy-four degrees, which also contributed to stretching my upper body.

Overall, these modifications produced almost a five-centimeter (two-inch) extension in my reach, enabling me to ride with a much flatter back and more relaxed arms. I not only became more aerodynamic, but also this position allowed my chest cavity to open up, making it easier to breathe.

Remember that these changes evolved over a five-year period, so my body had plenty of time to adapt. I don't recommend making sudden, radical position changes. When I returned to riding shorter American-style races, I moved my seat forward about three-quarters of a centimeter and raised the seat post slightly. You must always make adjustments slowly, or you risk not only stiff muscles but injury as well.

Another change I made in frame design when I rode in Europe was to lower the height of the bottom bracket (measuring from the ground to the underside of the bracket shell). In America, with its many criteriums, a higher bottom bracket facilitates safe cornering by offering more pedal clearance, but that tends to feel less stable when descending at speeds faster than fifty miles an hour. So in Europe, where riders descend at incredibly rapid speeds, frequently topping sixty miles an hour, I opted for enhanced stability that comes from having a lower bottom bracket and thus a lower center of gravity.

Back in America, I have decided to stay with the lowered bottom bracket, but have switched from 172.5-millimeter crank arms to the more standard 170-millimeter. This helps my pedal clearance and gives me more leg speed as well. Longer crank lengths have traditionally been used in time trials and for climbing. Many taller riders can benefit by having longer crank lengths, while very short riders might want to consider switching to 167.5-millimeter cranks. This can be an expensive change for a barely noticeable difference, but may be worth the try, especially if you can borrow some cranks to test-ride first.

Another adaptation I made to my bike for the longer races in Europe was to increase the fork rake, which is the crescent-shaped end of the frame where the front wheel attaches. The fork's rake absorbs shock from the front wheel. You might notice that some forks seem to reach farther forward (a longer rake), while others seem to drop straight down (a steeper rake). When you ride your bicycle over a bumpy road, you can look down at your front hub and see that the fork vibrates as it absorbs the bumps. A longer fork rake gives you more shock absorption and stability—both of which are essential for those daily grinds in the saddle. A steeper fork rake might make the ride bumpier because of the decreased absorption, but it will also be more responsive because it will turn more quickly. I have gone back to a shorter rake for more responsiveness and stiffness. Those are two qualities that I need for the American criterium circuit.

BIKE FIT

Saddle Position and Height

It is very difficult to give a standard equation for seat height, because of the enormous number of variables that must be considered. By using a relative percentage of your leg length (generally accepted to be in excess of 90 percent and not greater than 96 percent), you overlook pedaling style, riding posture, and foot length. Before you determine your seat height, you should have selected the shoes and pedal system that you will be using; otherwise, more fine-tuning will be required.

More angles. Consider two extremes in riding styles. A track pursuiter, who is a short time-trial specialist, has a seat-height position that results in a forty-degree bend at the knee when fully extended. This works for the maximum generation of power over a short period of time, but it puts great pressure on the knee. To the untrained eye, this position may seem very low, yet it is a position of great power.

On the other extreme, the American Academy of Orthopedic Surgeons recommends only a fifteen-degree bend of the knee when fully extended for patients with chondra malacia (a common knee ailment resulting from scarring under the knee-cap) which would give a racing cyclist greatly reduced power capability.

What angle should you strive for? For his patients, Andy Pruitt has settled on a twenty-five-degree bend, which is, practically speaking, as high as you can set your seat without rocking your hips from side to side.

Note the leg angle of about twenty-five degrees at full extension.
PHOTO CREDIT: BETH SCHNEIDER

Another factor affecting seat height, according to Pruitt, is muscular flexibility. Looseness of the hamstring affects seat height. Cyclists have to be able to touch their toes, or they risk not being able to ride a higher, more effective seat position. A good stretching program can help you maintain this flexibility, which is easy to lose in the limited confines of the cyclists' pedaling action.

So how do you go about measuring the knee angle? It is very difficult to do this, and at best is guesstimation. Yet formulas dependent on your leg length do not take into consideration the angles of your foot, ankle, knee, and hip when you pedal. How you sit on the seat, which is a factor of your pelvic tilt, greatly affects your bike fit and is clearly not part of the formula's equation.

Pruitt has found that a 25-percent angle is close to the seat-height equation given in Greg LeMond's *Complete Book of Bicycling* (Perigee Books, 1988). LeMond's formula (it is actually that of his former coach, Cyrille Guimard) is calculated as follows: take your inseam measurement and multiply it by 0.883 to get your estimated seat height. Your seat height is measured from the top of the middle of your saddle, down the seat tube to the center of the bottom bracket (the center of the crank-arm bolts). Davis's position works out to closer to 0.91 of his inseam and my position is closer to 0.90 of my thirty-four-inch inseam. Neither of us set up our position based on a formula, but on our individual pedaling style and anatomy. Greg's position works out to be relatively high because his saddle is pushed far back—almost five centimeters (two inches) farther back than Davis's. Moving the seat back makes the seat height effectively higher.

Our test. Start by making sure your saddle is relatively level. If your saddle is tipped down, the result is more pressure on your arms—to keep yourself from falling forward. When the saddle is tipped up, pressure shifts to the small of the back causing crotch discomfort. A level saddle is most comfortable. Start by checking this, and double-check it occasionally to assure that your seat is level. You can eyeball the seat or use a carpenter's level. Be aware that saddles with exceptionally high ridges on the back affect your leveling process and might give you a tip that is up too high. A new saddle will soften as you break it in, which will also affect seat height.

To adjust your seat height, put on your bike shoes and bike shorts. Sit on the bike, preferably on a stationary home trainer, and pedal for several minutes against resistance until you feel comfortable. Now put your right crank arm at six o'clock (where the crank is perpendicular to the ground) and your left up at twelve o'clock. Then take your right leg out of the clip or pedal and let the leg hang loosely down to the pedal. We like to see the heel of the foot graze the top of the pedal platform, or in a range up to one centimeter (two-fifths of an inch) off the pedal for riders using step-in pedal systems and up to two centimeters off the top of the pedal with the old toe-clip system. Note that measurements will vary depending on shoe thickness.

When you do this, be sure to sit on the seat as you normally do—avoid dropping your hip when you stop pedaling. In fact, try it a few times. Let someone else manipulate your foot to see where it falls. Try the same procedure with your left leg.

The position that Andy Pruitt recommends—the LeMond/Guimard formula (0.883 of inseam length), with a more forward fit—will result in a slightly higher position than feels comfortable. But remember, the majority of the people he works with are riding with some sort of injury or pain. As Andy says, "I like a high seat position because it keeps people out of my office."

Davis's seat height is high relative to his leg length but, again, it accommodates his toe-down pedaling style. He has found the pointy-toe style to be most comfortable, most efficient, and most natural. You must find your own natural riding style. Setting your bike up by someone else's standards tends to inhibit your best asset: your own anatomy.

How Can You Tell If Your Fit Is Not Right?

You can tell if your seat is too high if you feel your hips rock from side to side when you pedal, indicating that your legs are straining to reach the pedals on the bottom of the downstroke. It is especially apparent when you pedal fast and you are bouncing up and down. Another indicator is soreness in the crotch. A low saddle position will cause you to "dig," or drop your heel.

Over time, your bike position will change as you adjust and accommodate your

Positioning:

TOP: *The* reach *is dictated by the point where you find balance without the support of your arms.*

MIDDLE: *With your hands on the bars, you should rest comfortably. From this position, your bars should obscure the view of your front hub.*

BOTTOM: Seat height *is determined by hanging your foot down to the pedal, which is at six o'clock. Your heal should be no more than one centimeter off the top of the pedal.*   PHOTO CREDIT: BETH SCHNEIDER

musculature to the bike. This happened to me. I began racing after training for four years as a speed skater, which added bulk to my muscles. As I cycled and thinned out (losing ten to fifteen pounds over the course of my career), my position required a change. My seat was too low and contributed to a knee injury that had to be corrected by surgery. Afterward, I raised my saddle, and my knee problems never returned.

Juniors' note. Juniors must constantly evaluate their positions, because a growth spurt of even an inch or two—which is common—can necessitate radical bike-position changes.

Parents' note. Remember that buying an extraordinarily large frame will be unwieldy and dangerous for your child. Keep in mind that the used frame will be resaleable. A bike that is too large will hinder performance and do little to encourage your child's participation in cycling.

Leg-length discrepancies

The dangling method described above is helpful in determining whether you have a leg-length discrepancy that you might not be aware of. Many, if not most, of us have discrepancies in length between legs. There are a few ways to deal with this problem. Davis's right femur is slightly shorter than his left. For many years, he simply put a lift under the cleat of his right shoe to add height to his right leg. He has also tried orthotics, but without success. Belgian cycling legend Eddy Merckx (rhymes with *works*) recommended that he fashion a lift that makes up half the difference on the short-leg side and compensates the other leg by having the other foot go more deeply into the pedal. Eddy worked this approach out himself after he broke a leg in a racing accident that resulted in one leg becoming shorter than the other.

What if your leg length difference is due to your shinbone? Pruitt suggests that a shim in the shoe is most effective. If the difference is in the thighbone, he advises riders to compromise and take care when trying to set one leg up differently than the other. Don't try to make up for the entire discrepancy, but cater to the shorter leg. A rider with leg-length differences might also be advised to go with a floating-pedal system to minimize the injury potential.

Legendary Seat Heights

Eddy Merckx is also a fanatic about position on the bike. A video of Eddy during the Classic 170-mile Paris–Roubaix race shows him adjusting his seat height before and during the event. Even today, long after his retirement from competition in 1977, he always carries a five-millimeter wrench on rides to change his saddle height.

Eddy is arguably the greatest cyclist ever. In 1989, he came on board the 7-Eleven team as the official supplier of bicycles, which elevated the team's status enormously in Europe. He spent considerable time with each rider, going over positions in great detail.

Eddy also likes to do everything by sight. He rode alongside Davis during an early-season team ride and made observations about his seat height. "You need to raise your saddle a little," Eddy said. At the next traffic light, most of the riders dutifully got off their bikes and changed their saddle height. However, Davis is finicky about his seat height and would not change his position without careful thought and planning. While everyone else was adjusting, Davis only pretended to work on his bike—in deference to Eddy, who obviously possessed superior knowledge about the sport that he had dominated in the 1970s. Davis kept his saddle height unchanged.

After they resumed riding, Eddy came back alongside Davis and pondered the perceived changes. Finally, he suggested, "You need to lower your saddle a little now." Even Eddy Merckx didn't have the perfect "eye" for seat adjustments.

Fore and Aft Saddle Position: Using a Plumbline

Most people are so concerned with seat height that they forget to evaluate the position of the saddle relative to the bottom bracket. This is critical for the development of power. You will need to make two measurements using a plumb line, which is nothing more than a weighted string. You can make a plumb line easily by taking two feet of dental floss tied at one end to a wrench of any size.

It is best to have a partner make the plumb-line measurement while you have the bicycle fitted to a home trainer. Pedal several minutes to get comfortable on the saddle and to sit naturally. Don't drop your heels when you stop pedaling. Be sure to keep them parallel with the ground—or consistent with your pedaling style—when taking this measurement.

Start by putting your pedals at three o'clock and nine o'clock, dropping the plumb line from just below the front of the kneecap bone (the patella) that is at three o'clock. The plumb line should fall from the front of the kneecap to the front edge of the crank arm. These are easy and obvious points to locate.

This gives you maximum power by putting your knee directly over the pedal axle. This is a fairly neutral position which Andy Pruitt favors for his patients. It gives versatility to move forward or backward to accommodate different terrain and paces and, most important, lets you generate power through the maximum range of the downstroke. This is the longest range of power application through the pedal cycle. If your seat is too far forward or back, the result is a shorter application of power through the pedal stroke.

If you need to move your saddle, loosen the bolt under the saddle and slide it along the rail, which ordinarily accommodates several inches of movement. The plumb

line will show if your seat is too far forward by falling in front of the crank. If the line drops behind the front edge of your crank arm, move your seat forward until you find the optimal position.

Note: When you put your seat forward, you effectively lower the saddle height; when you put it back, you raise it. Measure your overall seat height again to see if a minor adjustment is needed.

Greg LeMond's position, which is farther back than we recommend, works for him because he has a great amount of hip and upper-thigh strength, combined with very long thighbones (femurs). Most people cannot generate much power from this position. It is a specialized position that enables Greg to push a big gear for long periods, which he has done for tens of thousands of miles each year for many years. He has adapted very specific strength in this position. For most people, this position is too extreme.

The second measurement is the distance the front tip of your saddle falls behind the bottom bracket. Drop the line from the front edge, or tip, of your saddle and let it fall near the floor. Measure how far the line drops behind the center of the bottom bracket. This measurement is a function of your bike-frame geometry (the angles) and your fore-aft position as determined above. Your position becomes a function of your anatomy (bone lengths), your bike frame (the angles and length of the tubes), and your riding style.

The longer the distance you ride or race, the farther back your seat should be. Sprinters tend to have their saddle set between zero and two centimeters (less than one inch) behind the bottom bracket, while pursuit riders, who compete up to 5,000 meters (3.2 miles), usually have their saddles back no more than two to four centimeters behind (less than one and one-half inch). These are very far forward positions. Road racers often have a position up to ten centimeters (four inches) behind, which means their seats are much farther back. Greg LeMond has a position almost eleven centimeters behind the bottom bracket.

Back in the late 1970s to the mid-1980s, when criteriums and team time trials were his forte, Davis rode very far forward on the saddle, about three centimeters behind the bottom bracket, because he rarely competed longer than 100 kilometers (62.5 miles). That position worked because of his physique. His leg strength came primarily from the upper thigh and gluteal muscles of the hips, and this, combined with his natural pointy-toed pedaling style, positioned him right over the top of the bottom bracket. Most sprinters seem to find this position is a good one for power and speed, although not necessarily for efficiency or long-distance comfort.

Triathletes usually have their seat two centimeters behind the bottom bracket, more like a track pursuit position. Triathletes are more forward because it is easier to get into an aerodynamic position and lay out over the bike without their knees hitting their chest. If triathletes come originally from running, which requires a lot of hamstring strength, they can take advantage of their hamstring strength and flexibility better if their seat is more forward.

The Reach: Handlebar to Stem

Reach is as important for your comfort as any other aspect of bike fit. If you are too hunched up, you cannot breathe and your back and shoulders will ache. If you are too stretched out, your bike handling will be compromised and your crotch will be more sore. Most bikes come set up for the typical body—but are you typical? Usually the stem length is too short. But for most women, it is too long. Your reach is a combination of your saddle position on the rails (fore/aft), your top-tube length, and the handlebar-stem length. Handlebar style also affects reach.

The Davis Phinney line of Serotta Sports Bicycles have top tubes that are slightly longer than those found on most bicycles. This helps stretch out a rider. Davis designed this with his own needs in mind and what he perceived were the needs of other long-distance riders. Very few frames offer this type of choice as standard. Usually you must make a custom order to obtain a frame that is longer than it is tall. Typical frame geometry results in a top tube that is shorter than the seat tube, so that a frame with a seat tube of 56 centimeters (22-inches) would have a 25-centimeter (21.5-inch) top tube. At the most, a rider might be able to find a frame that is "square"—the seat-tube and top-tube lengths are equal (for example, 56 centimeters by 56 centimeters).

Many cyclists tend to ride with their backs in a round hump because they are not stretched out enough. Stretching out opens up your rib cage, provides comfort and is more aerodynamic. We concentrate on flattening the rider's back, which is achieved with a combination of increasing the reach to the handlebar and a good flexibility program (back and hamstring stretching especially).

Checking the reach. After you have adjusted your seat position, sit on the bicycle with relaxed shoulders and arms. Rest the hands on the brake hoods, with a bend in the arms so the forearms are parallel with the ground. When you look down, the horizontal line of your handlebars should block your view of the front wheel hub. If your reach is too long, your front wheel hub will be visible on the near side of the bars (closer to you). If your reach is too short, your front wheel hub will be visible on the far side (away from you).

A good test to see if you are set up properly is to take your hands off the bars and maintain the same torso posture (unsupported) as when you ride. Find the point where you can suspend yourself without falling forward, since this is where you will be the most comfortable and is indicative of your ideal reach. A friend can help you find this by using his hands in line with or the same width apart as your brake hoods. Your friend can move his hands toward you and let you lean on them as they run the gamut of possible reach positions. You are looking to find the place where you are most comfortable. Davis can lie far forward with a flat back and take his hands off the bars and not fall forward. Not too many people can do this, but you should work toward it. Reach is something that evolves.

Handlebars should be as wide as your shoulders. Bikes are typically sold with a 40-centimeter-wide handlebar, which is too narrow for most men and too wide for most women. Handlebars that are too wide are less controllable because your hands are too wide apart. It is also uncomfortable to sit this way, because your elbows are more likely to be locked, instead of bent and relaxed. Handlebars that are too narrow constrict your breathing and increase your shoulder fatigue. You start to lose power if your shoulders are pinched or if your arms are too far apart. Find the neutral power position.

Handlebars should be fitted so that the bottom of the drops are parallel with the ground. To do this, open the stembolt and make a simple adjustment to the angle of the bars. Bars that are tilted up do not give your hand a comfortable resting place when you ride in the drops. Bars that are tilted down make you feel like your hands will slide out of the drops. Be sure that your bars are basically level.

Brake hoods. Racers and recreation riders alike commonly rest their hands on the brake hoods. Standard practice is to put the bottom of the brake lever parallel to the level part of the drops. They should be set halfway down the bend of the handlebars, so that when the hands rest on the hoods your forearms are relaxed and parallel with the frame's top tube. If the brake hoods are too high, you end up sitting upright too much. Placement of the brake hoods also affects access to the brake levers, which should always be convenient and readily accessible. Women, who tend to have smaller hands than men, may need smaller brake levers.

Stem height. When seat height and tilt is right and fore/aft position is correct, try to adjust your stem so that it is two to five centimeters (about four-fifths of an inch to two inches) below the tip of the saddle. Many people think that a lower stem makes them more aerodynamic, which it does, but at great cost to comfort and breathing. An elongated reach will give you a flat back for aerodynamics, and help you to open your rib cage for easy breathing. Adjust your stem height to give you comfort, especially for your lower back.

Your riding posture should enable you to ride with your shoulders relaxed and relatively square. When your cranks are horizontal to the ground, and your hands are in the drops, your elbow should be within an inch of your kneecap. This is one way to determine if your reach is properly adjusted.

Write it down. Keep a record of your bike fit. This will help you in the unfortunate event that your bike is stolen or lost. Record the frame dimensions (seat and top-tube lengths, and frame angles), your overall seat height, and the distance that the seat tip is behind the bottom bracket. Writing down these measurements might save you a lot of aggravation and guessing later.

SHOES/CLEATS

Getting a good fit starts with the fixed contact point with the bicycle: shoes. We advocate that riders wear cycling shoes on the bike. Cycling shoes have a rigid sole for effective transmission of power through the pedals. They are clumsy to walk in because they are designed for riding. Running shoes are designed for running, and their soft soles are not functional for cycling. Not only will you lose power due to the sole flex, but you will also cut off the circulation to your feet, causing them to fall asleep over the course of a long ride.

For the novice cyclist, the image of cleats and toe clips, or worse—step-in pedal systems—may be frightening. It's easy to imagine falling over at every stoplight, but this rarely happens once you get used to cleats. These systems are far superior to a touring shoe or cleatless system. The benefit in efficiency and comfort greatly outweighs the risk of falling over.

Selecting a cleat system is an individual choice, but the toe clip and cleat system is becoming less common as riders discover the benefits of the step-in pedal. Step-ins are more aerodynamic, more efficient, and definitely more comfortable, since the binding straps have been removed.

One primary drawback of the old toe-clip system is that the strap tends to be uncomfortable and can cut off the circulation, as Davis learned during a freezing stage of the 1985 Giro D'Italia. Decreased circulation combined with subzero temperatures almost forced him out of the race and resulted in complications that required minor surgery. His toes became infected from the cold injury, and the pressure caused intense pain. Sounds hideous, and it was. His toenails were black and tender for months after.

With the step-in system you have two primary options—static (fixed) and floating. The Time System is most well-known for its floating-pedal mechanism, which allows you to make adjustments in the cleat position while you are riding. As stated earlier, this type of system greatly reduces the likelihood of developing a knee problem by minimizing the rotation of the knee to accommodate a fixed foot position. Companies like Shimano of America offer fixed pedal systems, but they are developing floating systems. The fixed system is less expensive, but requires very accurate cleat setup. The static systems are less expensive, and are adequate for most cyclists. Some of you, however, will need to have more "play" in your cleats or risk significant knee injury. How do you know which category you fit into? If you have a history of knee problems or had cleated shoes previously and noticed that you liked them as they wore in and had more play, you may be a candidate for the floating system.

Take care to select a comfortable shoe first. It should fit snugly. Runners must buy their shoes large to accommodate the foot strike on the pavement, but cyclists must buy their shoes small because of the gentle nature of the pedal stroke.

Getting the cleat position right is critical. Start by sitting on a high flat bench or countertop, with your knees about shoulder width apart, and let your feet dangle. Notice what you see: what are your feet doing? One foot might point in, the other straight. Or maybe both feet point out, or one is out and one is in. Whatever you see, this is what you duplicate when you set up your pedals. When my legs dangle, my left heel comes in and my right foot is straight, so my cleats are set differently on the two shoes. It would be wonderful if everyone's feet pointed straight forward and their knees moved up and down next to the top tube, but that rarely happens. Pay attention to your own anatomy, not what you wish you were seeing.

The quickest route to injury is an improper cleat setup. Usually you can tell when the cleats are not set properly because you will find yourself pulling one foot toward the bike or away, and you will be uncomfortable.

The first rule of cleat adjustment is to center the ball of the foot over the pedal axle. This is your neutral position. The only exception to this rule is people who have very long feet, where the shoe might be set farther into the pedal (putting the ball of the foot forward of the axle). Sprinters often prefer having the foot set more shallow in the pedal (the ball of the foot is behind the center of the pedal), while some road racers prefer their foot deeper in the pedal (the ball of the foot is in front of the center of the pedal). If you have particular foot irregularities, like the tendency to supinate (where the feet roll inward), or pronate (feet roll outward), try a cycling orthotic, which runs the length of the shoe.

Experienced bike-shop personnel are adept at setting the cleat position for you. Setup works best if you find the neutral position and then spin on your bike in a stationary stand. There are other options available at many shops, like the Fit Kit Rotation Adjustment Device, (RAD), which allows you to step into the pedal and make the necessary adjustments.

Cleat adjustment. This is straightforward. Put your shoes on. Find the ball of your foot (the technical term is the distal head of your first metatarsal bone), and place a white dot there. Be sure to mark the point specific to the bone of your foot. Place the shoe into the pedal with the cleat loosened enough to allow easy fore and aft movement. Position the dot so that it is directly above the pedal spindle, with the front of the foot parallel to the ground. This is the neutral position, which is best for all but the big-footed rider. Tighten the cleat. If you have a flotation system you are done, since the lateral adjustment is not fixed.

The lateral position is best found after pedaling for a few minutes; your anatomy will dictate this position. Remember that your feet should be positioned in the same manner as the one they assumed when you let them dangle from a high bench. It may take a few tries before you get it right. When you pedal, you should not want to pull your heel in or out—if it feels this way, try the adjustment again. Aching knees or unusual muscle stiffness after a ride are good warning signs of the wrong setup. Take a wrench with you when you ride the first few times so you can find the perfect fit.

New shoes. Davis generally changes his cycling shoes only once a year—at the end of the season. By then, his shoes have been soaked in sweat and rain for months and look like they have been through a war. But they are comfortable. Shoes are very personal. Most cyclists prefer to stick with the same pair through the entire racing season, although you should always have a spare pair ready. When the season ends, get a new pair and make adjustments with the step-in system so that your shoes are broken in and ready for the next season. To help your shoes last longer, dry them between rides and pull the insole out occasionally to air them out.

Many riders are reluctant to switch shoes, because a properly fitting shoe is essential to good cycling performance. Davis's former 7-Eleven teammate Doug Shapiro used to wear his shoes for four years straight. Another teammate, Tom Schuler, lost the national professional road racing championships in 1985 because his leather Sidi shoes were so old and worn that his foot actually *pulled out of the shoe* during the final sprint, which he should have won. Jock Boyer used to say that he had a recurring nightmare in which he arrived at the starting line of a race without his shoes. This happened to Alexi Grewal during a stage of the 1986 Tour de France. Fortunately for him, he was able to borrow another pair for the start, and then switch midrace when his shoes were found.

When cyclists travel on planes, they take their shoes in their carry-on luggage and guard them protectively. You can set up a new bike easier than you can set up and break in a new pair of shoes. So if you plan to travel, take your shoes on board with you.

CLOTHING FOR PERFORMANCE AND COMFORT

Helmet

Your first investment should be a helmet. There is no logical reason to omit a helmet in the 1990s, because the advanced technology of helmet design has produced a wide selection of lightweight, fully vented, reasonably priced and stylish, yet safe, helmets. If you complain about the heat, you should know that laboratory tests have shown that riding with a helmet makes your body's core temperature no higher than riding without one. Racers should train with a helmet to help acclimatize themselves to the feeling of the helmet. If you always leave your helmet strapped to your handlebars after a ride, you will be less likely to forget it on the next ride.

Lycra Shorts

Your second purchase should be a good pair of padded cycling shorts made of Lycra or a revolutionary fabric like Fieldsensor (which has superior moisture-wicking characteristics). The comfort of good biking shorts cannot be overestimated. Until the late 1970s, biking shorts were made of wool and the crotch was not padded but was lined with natural chamois, which tended to dry and crack from use, and retained too much moisture during riding. Since the seat is a primary point of contact, this caused discomfort, chafing, and saddle sores. Today's shorts are far superior. Synthetic chamois materials and light breathable padding have helped to keep this area drier, and less likely to chafe. As a rule, synthetic fabrics do not crack or dry with use.

Biking shorts have traditionally been black, for several reasons: to hide road dirt, saddle-dye leeching, and grease. As regulations have loosened up in bike racing, there has been an increase in color in the peloton and in the bike shop. We still prefer traditional black with colored splices and panels. Bike shorts are long for a reason—to reduce chafing. You can try the shorter touring or mountain-bike variety, but remember that length is for function, not fashion.

Jerseys

Jerseys also serve many purposes, although they are one of the last items purchased. They come with rear pockets so you can stow a lightweight rain jacket and traditional cycling food like a PowerBar or banana. Synthetic jerseys are far superior in their wicking ability (taking moisture off your skin, so that it dries and does not chill you) to cotton T-shirts, which tend to become heavy with moisture. Look for a jersey that has a nice feel (in tech-talk: a good hand). Jerseys are snug for aerodynamics and long so that your lower back is covered.

Riding with nothing (or next to nothing) on top is not recommended even in the hottest weather, because you will become more quickly dehydrated. When you wear a T-shirt or jersey, some of the moisture is trapped, and that moisture can cool you on a hot day and reduce the amount of water you lose. Riding without a shirt is also foolhardy in case you crash, when you will be guaranteed to lose some skin. Even so, Davis loves to ride without a shirt to even out his farmer's tan.

In cold weather, layer your clothing, starting with a polypropylene-type base layer and finishing with a lightweight windproof shell. Silmond is an ideal fabric for cyclists, because it is highly water resistant yet light and compact, which means you can carry it with you.

Other

Of course, there are other important and fully functional items for clothing that you will want to consider. *Gloves* give you padding and protect your hands in case of a fall, which is the primary reason racing cyclists wear them. We prefer the lightest padding, since your hands should take a relatively light beating from your riding unless you have a death grip on the bars. Long-fingered gloves are essential for winter riding and should be selected for their warmth and water resistance. *Rain jackets* are also handy, especially lightweight shells that are easy to take along. *Socks* are good for wicking away the moisture from your feet. *Long tights* or *leg warmers* are essential for temperatures below sixty to sixty-five degrees. *Shoe covers,* many of which are made of insulated waterproof wet suit–type materials, make a difference in cold weather and enable you to ride in freezing temperatures— without freezing your toes.

High-Performance Technical Wear—for the Aero Advantage

The skinsuit has become standard wear in the peloton since the late 1970s. So-called "rubber suits" have been used in short time trials like the pursuit events on the track since the early 1980s. According to wind-tunnel testing, a nonporous (rubber) suit will give the rider an advantage of up to a half-second per kilometer. That's a lot of time. Traditionally these suits have been too hot for the road, where the events are longer. Pearl Izumi developed a composite suit with rubber material in places likely to come in contact with the wind, and breathable material in other places. This enables you to wear the suit for longer time trials and in warmer weather.

Hardshell helmets have been wind-tunnel-tested and proven to be more effective

Coors Light's Steve Swart wears Pearl Izumi's composite nonporous suit to gain maximum advantage in the time trial at the 1991 Tour Du Pont.　　　PHOTO CREDIT: JOHN KELLY

aerodynamically than no helmet, and an aerodynamic helmet can be even more timesaving if worn properly. Some riders drop their chin toward their chest, causing the tip of the aero helmet to rise into the air. If this is your style, you should opt for a regular helmet. The object of the aero-style helmet is to close off the space behind the neck, where ideally the point of the aero helmet should rest.

SECTION 2

RIDING TECHNIQUES (Davis)

The Basics

To say that cycling comes naturally is partially true. Most of us learned to ride as a rite of passage of childhood, and we still understand the basics of staying upright. But when you watch a professional like Miguel Indurain of Spain, 1991 Tour de France champion, you see someone who makes cycling appear to be very easy even under the most extreme conditions. Why is that? Because he has good technique—his style of riding is efficient.

Everybody understands that *technique* is required in golf or tennis. After all, it is common to take lessons from a professional to help you play better. But since everybody knows how to ride a bike, who needs lessons? And what would the lessons be for? Few people associate technique with cycling, yet it is an integral part of the sport, and a few adjustments may dramatically improve your cycling comfort and performance.

TENSION/RELAXATION EXERCISE

Try the following exercise. Tense your shoulders and pull them up near your ears. Now lock your elbows and make a fist, holding your fist out in front of you, about shoulder width apart. Stay tense. *Keep holding*. Imagine if you rode your bike this way? Would you be able to hold this position for three or more hours? Ouch. Believe it or not, many people ride like this, or close to it.

89

1991 Tour de France Champion
Miguel Indurain of Spain makes
cycling appear to be very easy
because of his relaxed, efficient
style.
PHOTO CREDIT: BETH SCHNEIDER

Now relax your shoulders, letting them fall down and be square—not tense or rounded. Bend your elbows slightly and unlock your wrists and your fists. Flutter your fingers lightly. Take a deep breath. *Whew!* You can breathe again. It feels amazing, doesn't it? Staying relaxed on the bike is not easy, but you can do it. Not only will it improve your performance by not wasting energy, but it also will increase your bike-handling skills and make your riding safer. Let's cover the basic riding position. We start with posture, because if you are riding as just described, you cannot use your legs efficiently.

POSTURE IN THE SADDLE

Basic riding technique starts with your posture on the bike. Posture affects how efficiently you will ride just the way a good grip on a golf club or a tennis racket affects these games.

Hand position. When you sit on the bike, you have to be comfortable and in control. When sitting in the saddle, ride at a moderate pace and rest your hands on the tops of the brake hoods. This position is favored because it is safe—your hands can easily reach the brakes and it is comfortable. Keep a relaxed grasp, not a grip. Occasionally flutter your fingers.

When climbing, always ride on the tops of the handlebars, because it facilitates breathing and helps open your rib cage. Many riders forget to sit on the tops when they come to a short climb. Riding up a hill in the drops is uncomfortable and inefficient, so sit up. When you are riding fast on the flats, you can still choose to stay on the tops, with your back flat and aerodynamic, and still have good bike control. I prefer to ride on the tops because I find them more comfortable.

Wrists. Let your wrists be straight, not locked in a bent position. Juniors typically ride with their hands up near the stem on the upper part of the bars and like to drop their wrists into a cocked position. Bike control is tenuous at best and overall comfort is diminished in this position. This is a lazy habit and easily broken.

Elbows. Let them be slightly bent, not locked in place. This is less energy-consuming because you will be more relaxed. Locked elbows make your steering rigid, so keep your arms bent, relaxed, and ready to respond.

Shoulders and back. When you sit upright, keep your shoulders square, not rounded. This facilitates breathing. Do not let your shoulders hunch up to your ears, but keep them relaxed. To keep your back from being rounded or hunched, concentrate on stretching from your lower back. Think of having a rope tied from your lower back through your belly button to the middle of your top tube, which would pull you forward and lengthen your back.

Your goal is to have an elongated flat back, square shoulders, bent elbows, and a light touch on the handlebars. With this position, you are more aerodynamic, more comfortable, and more in control. That means you are safer, faster, and able to ride longer.

Full range of hand positions on the bars:

1. This simulated aero-position illustrates the best position for me, featuring an elongated and flat back, which enables me to breathe easily. Keep your head up but let your shoulders stay low and relaxed.

2. In the drops—notice the bend at the elbow, and the hands, which are deep in the drops. Assume this position for optimal speed and power on flat terrain.

The drops. When you ride faster, whether you are solo or in a fast group ride, racing or descending, you will want to be in the drops of the handlebars. Riding on the tops under high-speed conditions is also acceptable, but the drops give you a power position. Put your hands deep into the drops, keeping within fingertip reach of the brakes. Keep your wrists in alignment with the horizontal part of the bar or just to the outside at a slight angle—don't lock them or cock them to the inside of the drops, which is uncomfortable and breaks the connection between your arms and hands. A common mistake is to ride with the hands on the far back flat part of the handlebar drops, which puts your hands too far from the brakes and is not as efficient as in the hook of the drops. This position also effectively shortens your reach, which will constrict your torso and restrict your breathing.

3. *An ideal position for climbing—hands relaxed on the tops of the brake hoods, head up, and shoulders square.*

4. *Another good climbing position with hands on the tops of the bars and arms relatively straight.*
PHOTO CREDIT: BETH SCHNEIDER

Wear protective eyewear. Bugs and gravel in your eyes will do more to hinder your descending than anything else, so take precautions.

When descending at warp speed, never sacrifice safety for aerodynamics. Find a tuck position that works for you, but don't find such a radical position that you lack access to your brakes.

OUT OF THE SADDLE

Riding out of the saddle enables you to do two things: you involve new muscles, which are more rested than the ones you have been using; and you generate more power in a bigger gear. Standing is less efficient than sitting because it requires more

Never sacrifice safety for aerodynamics. Notice that Andy Hampsten's position is aero-dynamic, with his hands deep in the drops of the handlebars, allowing him fingertip access to the brakes. Note also the protective eyewear.   PHOTO CREDIT: BETH SCHNEIDER

energy to do the work, but standing can be very powerful for short-term effort and acceleration of speed, which is why people primarily sprint out of the saddle.

Most newcomers to cycling are very awkward out of the saddle, due to lack of practice and poor bike fit. Both are easily overcome.

Standing basics. Before you stand up, put your hands in the hooks of the drops (for sprinting) or on the tops of the brake hoods (for climbing). When you first come up off the saddle, rise up and move toward the handlebars. Your shoulders should be just above the linear plane of the bars, supported by your arms.

If your arms are weak, you might drop your shoulders and head too much, which will compromise your breathing. Try to keep your shoulders and head fairly upright. Pull your weight slightly *up* and over, and from side to side so that you get your weight on the pedals. Keep your bike motion to a minimum.

CADENCE AND PEDALING STYLE

Cadence, or pedal revolutions per minute (RPMs), is a controversial topic. Scientists claim that riding at a cadence around 60 or 70 RPMs is most efficient. This may be true for the novice cyclist, but experience has shown that a cadence of at least 90 revolutions per minute works for racing cyclists. A higher cadence enables you to recruit your long-lasting slow-twitch muscle fibers, which are designed for hours of use. This cadence also helps you build a quality called suppleness, which is a trained-muscle characteristic that enables a cyclist to accommodate speed changes. Juniors tend to ride at the highest cadence, not only because of gear restrictions, but also because they have developing muscles that favor smaller gears. Professionals ride bigger gears, and thus ride at a lower cadence, primarily due to the sheer volume of miles ridden. Triathletes also ride a lower cadence because they turn over a bigger gear in time trials and they have less need for suppleness in their three-sport event. Tourists will also have lower cadence when loaded down with camping gear.

The acceptable range for cadence on the flats for a racing cyclist is 80 to 110. Finding your optimal cadence is a function of your own pedaling style, the demands of your specialty, and the time of year. The average optimal cadence seems to be in the low 90s. However, don't get locked into statistics—find out what works for you.

Hills—up and down. Your cadence will obviously drop on uphills, depending on the length and grade of the climb. Shift gears to maintain a cadence of more than 60, blending power and cadence. On descents, sit and spin. Practice increasing your leg speed to 120 to 140 RPMs to improve your technique and enhance your pedaling style. You won't do this in a race, when you will be in a big gear, but it is great training for your technique and the responsiveness of your muscles.

Spinning up hills is acceptable in the early season or during recovery training, but in general you must train yourself to ride a bigger gear on the hills to develop power. Many riders, especially women, favor smaller gears on hills and consequently never develop power. Work on this. Mountain biking gives you a great cardiovascular workout with one primary disadvantage—you tend to ride in small gears, which inhibits your ability to develop power.

Conversely, many riders are lazy descenders and never develop high-speed spinning, which is good for recovery because it promotes circulation and develops smooth pedaling style. At first, you may feel awkward when spinning, but with practice your style will smooth out and you will no longer feel as if you are going to bounce out of the saddle. Track sprinters are so smooth at spinning that they can spin in excess of 140 RPMs with very little torso movement. It looks almost comical to see this large muscle-bound species of cyclist spinning a tiny gear, but it is a testament to their efficiency that they can ride this way.

Pedaling style is a function primarily of your anatomy. I pedal with a "pointy toe" or toe-down style that is typical of sprinters who have bulkier, compact muscles and shorter tendons. Steve Bauer is a typical "flat-footed" pedaler. His Achilles tendon is probably longer than mine, and despite appearing to have similar body types, we clearly don't pedal the same. Bauer's style may well be learned, since he emulated the great Canadian cyclist, Jocelyn Lovell, also a very flat-footed pedaler. Neither style is more correct than the other. Instead, they are products of anatomy and drilled in by practice.

Strive to pedal with as smooth a stroke as possible, by spinning and consciously thinking of dropping your heel at the bottom of the stroke and pulling back and up on the top side. Your goal is to have a circular motion, although there are exceptions: Alexi Grewal favors a very up-down approach to pedaling, and Greg LeMond favors a down-and-back stroke. Find out what works for your anatomy, but work on it when you ride on the road and on the home trainer. Consciously work to drop your heel as you pedal, but don't stab with your heels or your toe. Watch your gearing, too, since overgearing tends to lead to less-efficient, ratchet-style pedaling, early fatigue, and knee injuries.

To illustrate how important pedaling action is, look at Miguel Indurain, who won the 1991 Tour de France. His time for the 2,445-mile event was 101 hours and one minute, which translates to 6,061 minutes of riding. If his average cadence was 90, his total revolutions (counting one leg) were in excess of half a million pedal strokes (545,490 to be precise) for that twenty-two-stage race over three weeks. Counting both legs, that's more than a million arduous pedal strokes. Pedaling efficiency is not only critical to performance, but it is an integral part of the whole picture. Function follows form: you cannot go the distance without good technique.

Pedaling squares is a term used to describe a rider who is dying and losing form. This is apparent in very choppy pedal strokes and diminished cadence. So when you hear someone say, "He was pedaling squares," you will understand the meaning.

Terminal threshold? My 1984 Olympic teammate Thurlow Rodgers is the king of spin. He always rides a small gear at a high cadence. We used to joke that the body has a terminal revolution threshold and when you hit your limit, however many billion pedal strokes that might be, that was it and you were done and could go no farther. We joked that Thurlow was going to hit the point well ahead of us.

You don't necessarily need a handlebar computer to measure cadence. Calculate your cadence by counting the downstroke of one leg for ten seconds, using your wristwatch (which you can easily mount on a padded section of your handlebars for easier viewing), and multiply that number by six to get your RPMs. A count of fifteen will give you an RPM of 90; seventeen will translate to 102 RPMs. Once you get the feel for your cadence, you can guess it fairly accurately, which helps you make easier and wiser gearing selections. This is important in races when riders obviously become tired; with fatigue comes the necessity to determine the optimal gear. But with fatigue also comes inefficient shifting, which only further increases your fatigue. One of the reasons I favor the STI handlebar shifting is that it allows me to shift more often—standing or sitting—and this helps me to keep my cadence at the most efficient level which maximizes my performance.

Minimize extraneous movement on the bicycle at any cadence. Keep your torso steady. Let your legs do the work. On a properly fitted bicycle, your hips should not rock or bob from side to side. Keep your shoulders square, back elongated and flat.

Videotaping is ideal for analyzing your bike position. Your mental image of how you ride may not exactly match what the camera captures. Most of us get the chance to see ourselves only in glimpses in the reflection of a storefront window. A video camera gives you the chance to see yourself for an extended period of time in a variety of positions—standing, sitting, sprinting, and spinning. Don't be put off when you first see yourself. It can be a shock to realize that you don't look like the professionals on the cover of *Winning* magazine. Study pictures of top riders; it helps to ingrain the right image in your mind and gives you something to work toward. The next videotape audition will certainly be more inspiring.

CORNERING—CARVING A TURN

Cornering comes naturally to some riders, and with practice for others. We all know how to go around a corner, but what about at speed through a tight turn? The basic equation involves two factors: how tight the turn is and how fast you want to go through it. Other factors come into play, including the road surface, road conditions, and what comes up after the turn.

For me, the goal is in being able to handle any corner and any situation on the fly, with as much speed and safety as possible. That starts with basic practice and understanding the fundamentals. At the Carpenter/Phinney Cycling Camps, one of the most productive sessions we have is to ride around a series of tightly spaced orange cones in a parking lot. By learning to corner at a relatively slow speed through tight turns, you learn to feel what your bike and body are capable of. Subtle maneuvers have a big impact. This exercise trains you to be in sync with your bicycle.

I developed my cornering technique by watching other racers and utilizing methods of turning from other sports. From motorcycling I have adopted the principle of *countersteering*. From downhill skiing, I have adopted the principle of *angulation*.

The Basic Tenets of Any Turn

Inside leg. When you approach a turn, it is essential that your inside leg be up. Let your inside knee point naturally in the direction of the turn.

Pedaling through a turn at speed is not recommended for novices, and should be done only when you know you have enough clearance to avoid catching your pedal. As your speed increases through a turn, so does your bike angle and the risk of scraping your pedal. When you barely scrape your pedal, you can hear it and it might jolt you a little, with no consequence. Catching a pedal sharply causes your rear wheel to bounce or skip to the side sharply, which might cause your sew-up tire to roll off, causing you to fall or swing your bike out from under you.

Outside leg. Think about your outside leg as you go through a turn. Your outside leg will give you great stability if you concentrate on weighting it, by pushing your leg through the pedal, so that you actually feel the pressure on the outside pedal.

Body position. Rather than sitting rigidly on the saddle, I like to push my pelvis back on the saddle, which weights the rear of the bike and gives me better control. Keep contact with the saddle, and use your body to add steering power. Pressure the saddle with the inside of your thigh toward the direction that the bike is leaning. I let my upper body flatten out across the top tube, especially in tight turns. This exerts weight on the front of the bike, which will help you maintain a low center of gravity for added stability and balance. Your hands should be deep in the drops, giving you good access to the brakes and ensuring maximum control.

When descending off-road, you also move your weight back, but for different reasons. Sitting far back off the saddle of the mountain bike allows your front wheel to float over the rough road surface (rocks, roots, etc.), increasing your stability and control.

Countersteering. This technique comes from motorcycling. As you go around the turn, straighten your inside arm and actually push your arm into the bar. This effectively turns your wheel away from the turn but lets your bike fall into the turn, enabling you to go around it. At slow speeds, this technique does not apply, but the faster you go and the stronger you push against the wheel, the tighter the turning capability at speed. Your body will naturally align itself across the top tube and your head should be in a line across your outside brake hood.

Countersteering takes practice to develop. Even at slow speed, when you don't get the opportunity to really push the wheel away, you still get the sensation of pushing the inside handlebar and feeling the bike drop over in the direction of the turn. While this is difficult to explain, it's much easier to feel, so try it for yourself.

Greg LeMond takes a sharp turn fast during the 1991 Tour de France prologue time trial—notice his inside knee pointing into the turn and his upper body cocked low and flat across the bike.
PHOTO CREDIT: BETH SCHNEIDER

Angulation. In skiing, a turn is initiated from the ground up. The faster you go, the farther your skis get out from under you and the more you have to angle into the hill. This is called *inclination*. In skiing, it's important to keep the middle of your mass centered, or you fall. Skiers angle into the hill with their ankles, knees, and hips. The angles decrease in the upper body, which helps keep your mass centered, giving you a manageable center of gravity.

Lowering your center of gravity and initiating the turn from the ground up also applies to cycling. Your tires do not have metal edges like skis do, but they can be angled over quite far and still grip the road. Some people argue with me over the physics of what I say, but this technique has worked for me over hundreds of thousands of miles and thousands of descents.

Angulation. Swiss ace Marc Giradelli shows how angulation gets him through a turn—legs are angled, upper body is upright.   PHOTO CREDIT: BETH SCHNEIDER

You be the judge. One common turning technique teaches the exact opposite of what I propose here. This technique involves keeping the bike as upright as possible, which theoretically gives the tires more contact and more grip on the road. Further, it is suggested that you steer the bike as you would a car, using your handlebars like the steering wheel while leaning with your head into the turn.

From my experience, this is a less effective way of turning, because the upright bike makes it more difficult to turn. As you turn the wheel toward the turn, the bike actually pulls in the opposite direction. To make the turn, you have to lean so far over that you are actually less stable because your center of gravity is well outside the plane of the bike and you are initiating the turn from the point farthest away from the road instead of closest to it. When you do this, you limit your ability to make adjustments on the fly. You cannot tighten the turn or accelerate from this position. Should you encounter an obstacle you will have to brake sharply, forcing you to either stop or go flying off the road.

With countersteering, you can throw your bike more sharply into the turn and still make it through the turn *at speed*. In the worst case, you can let the bike go upright by straightening your body and letting the bike come straight, which will flatten out the turning radius. Countersteering gives you more variety, more choices, and a greater ability to react. In motorcycle racing, riders lean their bike over to the very edge of the tire, often hanging off the bike. This is not possible with a twenty-pound bicycle and three-quarter-inch tires, but the lean principle does carry over. Your body compensates on a bike by keeping the body mass more centered over the bottom bracket.

My old teammates, like Andy Hampsten, Alex Stieda, Ron Kiefel, and Roy Knickman, have integrated this type of cornering into their repertoire and are big proponents. Why? Because they have found it works. Try it on the road, and you decide.

Braking. Braking affects the handling of the bike through the turn, because it straightens the bike. The more you brake, the more upright the bike will be. Therefore, the best way to brake for a turn is to brake prior to the turn. Hit both the brakes fast and hard just before entering the turn. Feather the brakes to control your speed once you are in the turn. Try to limit braking in the turn so that you accelerate out of the turn. Good use of your brakes will save you time and energy.

Use fingertip control of your brakes. Ideally you want to feather the brakes, not

Countersteering practice in a closed parking lot during a Carpenter/Phinney Cycling Camp. Notice how my left leg is extended, inside knee is falling toward the turn, and my bike is at an extreme angle. I keep my upper body more upright, like a skier. I knocked this cone over with my handlebars to illustrate how far a bike can be angled over without losing traction. Notice my inside arm is straight—this is the essence of countersteering.

PHOTO CREDIT:
BETH SCHNEIDER

You be the judge. Roy Knickman's inside leg is up and pointing into the turn, his outside leg is extended and weighted, his hands are deep in the drops, and his inside arm is pushing, or countersteering. Look at the angle of the bike. He can carry a lot of speed with this technique.

PHOTO CREDIT: BETH SCHNEIDER

grab them and lock them up. Most people are afraid to use the front brake because they think it will send them over the handlebars, but the front brake is very effective if used properly. The biggest drawback to the front brake is that a front-wheel skid is less controllable than a rear-wheel skid; it's more likely that you will go down if your front wheel skids. Your rear brake is softer, but you can apply more leverage if your weight is back. Further, a rear-wheel skid is more controllable, but the rear brake is less precise than the front. You might be surprised to learn that if I could have only one brake, the front brake would be my choice. The rear brake simply does not have the stopping power of the front.

In steep straight descent on a mountain bike, put your weight far off the back of the saddle and clamp on the front brake. Your rear brake is used, but you will skid if you brake hard. The front brake is best for optimal control and stopping power on very steep descents like those found on the Slickrock Trail in Moab, Utah.

Rain turns. Riding fast in the rain can be intimidating. Your biggest danger is oil-slick wet roads, which make bike control extremely difficult. On rough surfaces, rain often does little to impair your tire adhesion and you can maintain surprising speed. While turning on wet surfaces, maintain a neutral posture. Instead of pushing the bike so far over, just angle it so that the line of your body goes straight through your bike. You're still angled over, but the bike is at less of an extreme angle and your body is in line with the bike. Imagine a plane going straight from your head through to your tires. This will put more tread in contact with the road. Don't hold the bike straight up and turn in with your body; while this seems like a safer way to make a turn, it is slower and gives you fewer options. When the bike comes upright, it will flatten out the line of your turn, forcing you to compensate at the outer edge of the turn, but buying you time to get you out of your skid.

Moisture makes your brake blocks grip the rims more softly, so you won't stop as quickly, but that does not mean you can be more heavy-handed; the brakes can suddenly lock on you, which will definitely send you into a skid. A light touch on the brakes is therefore essential. Take extra care to brake before the turn.

The primary reason people fall in the rain is that they tense up. Tensing up leads you to overreact. You want to be able to act and react, but don't overdo it. Remember: the more relaxed you remain, the easier your job. If you have to make a speed adjustment and brake in the turn, don't panic. Try lightly feathering your rear brake. If possible, avoid braking at all in the turn.

Riding on oil or gravel makes the surface slippery and unpredictable in much the same way that riding on wet surfaces does. Once again, try not to overreact and try to anticipate by braking before you panic. If you come into a gravelly turn fast, try to keep your bike a little more upright to increase the friction between you and the road. Don't brake, or you will skid. If you are relaxed on your bike, you can quickly straighten the bike up and then bank it over again after you've passed gravel or oil.

Correct line. Choosing the correct line to take through the turn is essential for good cornering, whether on a fast twisty descent or taking ninety-degree turns in a race through city streets. In a sharp left-hand turn, you want to approach the turn from the far right side of the road. Anticipate the turn to have most of the turn accomplished before you pass the apex. This way you aren't forced to drift wide, but you can drift if you need to, giving you a greater margin for error and more speed out of the turn. If you set up correctly, you are in effect turning before the turn, or preturning. (See diagram on page 104.)

Review

If you're comfortable with your cornering techniques, you feel much more confident when something unexpected happens in a turn, or when you encounter a turn at high

CHOOSING THE RIGHT LINE

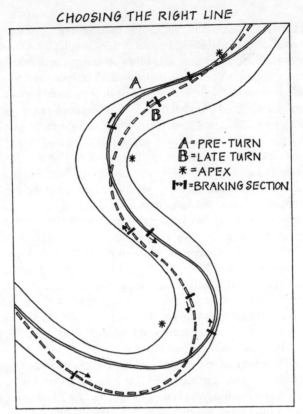

A = PRE-TURN
B = LATE TURN
* = APEX
|←→| = BRAKING SECTION

Rider A makes the turn early or preturns, allowing him more roadway if needed. He brakes before the apex of the turn, which allows him to accelerate out of the turn. Rider B brakes late, forcing him to go wide out of the turn, which leads him to lose speed and puts him in the wrong spot to start the next turn. Clearly, rider A is taking the preferred line through the turn.

speed. You will have little time to think at fifty miles an hour, so think ahead of time. With practice comes confidence and a mastery of the situation. Knowing you can make it through a tight turn at speed goes a long way toward getting you through it. Take a little time to play with the basics, then learn a few tricks that work for you. Above all, don't take your turning for granted, but study and practice. If you have trouble with a particular turn, watch how others corner, model them, and then analyze what you have done. Why did it work? How can I make it work?

Mountain biking or cyclo-cross riding on gravel roads is excellent practice for getting used to the feeling of sliding without falling. Thicker mountain bikes or cross tires give you more room for error and, thus, time to respond. Sliding is scary at speed, but don't let your bike control the situation. Instead, *you* control your bike.

DESCENDING—A LITTLE HISTORY

It was imperative that I *learn* to be a good descender. I had always been good at cornering, good in criteriums, but when I went to Europe I discovered sixty-mile-an-hour mountain descents where what lay around the next corner was a mystery. I started out at the front of the group and wound up almost getting dropped because I wasn't comfortable turning that fast and didn't know how to control my bike at speed. My whole comfort zone was too slow, so I had to study ways to be a better descender.

I first started going to Europe in 1979 as an amateur, but when I started racing stage races with major climbs in 1982 and 1983, I realized unexpectedly that one of my weaknesses was descending. In American events, we simply didn't often have the opportunity to ride down the kind of steep, narrow, rough roads that are a typical part of European road races. Despite the fact that I was from Colorado and my backyard was the Rocky Mountains, I hadn't practiced enough high-speed descending.

Part of descending well is the ability to judge corners without any sort of preview, and adapting your comfort zone to higher speeds. Initially I found myself inadvertently riding the brakes because I wasn't used to the speed. I lacked confidence and control over my bike while flying through turns at speed.

In 1984 we had a Polish rider, Stanislaw Szozda (pronounced *shows-da*), who was working with the national team in Italy. Szozda had been a great amateur rider in the 1970s and was reknowned for being one of the best amateur descenders in the world. I wanted to pick his brain. Szozda was the one who introduced me to many of the ideas and techniques I now use.

Szozda explained to me that he once had the same problem, so he studied other forms of descent: downhill skiing, motorcycle racing, as well as cycling. He broke down the elements of what it took to go down a mountain fast, including turning, body position, and center of gravity.

He introduced me to *countersteering,* which was a totally new concept to me. Pushing the handlebar in the opposite direction you want to turn was something I had not thought of or tried. But he was right: the harder the push, the more the bike banks, and the tighter the radius of the turn. Because a bicycle is considerably lighter than a motorcycle, he explained, a bicycle rider's body naturally assumes a certain position that is opposed to the angle of the bike, so the bicycle rider's upper body is going one way and the bicycle is going the other. But a cyclist needs to keep his (or her) center of balance right over the bicycle's bottom bracket (where the pedal axle goes through the frame).

He took me out and showed me these techniques down descents. I couldn't even stay with him for two corners. The guy was phenomenal. I realized how much I could learn from him and that I really needed to work on this. I spent years perfecting this technique.

Sprinters are generally poor climbers and often wind up being left behind. Muscles that power a sprinter also add weight and become extra baggage to lug up hills. So sprinters have to be good descenders. That's the way sprinters catch up, especially in Europe. All the best descenders are sprinters, because they have to hang it out the most to catch up after the climbs.

As I found my niche in Europe and wound up in the sprinter's groups, we would always ride together. I trusted these guys the most, because they were the best descenders. I gradually learned my own technique, and wound up expanding my own comfort zone enough to hurtle down mountains at more than sixty miles an hour, literally bouncing from brake point to brake point, especially in the Pyrenees in southwestern France. There the roads are steep and so rough and narrow that you feel you are dropping straight out of the sky—except for a U-turn every half-mile or so, as the roads snake along the mountainsides. You skid into the turn, throw your bike, and shoot out of the turn. You hope you do it all right and don't shoot over the edge.

In fact, I once did go shooting over the edge, in 1983 when I was racing in the Tour de l'Avenir (Tour of the Future, which was the amateur Tour de France). That was before I started working with Szozda. I had punctured on the first climb on one of the last days of the fourteen-day race, and I was giving everything in the descent, trying to catch up. I was flying through the following-car peloton, passing cars, getting in their draft—boom!—flying by them. Every once in a while, I would come around a turn and there would be a rider who had crashed. It was a very dangerous descent. I was reckless, because I had to get back up with the pack again.

Up ahead was a group of four or five riders. It was a straight road, so I put it into my biggest gear and spun out trying to catch them. I got low on my bike and went into a tuck. I was flying and catching them quickly. Then they started to slow down and I thought I had them.

It turned out that they were slowing to make a hairpin turn. I had no prayer of making the turn. I got maybe twenty or thirty degrees into it before I went straight into a cement retaining wall. I catapulted over the side. My bike went flying about fifty meters down the road into a vineyard. I fell about twenty or thirty feet and was caught in brambles, hanging in them. When I got free, I had scratches all over and looked like I had had a fight with twenty-five cats.

Somebody had seen my spectacular fall over the wall and stopped my team's following car. Otherwise I would have been left for dead. My bike was so far down in the vineyard that the search for it took several minutes.

That was part of the incentive for me to learn how to descend at speed. If I'm going through a turn that is tighter than I expect, what should I do? You can change the angle of your turn, even radically at a moment's notice, if you've got the right attitude on your bike and the right physical counterbalancing of the bicycle.

I felt I had really arrived when I was in the Tour of Italy, on an incredibly long stage that wound up lasting eight and a half hours. On the last climb, I was in a group of sprinters. At the top we were pretty relaxed and having fun. A couple of the riders were fans of motorcycle racing, so we started joking that we were motorcycle road racers. We were hell-bent-for-leather, going faster and faster. Everybody fanned out—five or six abreast—speeding into the corner. The rider willing to hang it out the most would brake last. The rest of us would file in behind and he would lead us through the turn, just holding it on the bare edge of the tires around the turn.

Then—*boom!*—we would fan out and another guy would lean through the next turn. We were just flying down this mountain. It was unbelievable how intense it was. Nobody backed off. But I felt safe with these guys, because they were so good. I felt comfortable hanging it all the way out. I felt I had complete control of my bike, even to the point where I had both wheels sliding a little bit as I was going through the turn. I was that comfortable. We had an incredibly natural high after we came off that mountain. We gave each other high fives all the way around. It was a real thrill. That was pure bike racing.

I had gone from being dropped and fighting to just stay with the peloton, to being able to go with the fastest riders—and even scare them.

NIGHTMARES (CONNIE)

I had a similar problem in my first World Championships in 1976. I made the team after winning the women's national road race championship in Louisville, Kentucky. I succeeded on pure strength and instinct, not on bike-handling skills. Several weeks later, I found myself training on the road course for the world championships in Ostuni, Italy. The world's course featured a fast descent with a few high-speed hairpin curves. I had been racing for only six months. Having been raised in the rolling farm country of Wisconsin, I had never descended anything mountainous. I was petrified. When we went home that night, I had nightmares.

Our team mechanic, Steve Aldridge, couldn't believe what a state of disrepair my bike was in. I had bought it used from Jim Ochowicz, a two-time Olympian in the 1970s who would later become Davis's team manager (and boss) for 7-Eleven. It was a good bike, but the frame was a little bent. Over the summer, some of the spokes came loose and the wheels were not "true." "No wonder you couldn't make the turn," Steve declared. He spent hours straightening the frame, adjusting the brakes and other components, and truing the wheels.

My mentor, rival, and teammate, Miji Reoch, agreed to help me learn to descend. We returned to the course the next day in the team van with the coaches. With my realigned and tuned-up bicycle, and my resolve not to careen into the woods, I set off down the hill behind Miji.

"Remember," Miji counseled, "if I can make the turn at this speed, so can you."

I followed her down the first time and stayed close. We took the van back to the top and did it again. And again. We kept doing it many more times until I mastered the descent. In the race, it was like a dream. I was one of the first to fly through the turns and I was never afraid again.

The moral? First, make sure your bike is correctly aligned. High-speed wobbles are usually taken care of mechanically. Second, build your confidence by learning from someone who is better than you. It is true that if everyone else can make it through the turn at speed, so should you. Finally, practice. Cornering does not come naturally to everyone, but if you learn a few tricks, watch out—all of a sudden you can fly.

Relaxed riding requires practice. You don't need a steep mountain descent to train on to feel comfortable, although that certainly helps. In our training camps, we put orange pylons down in a parking lot for riders to negotiate as they work on technique. Then we stand at the farthest edge of a turn, where people are prone to overshoot, and we say, "I'm a thousand-foot cliff right here." One of us stands right there to emphasize the fact that you make it—or else. That forces our campers to push their bikes down to make the turn in a playful setting without harsh consequences.

But we notice that if a rider has an out, or easy exit, he or she won't try to make it. They back off. They have a sense that angling their bike over will cause them to skid out and fall. Making it around the turn has a lot to do with your attitude, or body language, and counterbalancing your upper body.

Take the time to set up this kind of a course. On a weekend morning, most parking lots are empty and all you need are a few markers (water bottles or cones will do). Vary the course a few times. Find out what works.

Winning

Let me tell you another story about Szozda, who adapted his style of cornering to win races. For an amateur in the 1970s, the biggest cycling race in the world was the Peace Race, an Eastern-bloc race from Berlin to Warsaw to Prague. To Szozda, from Poland, this race's importance was huge.

Peace Race stages often finished on a cinder running track—flat 400-meter tracks that lack the banking that cyclists need to speed through turns. One-hundred-mile stages would take the riders through a right-angled turn to enter the stadium from the road, then another right-angled turn onto the track.

Szozda developed an innovative method that allowed him to pedal and corner simultaneously. When everyone else was braking, he would sprint into the corner.

By utilizing a severe bike-throwing motion, he was able to continue pedaling. He threw his bike upright as the inside pedal was going down, thereby keeping the pedal from striking the road; then he threw the bike back the other way, bringing it upright when the pedal came around again, skipping his rear wheel around the whole way.

Track sprinters actually use a variation of this technique when they are going very slowly on very steep banking (in excess of thirty-five degrees). By leaning to the left as their right pedal comes down to the steep banking, they can keep from catching the pedal, which would cause them to fall.

Szozda mastered this technique. He would fly into these sharp corners and gain four bike lengths on the pack on the first corner. On the second corner, he would have ten lengths. No one could stay with him. He racked up the greatest number of stage victories until only recently, when Olaf Ludwig of Germany, gold medalist in the 1988 Seoul Olympics road race, won more stages. This technique might be a little too radical for most of you, but it illustrates one major point: experiment to find what works for you. You might be surprised with the results.

CLIMBING

The saying goes that climbers are born, not made, and this is true. I do not have the anatomy or physiology of a great climber, but I have improved my climbing dramatically over the span of my career. How? By working on it. There are basics that everybody can work on to improve their climbing technique. You *can* improve. Believe me, I did.

Climbing Basics: Sitting in the Saddle

Cadence. Keep your cadence above 60 RPMs even on the steepest climbs. Ideally, you should aim for an RPM of 75 to 85, but this is not always attainable. Overgearing bogs you down. Heavier riders are especially guilty of this. Undergearing can be equally fatigue-inducing, because a high cadence is simply not sustainable for a lengthy period of time.

Hand placement. Place your hands lightly on the tops of the handlebars, a few inches on either side of the stem or on top of the brake hoods. For long climbs in the saddle, rest your hands on the flat part of the tops of the handlebars. Keep your wrists flat and level, not cocked below the level of the bars. *Never* climb with your hands in the drops—they are for the descents and riding at speed on flat terrain. (One exception to this is at higher speeds, in excess of twenty miles per hour, when aerodynamics becomes a factor.) Climbing on the tops enables you to breathe. Stay relaxed, sit up, and keep your shoulders square.

In the saddle. *The big guns climbing in the 1991 Tour de France. Notice their hand positions on tops of the handlebars, relaxed bend in the elbow, and their upper-body positions— upright and relaxed under the duress of the climb. Greg LeMond is in the leader's jersey in the middle, with glasses but no helmet.*   PHOTO CREDIT: BETH SCHNEIDER

Saddle weight shift.   Notice that riders shift their weight around in the saddle. Many cyclists, like Connie, push their seats back toward the rear of the saddle to gain more leverage when climbing. Others, like myself, tend to pull forward over the nose of the saddle to get the weight right on top of the bottom bracket.

I pull forward because I have strength from my upper thigh (quadriceps) muscles, which I can take advantage of when I am directly over the pedals. I like to move from sitting back on the saddle, to sliding forward and riding the tip, (or *tipping*), to standing off the saddle. This enables me to rotate my positions and muscle use. I try to maintain the momentum of the chosen gear. On steeper climbs, I climb out of the saddle because I have more power standing, and use the added strength of my arms. If you are constantly pushing in one direction, check to see if your bike is properly fitted. With proper positioning, you should be riding primarily on the center of the saddle and pushing back on climbs.

Three examples of saddle weight placement:
TOP: *I call this "tipping" because I pull myself forward onto the top of the saddle, which gets my weight directly over the pedals. Note the angle of my knee over the pedal and how much seat is exposed behind me. I use this position for fast climbing.*

MIDDLE: *Notice how far back my weight is, which forces me to almost push forward—instead of down—on the pedals. The angle of my shin is almost vertical.*

BOTTOM: *My weight is centered nicely over the pedals, which is the more neutral position and is best for all-around riding.*   PHOTO CREDIT: BETH SCHNEIDER

Out of the saddle. On steeper hills and on long climbs when you need to rest your sitting muscles, stand up and out of the saddle. This enables you to use your arms, stretches out your legs, and gets your full weight on the pedals. Pull yourself forward so that your hips are no more than three to four inches in front of the nose of

Out of the saddle. *Steve Bauer powers up a hill ahead of me in the 1985 Coors Classic. Note the weight transfer over the working leg and onto the pedal. Toe, knee, and nose are aligned. Head and shoulders are up—not dragging. Look at Steve's left hand; it's relaxed as his right side does the work.*   PHOTO CREDIT: MICHAEL CHRITTON

the saddle. Ideally you can feel the saddle tip as you move from side to side, but on steeper slopes your hips stay farther back for traction and your upper body is down closer to the bars to keep your front wheel from pulling up. Keep your head and shoulders up; you can always spot a really tired climber, because his head is hanging down.

Weight transfer. Notice that, when seated, you naturally bend your elbows slightly, first your right when you push on your right pedal and then your left elbow as you push on the left pedal. Follow the elbow with your shoulder and your head. This movement gets your weight over the pedal without excessive bobbing. Avoid throwing your head from side to side. Bobbing also occurs when you are overgeared. Move in a horizontal plane from side to side, not up and down. Some riders, like Andy Hampsten and Miguel Indurain, are incredibly smooth climbers, while others, like Greg Lemond, have more upper-body movement. Which is right? Each person has his (or her) own particular style based on what works best for him. Of course, it is better not to waste energy, but many of the world's top climbers have a style that can best be described as "all over the place." As you get tired, your form will become more ragged, so the smoother you are in general, the less chance that you will fall apart under stress.

As the grade steepens or the hill length increases, get out of the saddle. Think of bending and *slightly* dropping your right elbow and letting your weight (shoulders and hips) follow horizontally. Then shift your weight to the other side by pulling up and over, again following the bend in your elbow to get a full weight transfer. Pull with one hand while relaxing the other (consciously let the relaxed fingers lift off the brake hood as you weight the opposite side). Keep your head up and try to keep from throwing your head from side to side.

Move your hips from side to side and try to avoid dropping them from one side to the other. Power comes by extending your leg, not by collapsing your weight onto the pedal. Many riders have a snakelike climbing style, twisting from their head and shoulders down through their hips as they move from side to side. You can see this style even in the professional peloton. Weak arms and shoulders, the root of this problem, force the rider to drop his shoulders—instead of pulling with the arms from side to side. Moving in a horizontal plane is more effective. Hips and shoulders follow the elbows out from side to side, to get the weight over the pedals without excessive movement.

Standing. Try not to let your bike slip backward when you stand up, what I call a drop-kick. Avoid doing this by keeping pressure on the pedals as you stand. When you stop pedaling—even for a fraction of a second—the bike shoots back. Keep your eye on the rider in front of you, because if his wheel shoots backward when he stands up, it might clip your front wheel and send you down. Be alert. Most people

A rider climbs a steep grade in San Francisco with a snakelike style. A more effective style would have the rider's hips move over the pedals from side to side.

PHOTO CREDIT: MICHAEL CHRITTON

don't realize that they drop-kick their rear wheel, so check to see if you do before you start reprimanding everyone else.

When to stand. Sitting for long climbs is much more efficient than standing on the pedals. Stand to get over a short steep section, or to rest the muscles used while sitting. Your RPMs will go down when you stand, so remember to shift if the grade of the hill has not changed to keep your cadence up. If you are a better out-of-the-saddle climber, discipline yourself to sit more in training.

Don't stand for too long—anything over a few minutes is too long and becomes inefficient to maintain. There are exceptions to this. Some South American climbing specialists, like Lucho Herrera of Colombia, have trained themselves to climb forever, or so it seems, out of the saddle. Few cyclists develop this capacity, so sit down within a reasonably short period of time.

Breath play. On long, hard climbs, it helps to control your breathing. Try to exhale on the downstroke. If that seems too rapid, try every other downstroke. But the key is to get control. By concentrating on exhalation you will force air out, leaving more space to be filled. Don't be afraid to blow out forcefully—loud enough so that you and people around you can hear it. Don't worry about concentrating on inhalation. You won't forget to breathe. In races, notice how others are breathing. Sometimes it helps to hear other riders' labored breathing, especially if your breathing is under control. You are not the only one who is working hard and feeling it.

ADVANCED RIDING TECHNIQUES

Sprinting

Even if you never plan to race, sprinting can be a lot of fun and a great way to add spice to your workouts. Who knows, you might be so good that you decide to race.

Come up and out of the saddle with hands deep in the drops, weight centered, and back flat. Keep your head up.
PHOTO CREDIT: JOHN KELLY

Basic Position. Start with your hands on the deepest part of the hook of the drops. Your hands are close to the brakes (if necessary, you can reach the brake with your index finger) and the lower part of the handlebar fits nicely into the palm of your hand, the way a hoe fits into a farmer's hand. Your wrists should be outside the handlebar, not bent inside. This aids in two ways. First, you keep a direct connection between your arms and the bars. Second, you can bend your elbows to the outside, following the line established from your wrists, which will make you more stable if someone bumps against you and also support your weight over the pedals. Your shoulders should be relatively horizontal throughout the entire sprint.

Acceleration. Come up and out of the saddle smoothly without throwing your bike back. To achieve maximum weight transfer on the pedals, let your bike move from side to side underneath you. As your pedal stroke increases, let the bike become stable. Your body position will come forward, your elbows will drop out more, and your head may drop down. Let your head find a comfortable but aerodynamic position that allows you to see where you are going. Stability also comes from knowing where you are going, so be sure to keep your head up; looking up and down constantly is unnecessary and dangerous.

A common mistake in sprinting is moving forward too quickly. That can cause you to bounce your rear wheel from side to side. If your front wheel skips, be sure your arms are not too rigid, and check to see that you are not pulling up with both arms simultaneously. Instead, as you pull your weight over to the left side and onto the left pedal, relax your right arm as you pull up with your right leg.

Concentrate. Sprinting requires complete concentration. Everything in the race leads up to the final sprint. You've already made considerable investment in getting that far, so make it count.

Breathe. Don't forget to breathe. This may sound silly, but many people hold their breath when they sprint. Exhale on the downstroke, like a boxer exhaling when throwing a punch. Practice forcefully exhaling in training sprints to develop this habit.

Be consistent. Try sprint training at least once a week, from early spring to the end of the season. Begin with spin sprints first, at RPMs faster than 120 in the small chainring for at least 200 meters. Progressively work up to bigger gear sprints while keeping a high rate of pedal revolutions. Later, you will be ready for uphill sprints.

Be aggressive in your sprint training. I remember sprint sessions with former world champion Sue Novara-Reber of Flint, Michigan, who would do anything to

My sprint position has not changed much in sixteen years—note my style in 1976 (above, far right) and today. Shoulders square, head up, and heavy reliance on my strong arms.

PHOTO CREDITS: PERSONAL ARCHIVES
AND JOHN KELLY

win a sprint—even in training. Sprinting against her made me really sharp. Sue hated to lose, which made her very feisty—even in training. We'd sprint for a city limit sign and if you tried to come around her, she'd throw something extra at you— a hook, a lean—anything to win. She was a purebred sprinter. Connie improved her sprinting dramatically by sprinting regularly against me and Sue.

Leg speed. Never compromise your leg speed. Sprinting requires both speed and stamina. In Europe, I found that I was not nearly as fast at the end of races longer than four hours as I was after shorter races. Part of the reason I was able to win a pair of stages in the 1988 Tour de Trump here in the United States was that their length of about two hours each suited me. I once asked the legendary Eddy Merckx of Belgium how to improve my sprint for European races. Merckx answered with a

Two-time world sprint champion Sue Novara-Reber winning the 1982 Washington Park criterium stage of the Coors Classic. Sue was a purebred sprinter; her feisty attitude in training paid off in race wins under any conditions. PHOTO CREDIT: BETH SCHNEIDER

laugh that was rooted in his experience of more than 400 victories, including four world championships and five Tours de France: "Ride for six hours and go hard in the last hour. It is the strongest racer who will win in the long races." That was Eddy's idea of sprint training.

Greg LeMond is not a great sprinter, but after a long, hard race, he is very fast. The 1989 world professional championship in Chambéry, France, was 164 miles long on a difficult course. On the final lap Greg was in a lead breakaway of five riders, who were faster than he under normal circumstances. But after seven hours of racing, Greg was the strongest and the fastest—he outsprinted his rivals to win by a wheel. Sprinting is relative. How you perform after a difficult race is a function of your level of fatigue, the other riders' fatigue, your tactics, and your motivation.

CLIMBING

Gearing. One of the biggest mistakes people make climbing involves their gearing. When you come to a hill, shift to the gear you think you might need, but err on the easy side. Then, as you get into the hill, you can shift to a bigger gear and power up the climb. Practice this in training to get used to it, because shifting under pressure can cause problems and takes some physiological adjustments. Once you have mastered this shifting and have the power to back it up, you will be much stronger climbing.

Climbing magic. Stanislaw Szozda was not a great hill climber, so he figured out how to get better. He felt his weakness was cardiovascular, especially his lungs. So he set about improving his performance in anaerobic conditions. That's a big undertaking.

In the winter, he would swim in an indoor pool. The objective was to swim underwater as far as he could. He was teaching his body to function anaerobically, and he was teaching his lungs to use every bit of oxygen possible. More than that, he was teaching himself control—not to panic when he felt a desperate need for more air. He gained confidence from this. He continually worked on expanding his lung capacity, which is something that hardly anyone thinks about, much less works on. Physiologists might scoff at this, but it worked for Szozda.

Our lungs have a surface area that would cover a tennis court. Each of us consumes considerable air—about 20,000 liters daily. But our lungs use only a small portion of the air we breathe. Szozda wanted to train his body to be more efficient with the air he inhaled.

Incorporating this in his cycling, Szozda was not afraid to ride 110 percent on the climbs, forcing his body to work with less oxygen. When he got into a race, he would wait until the point when everybody was dying, including himself, but he would have that little bit extra. By training certain responses in his body, he took his climbing to a new level.

Power climbing: five-time Tour de France winner Bernard Hinault is a study in power and concentration. Look at the perfect alignment of his toe, knee, and nose.

PHOTO CREDIT: DOUG CONARROE

PACK RIDING

The old adage "safety in numbers" does not apply to cycling. One of the reasons that mass-start running races can take place is that running is a relatively safe sport. The dangers inherent in riding wheel to wheel make mass-start cycling races unfeasible.

Group riding is great fun and extremely energy efficient, but it can also be intimidating. The key to comfort and safety is to ride with people you know and trust. Of course, in a race or large tour, this is not possible. By working on your own skills and by learning to recognize safer riders, you will improve your chances of a safe ride.

The United States Cycling Federation has a categorization system for racers based on bike handling, experience, and fitness. Beginning racers have traditionally started as Category 4 (a Category 5 was added in 1992) and work up to the highest category (Category 1) through a points system. Often the difference in riders' abilities is in their bike handling, not necessarily their fitness. It takes time to develop as a racer.

A good way to work on fundamentals is by participating in club riding. New riders can't imagine their elbows being bumped while out riding, or having someone touch their handlebars, without instantly falling down. These cyclists tend to ride alone, something that is particularly characteristic of triathletes whose competitions are by definition solo efforts. But a lot of riders, no matter how strong they are, freak out when they get into a bicycle race where everybody lines up in a mass and competes together. This is true of many triathletes who shy away from large groups and have a difficult time if they do try pack racing.

Group riding is fundamental to bicycle racing. Use the group to your advantage to see how much faster you can go than plugging away solo. The reason that you can ride so fast is that it costs you much less energy to ride in the draft of another rider or a group of riders. By riding behind a car or truck you can really feel the benefit of the draft. You are literally riding in a pocket of air that seems to pull you along.

According to a recent study, riding in the shelter of a pack traveling twenty-five miles per hour requires you to use almost 40 percent less oxygen than if you were at the front of the pack. This is an incredible savings. The more sheltered you are, the greater the advantage. The faster you ride, the greater the advantage. This is why it is not as advantageous to *climb* in someone's draft as it is to *sprint* in someone's draft; the advantage is relative to the speed you are traveling.

Benefits to riding in a group extend beyond simply riding faster and with less effort. Riding in a group is challenging and fun. Getting comfortable in a pack is all a matter of practice, which is what many clubs help to provide on weekend club rides. Seek out the smaller, more structured rides that are bound to be safer and more instructional. The Morgul-Bismark Bike Shop weekend bike rides that we routinely conduct in Boulder are geared toward all riders. We make an effort to keep the groups small, disciplined, well-mannered, and safe, while still providing a vehicle for fun, fast riding.

PACK BASICS

Stay relaxed. How many times do we need to say it? Stay calm and stay relaxed if you want to be safe and comfortable. The instant you start to tense up, you will find yourself losing control of your bike. Your arms serve as shock absorbers. Let your arms absorb some of the road shock instead of your wheels and bike. This will help your equipment last longer. Keep an eye on form, from the hands up to the shoulders. Relax.

Overlapping wheels. Remember to guard your front wheel, because it is the least stable. Let's say the wind is coming from the right, so you are slightly overlapping the rider's rear wheel in front of you to the left. Suddenly, he swerves left. Where does that leave you? Probably in the ditch if you aren't prepared. You need to be aware of sudden movements and try to anticipate them. If you have a little experience, you will not overreact and crash. It is common to lean into the wheel you are making contact with. When the wheels separate, you are leaning too far and you fall over. Another reaction is to turn the wheel away too sharply. Learn to lean or pull away from the other bike to stay upright. Don't panic if you feel someone touching your rear wheel, because while it may be distracting, your rear wheel is very stable.

Overreacting. This is common in many situations. Use both brakes sparingly. Remember that the front brake will stop you more quickly and the rear brake will skid if used heavily. Use moderation. If your brake adjustment is loose, you can grip the brakes harder—the common reaction in a crisis—and they won't skid. Don't swerve unnecessarily or too quickly, which might send the rider behind you down. Be fair to those around you and try to hold your line within the pack. If you are trying to move up or around, do so when it is safe for those around you.

Focus a few feet up the road instead of only on the spinning wheel in front of you. By looking up the road, you get a better perspective of what is coming down the road. If you look at the rear wheel in front of you, you are more likely to fail to react to group movements. Besides, it's hypnotic to stare at one thing so close to you, making your focus too narrow.

Recognize safe riders. Have you ever been in a situation where you see a rider that seems to wobble in front of you? That's an indication that the cyclist is riding the brakes. Stay away from him. Also be wary of the rider who fails to ride the paceline smoothly and is always popping out into traffic. This rider is probably uncomfortable in a pack, and you don't want to be behind him. The term "squirrelly rider" applies to a rider who darts all over the road. Stay away from these kinds of riders. Safe riders sit solidly on their bikes, do not make erratic movements, and are generally reliable.

DRILLS TO PRACTICE FOR SAFER RIDING

Wear your helmet and gloves for these exercises. Be sure your handlebars are tightened down at the stem. Ride within your comfort zone and be careful.

Bumping. One common practice is bumping with some friends in an easy gear on a large grassy field. Bumping is simply riding close together, leaning shoulder to shoulder, elbow to elbow, handlebar to handlebar. Your contacts can be brief or prolonged; the art is not in touching, but in feeling how you can extricate yourself from the contact. You need not fall down (though you might, and that's why you want to do this on a grassy field and not on the road). Stay relaxed. When you touch, lean in a little and use your body to pull yourself away. Don't make radical movements or jerk away quickly; this will likely throw you off balance. Lean away, and steer straight ahead. Switch sides with your partner, so that you feel comfortable on both your left and right. Finally, try a three-up bumping exercise—we call this *the sandwich*.

Wheel touching. While you are on the grassy field, practice touching your front tire against the rear tire of the rider in front of you. Pull up about two or three inches past the plane of your partner's rear wheel and steer into him sharply, then promptly turn away. This is called *overlapping wheels*.

Slow race. The slow race at our camps is really a lot of fun, because it requires tactics and bike handling. We start out with everyone in a large square on a grassy field. If anyone puts a foot down or falls over, they're out. All form of contact is allowed—head butts, body leans, straight arms—as the riders slowly ride around. Sneak attacks—from the rear—are encouraged. As the group size shrinks, the size of the square is brought in tighter. As we get down to a few riders, the tactics are very creative, and it is always great fun to watch as the final rider is left upright. This type of practice encourages you to be creative and stable on your bike, hopefully in an upright position. Your bike is very capable of staying upright at any speed, and so are you.

Pack-Riding Form. We emphasize group riding at our bike camps in Beaver Creek Resort. We especially encourage riding two abreast when the roadway, traffic, and local laws allow it. Riding two abreast is good for your bike handling and pack awareness and provides you with a method to ride faster: the paceline. A paceline is nothing more than a group of riders, each taking pace. This can take the form of a single or double (two abreast) paceline.

Riding etiquette. One of your obligations when you ride in a pack is to point out or call out road hazards. Don't just look out for yourself; be courteous of those behind you. If you spot a rock or rough road surface and it is easy to point out—do so. If it endangers you to point, call out loudly. But don't be like the boy who cried wolf—you can't call out every speck of gravel. Your obligation is to call out threatening obstacles. It's your decision, but if you keep calling out nonhazards no one is going to listen to you when something important comes along.

Another obligation is to prevent *gaps* from opening between you and the rider in front of you. Of course, there will be times when you cannot sustain the pace—but if this occurs on a regular basis and you are riding like a yo-yo, you might better spend your time at the back of the pack learning to ride comfortably behind the wheel in front of you. That way you won't have to worry about the riders behind you, since there won't be any.

When it is your turn to *pull through* (take the position at the front of the paceline), maintain the same speed as when you were drafting. The normal temptation is to speed up. Nothing destroys a paceline faster than an ever-escalating pace. If you have a handlebar computer, monitor the pace until your sense of pace is well-established. You won't prove anything with an overzealous pull at the front during a training ride.

You should always pull through, even in a race, because it helps to keep the pace going. That does not mean you are obligated to pull long; if you are struggling, you can go to the front and pull off quickly. If you truly cannot maintain the pace, you are better off sitting on the back of the group. This practice of sitting in, or *wheel-sucking* as it is called, will make you pretty unpopular in a race—especially if you are in a breakaway or a motivated chase group. Your riding partners want you to work, not rest. However, it is a better tactic to sit on the back than to die and get dropped because you pulled at the front. Just be prepared for some venomous words from your riding partners.

Don't *half-wheel* the rider next to you. When you ride a two-by-two, your goal is to ride even with your partner, hub to hub, handlebar to handlebar. Many riders have the annoying habit of always riding about a half wheel ahead of their riding partner. Most people don't even realize they are half-wheeling. This is aggravating. Your partner might continually try to ride next to you, but you keep inching forward, escalating the pace and driving your riding partner nuts. This is an easy habit to break once it's recognized.

Even the pros are guilty of half-wheeling. On one early-season 7-Eleven team ride from Santa Monica to Santa Barbara, Bob Roll and Jock Boyer were riding two abreast at the front of the group. Jock started to half-wheel Bob. Nobody half-wheels Bob and gets away with it. Bob kept forcing the pace by trying to ride next to him, and the pace escalated for almost an hour until Jock finally had to drop back. He sat behind everyone—like a puppy with his tail between his legs—for the rest of the ride.

Conversational rotation. This is a standard group riding formation and should be employed in most casual riding situations. It is also the basis for the more complex and faster-moving echelon formation that is essential practice for pack-style racing. You start out two-by-two. The first rotation begins when the rider on the front left pulls up in front of the rider on his right. He moves forward and, when past the rider's front wheel, he pulls to the right. That cyclist is now front right, and the rider who was previously behind him on the left moves up to front left. In this way, the riders on the left move up and the riders on the right are moving back. Ideally, if the wind is from the left, the line moves from the right across to the left.

Another rotation commonly practiced is to ride two-by-two and have the front two pull to the outside (the rider on the left pulls to the left and the rider on the right pulls to the right), to let the second pair pass through to the front. The leaders then drop to the back. This rotation takes up more road space and is less useful overall than echelon work, but is commonly practiced out of habit. It is a lazy way to ride. The conversational rotation, a precursor to the echelon, gives you more opportunity for, well, conversation.

Echelons. These types of pack formations are simple and essential, but everyone seems to make a big deal out of performing them correctly. Let's say the wind is coming from the right as you ride down the road among a small group—say, six riders. You are riding paired, but your formation takes on more of an oval shape since you are staggered from the lead right to the rear left. The lead rider is to the far right edge of the road. The rider to your left will pull in front of the leader and almost immediately start to ease off to let the third rider do the work of moving into the wind, in front of the second rider. The first rider is sitting directly behind the second rider—to his left, resting as the right line drops back and the left line works up the road in a circular fashion. Each rider works for a short time in a true echelon, often only a few seconds and certainly less than a minute, when the next rider takes the lead.

The most common mistake in an echelon formation is failing to follow the rider in front of you all the way back (on the line that is dropping back). You need protection to recover, and this is what keeps the group tightly formed. The second most common mistake is to pull too hard at the front. You are aiming to keep a consistent pace. When the pace is erratic, it is more difficult to maintain and gaps open up.

When the wind is coming from the left, the lead riders move out to the left, providing enough shelter for those riders in the working group, without being stuck in the proverbial "gutter." Riding the gutter, or extreme right side of the road, is tricky and dangerous. It provides the least protection in a big group of riders echeloned across the road from the left to the right and followed by a train of single-file riders running down the gutter. The danger of being in the gutter is not only from rough road, making handling difficult, but also from the riders in front of you who grow tired and open a gap. Gaps are extremely difficult to close in windy situations.

When you ride or race in a strong crosswind, the pack generally splits up quickly and you have to stay toward the front. Once you are dropped in a strong wind, only the rare rider can make it back up to the front group. Bike handling can become erratic with high winds, so keep a firmer grip on the bars and ride defensively.

The safest approach is to be up front in the echelon, or to form a second tier of echelon behind the first. You benefit from the front tier, and stay out of the gutter. Echelon riding is especially important for any small-group fast riding, and comes into play especially in the windy flatlands of Holland, Belgium, or the American Midwest.

TIME TRIALS

Time trials are called the races of truth, because you race the clock and the clock never lies.

In today's high-tech era, however, this perception is being challenged. Time trialing used to be simple even ten years ago. The technological revolution brought about in the last decade has taken time trialing from the simple—man against clock—to the complex—man and machine against clock. The key to gaining an advantage in the time trial is a few well-chosen pieces of equipment, properly set up.

Aero Anatomy: Optimal Time-Trial Bike Setup

Aside from having aerodynamic equipment, it helps if your body is aerodynamic. Wind-tunnel testing has shown that some riders sit on the bike at a greater aerodynamic advantage than others. Some of this is determined by anatomy, some by bike positioning. Greg LeMond, one of the world's best time trialists, sits on the saddle with his pelvis tilted forward, which enables him to get his head, shoulders, and back down in the most advantageous—or aerodynamic—position. The combination of tilting the pelvis forward and using aero bars to drop your head and narrow your shoulders enables you to close the wind pocket around your hips and midsection, allowing the air to flow more easily around you, not smash into you.

Your goal is to find a position that enables your head and shoulders to drop below your back, reducing your frontal air resistance. This is not practical for everybody and you may be limited by your anatomy. Use a video camera to assess your own position. If you have access to experts, try consulting them; with myriad new equipment options, it is often difficult to know what to do or where to begin. I started by consulting Leonard Zinn, a Boulder frame builder who has studied aerodynamics, about bike position. He advised me to get my forearms and elbows out front and as close together as possible, which would effectively close off the hole between my shoulders and hips. This is the position I adopted for the 1991 season, which I found to be effective. My chest cavity is elongated in this position and I can breathe easily, while still being as aerodynamic and powerful as I can be.

Many riders use the aero bars but make the mistake of mounting them in a position that does not give them any functional advantage because they are still sitting too high. You have to try to get your head and shoulders low, while keeping your back and chest long and relaxed. If you can't relax and breathe, you still won't go any faster no matter what equipment you use. If you are too stretched out, you will lose your effective power position.

Aero bars do make a difference. This is illustrated by an experience I had before the 1989 Tour de Trump race. I was out training on my time-trial bike and testing out a pair of then-new Scott aero bars. Alex Stieda was motorpacing, and I joined him, so that two of us were taking turns sitting behind the motorcycle and each other. When he sat behind me, he had to work really hard to keep up, almost getting dropped many times. But when I sat behind him, I was almost coasting. The difference was the bars, which had made my position more aerodynamic and greatly reduced my work. Wow, what a revelation! Andy Hampsten wanted to save these bars as a secret weapon for the Tour de France, but we knew we would need them in the Tour de Trump, which finished with a time trial.

In the penultimate Tour de Trump time trial, Greg LeMond used regular bars and beat me by only a few seconds for tenth place (the closest I will ever be to him in a time trial). Four of my teammates who used the bars finished in the top ten. And Ron Kiefel won.

Greg went on to use the bars to win both time trials in the 1989 Tour de France. He won the Tour on the last day's time trial due to several factors: his great ability, desire to win, and his equipment.

One obvious drawback of aero bars is the increased distance between your hands and the brakes, making these types of bars impractical for road racing. But in a time trial, where your brakes are seldom used, this is less of an issue. Contrary to some cyclists' fears, this position does not restrict breathing. Instead, the lengthening out

*Aero bars make a difference. Dave
Farmer slices through the air by
narrowing his frontal resistance
and closing the air flow into the
chest/hip cavity. Aero bars also
enable you to stretch out your back
and open your rib cage, which
enhances your breathing.*
PHOTO CREDIT: JOHN KELLY

of your torso has a positive effect by enabling you to open up—not close—your rib
cage.

Disc wheels. Disc wheels are a great advantage in time trials, and may give you
an advantage of a second or more per mile over normal spoked wheels. Since the
disc wheel first appeared in 1983, it has become less expensive and more widely
available. Companies like J-Disc have developed a disc wheel that is simply a light
road wheel with a light covering over the spokes. This gives you the same feel and
control as does a road wheel, and the added advantage of being more reasonably
priced. The Coors Light team used the J-Disc for the prologue at the Tour du Pont
and placed three riders in the top ten. These wheels are also being used for open
races, with good results.

Trispoke wheels have three thick spokes that are flat. Trispoke wheels are becoming increasingly popular. They have many of the characteristics of a disc wheel, with the increased responsiveness of a road wheel.

The question of whether to use a double disc (front and rear) arises frequently at the elite cycling level. Sean Yates was the only rider on 7-Eleven (now Motorola) who could ride a double disc with aero bars, which he successfully used to win the 1989 Grand Prix Eddy Merckx in Belgium. I find that the front disc makes me feel like I am riding on a train rail. I can ride straight, but have limited handling ability. It's not easy to get used to. Most riders opt for a lightweight spoked front wheel, which is easier to handle. Front discs generally require you to have a special time-trial bike—which most people do not have.

Handlebar information. A good handlebar cycle computer will help your time trialing by enabling you to constantly monitor your speed and cadence.

More and more athletes are using a heart-rate monitor to accurately assess the body's response to work and recovery. A heart-rate monitor has two parts—a

Andy Hampsten shows good positioning and good equipment choice. Note the handlebar setup, the sloping top tube, disc wheel, aero helmet—all designed to help Andy gain valuable time.   PHOTO CREDIT: BETH SCHNEIDER

beltlike strap that fits around your chest, and a receiver-monitor that you can easily mount on your handlebars. Electrodes in the belt send your heart's impulses to the receiver-monitor, where you can read your heart rate. Many heart-rate monitors have a memory function that allows you to review the day's response to the training or race following the event.

Caution. Loading the handlebars with the latest microchip technology is not always a coach's dream. One pitfall is that you become too reliant on this technology and fail to listen enough to yourself. Here you are with these gizmos that beep and flash on your handlebars and what have you learned? Don't be like the child who only learns to "tie" shoes with Velcro straps. Sometimes it pays to do things the old-fashioned way.

You have to learn to *feel* the cadence and the speed, not just read them on the computer. And you must know when your heart rate is high or low by feeling it, not simply seeing it on the monitor. Using the computer and the heart-rate monitor will enable you to get more out of your training and racing when used properly, but you can't program them to tell you how fast to go; you will have to do that for yourself.

THE DOWNSIDE OF RACING: CRASHING

Crash Prevention

Crashing is part of cycling, but good riders crash seldom. And it isn't just luck. Golfer Gary Player said, "The more you practice, the luckier you get." It's true. You make your own luck. Most riders that crash swear that they could not find a way around it.

When you crash, evaluate why. It might be true that you just got stuck behind the wrong rider, but maybe you should have avoided that rider. Stay away from known crashers, stay toward the front, and stay alert. The number-one goal is to train yourself to avoid a crash in the first place. The drills offered in the pack-riding section are excellent for crash-prevention training. The more comfortable you are on your bike, the more you can react, and avoid *over*reacting. Control on the bike will also give you confidence to get around a crash.

Much can be done to prevent falls. When you're in a precarious situation, you have to concentrate and relax. It's a matter of experience to know that your wheels can slide and you can adjust your body position to compensate so you don't fall down. If a group of riders fall in front of you, you have to react by stopping quickly or swerving to avoid the pileup. This takes split-second reactions. Experience, concentration, and alertness will buy you time to avoid a crash.

Another helpful measure that seems so simple that it is easy to overlook, especially for adults, is to practice rolling and tumbling on a lawn, or indoors on a mat. I grew up with a trampoline in my backyard, which I feel increased my agility and aided my crash reactions. Landing on an extended arm, or a hit on the shoulder, can break the collarbone or a tiny bone in the wrist called the navicular, which is very slow to heal. These are common cycling injuries.

To avoid falling, position on the bicycle is important. At high speeds, be sure you put your hands deep in the handlebar drops and keep your fingers accessible to the brakes. Put your weight a little back on the saddle, but not fixed to the saddle; you should be able to adjust your body position around a turn. Use the skills you've learned to finesse your way around a pileup.

Riders who come into the sport from mountain biking or BMX (Bicycle Moto-Cross), such as Greg Oravetz and John Tomac, have amazing reaction ability instilled in them to prevent crashes. Riding mountain bikes on irregular terrain that causes wheels to slide and changes the rider's center of balance helps sharpen handling skills that prevent crashes.

Andy Hampsten rarely crashes. He is an example of someone who has managed to avoid them. It's a matter of having some experience with what happens when you get in a bad situation, such as overlapped wheels, or oil on a turn. Prevention stems from what you have previously practiced. You develop learned responses that come into play in threatening situations.

There are many ways to fall off a bike, but the bicycle is extremely stable. The fundamentals of cycling are crucial. When you practice what might happen, you're prepared for the unexpected. You can see this when you take your hands off the handlebars and sway the bike back and forth. I've seen some riders do amazing things to keep from falling because they have developed the skill of keeping themselves on top of the bicycle. Get used to the bike; don't be afraid of it.

War Stories: You Gotta Get Back Up

Crashing, a fact of racing, makes for good stories even before the wounds heal. I'm always careful, yet there are times when I've got to go for it and ride aggressively. When I make a mistake, I pay for it—usually with my hide. My crashes are noted here because I have had some that were spectacular. They become part of my repertoire of war stories, which are hell to live through but fun to tell about later.

During the 1983 Coors Classic, in the North Boulder Park stage—in front of my hometown crowd—I made the breakaway. We were lapping the field, and I was raging. Then I clipped my pedal on a pylon while making a turn leading to the back stretch. I fell, and everybody behind me piled on top. I lay under the heap with a badly sprained wrist and my entire side scraped raw. We all quickly got back on our bikes anyway, and I went on to win the stage. *Sports Illustrated* covered the race and ran a photo of me with my hand, knee, and hip piled with huge ice bags. Teammates were holding me up, because I was ready to pass out.

Several times in my career, I've crashed and really gotten scraped up, but I often got back on my bike. I never let a crash bother me. Once in the Tour of Texas, Steve Bauer and I were having one of our epic battles at the end of a race in Fort Worth. I was drafting snugly behind his rear wheel and he was trying to shake me by snaking back and forth across the road. Steve cut through lane markers that were like cannonballs submerged in the pavement. He narrowly missed one lane marker, but I hit it squarely with my front wheel. I fell at thirty miles an hour. Another rider who had been sitting on my rear wheel fell, and as he landed his pedal punctured my right calf muscle.

I was in pain by the time I got back on my bike. Right after I finished I went to the hospital, where my calf was stitched together. It left me with a scar that forms a nice *T* for Texas. Doctors told me not to ride for about a week because the cut was so deep. I promised Connie that I would not race. But on race day, I got in my uniform and warmed up. Connie saw me and really let me have it. But I raced and won in Dallas. A photographer shot a photo of me that was featured on the cover of *Competitive Cycling*. My legs and arms were covered with bandages and surgical netting.

I don't like to be remembered for my spectacular crashes, but rather for overcoming them. Crashing is literally the downside of cycling—do your best to prevent it, but it does happen. When you crash, you have to get right back on the bike and start riding again.

ROAD RASH—WHAT TO DO

One of the primary reasons racers shave their legs is that if they have road rash from a fall, cleaning the wound is easier without hair. Cleaning out road rash is no fun, but it's basic first aid. Often there is road dirt and even asphalt mixed into the abrasion, and the wound has to be cleaned to prevent infection.

Scrub the rash area hard right away with a clean soapy washcloth to clean it out completely. If you are going home, do it in the shower and be thorough. And be careful if someone else cleans you up; make sure you are dirt-free. Not all emergency-trained personnel are experienced with road rash—I have had some use rubbing alcohol on the wounds, which is extremely painful—and are hesitant to scrub hard enough.

We use hydrogen peroxide, because it greatly reduces the chance of infection. There are medicated brushes you can purchase that are also effective. Regular applications of hydrogen peroxide during the first few days after the injury can speed recovery on areas like the hands that are more difficult to bandage and more likely to get infected. Put on a medicated antibacterial cream, like Bacitracin or Neosporin, and a gauze pad and tape it up. Change the dressing frequently, because they soak through. The gauze pad shouldn't stick to the abrasion, so use the cream generously. Milder abrasions can be left to dry out after a day or so, but the deeper ones need more attention to be sure they are not infected. Signs of infection include excessive weeping or oozing of yellow pus, excessive redness, tenderness, and fever. Soaking the wounds in warm water can help. See your doctor immediately if you are concerned.

To help reduce scarring, Vitamin E oil and pure aloe vera cream are effective. That treatment, combined with liberal sunscreen applications to protect the damaged skin from sunburn, greatly reduces the scarring.

Overcoming Crash Phobia

Often I get questions from people who have crashed and are spooked about getting back onto their bicycle again. One of our Carpenter/Phinney Cycling Camp riders was an older rider who fell and was afraid to ride again. The same thing happened to me after I crashed at speed in April 1988 during the 170-mile Belgian classic, Liege–Bastogne–Liege. I went headfirst into the back of a station wagon. At the hospital, a surgeon had to break my nose to reset it properly, and close cuts on the left side of my face with more than 150 stitches. Just before centerpunching the station wagon, I had raised my left arm up to protect my face, and my forearm received many cuts as well.

A cyclist who suffers a hard crash is confronted with the same problem as somebody who falls off a horse or gets hit by a baseball. You have to get your confidence back. *Don't wait too long.*

What you lose when you are spooked is that ease with which you do something. You're accustomed to acting from learned instinct. Responses come naturally. But when you're scared, you overthink, and it makes you second-guess yourself. It takes the joy away, and the only way to overcome that phobia is to get back on your bike and get going right away.

Two days after smashing into the station wagon, I went out riding. The window glass had cut a muscle in my left wrist, so I had a big cast on my arm. After a week, I cut the cast off and went on a six-hour ride. I was terrified the whole ride. Belgium has narrow roads. Every car that came around a corner scared me. This was a fear I had to overcome by putting myself back in the environment, or I would have had to quit for good—and I wasn't ready to do that.

I had 150 stitches in my face after I crashed into the back of a station wagon in a Belgian Classic. Less than six months later, I won the Coors International Bicycle Classic. You can't let a crash keep you off your bike.

PHOTO CREDIT: JOE DANIEL

I rode my first race ten days after the accident. I was jumpy the whole way, but as the race went on, my confidence began to return and I gradually relaxed. Still, it took three or four races before I felt as if I was back emotionally and wasn't preoccupied with falling. In a month's time, I won a stage of the Tour of Romandie that finished in Geneva, Switzerland. I had made it over the hurdle, probably the biggest one of my career.

Rebecca Twigg of Seattle, silver medalist in the 1984 Los Angeles Olympics women's road race, is an example of someone who took too many falls and never rode comfortably in the pack again. In 1986, she fell on the rain-slick course in the finishing stretch of the worlds, while on a two-up break with Jeannie Longo. Then she suffered a training accident. After that she couldn't even ride in the pack. She would hang five to ten feet off the back for the entire race, until she felt she could make a race-winning move, or chase after a break that was going. Then she would shoot past everyone and either go away solo or return to the very back of the pack. Nobody is strong enough to do that for long, not even a rider of her exceptional caliber. In 1988, she retired quite unceremoniously, after not making the Olympic Team.

Much of your ability to recover depends on your personality and temperament. How much is cycling worth to you? It is dangerous at times. Anyone who says it isn't is a liar. But you cannot dwell on the danger. Connie had a bad accident in 1984 and knew that if she thought about it, she wouldn't make it to the Olympics. So she put it behind her, but she also knew that the kind of risk-taking that makes a good cyclist was starting to fade out of her. You have to know yourself. Cycling isn't a sport to do in half measures.

Often you see riders sitting so rigidly on their bicycles that when they hit a bump the front wheel turns sideways and immediately they're down. Or they are rigid on descents, and when they hit gravel they fall right over, rather than relaxing and compensating with their body to pull the bike back under them to prevent a crash.

We counsel that whenever you ride, including races, be sure to focus on what you are doing so that you can respond properly. Leave your Walkman at home. You need all your senses to ride a bike well, especially at speed. If you're thinking about something else and people fall in front of you, their crash may be your crash. Most crashes are preventable.

Not all crashes are limited to races, either. Once I fell just two blocks from home, on the way out for a training ride, because I hit a pothole while adjusting my shoe. On the other extreme, at the end of a 7-Eleven training camp in northern California, in Rancho Murieta, right before we went to Europe as professionals in 1985, I had a classic fall that could have been avoided. It was at the end of a six-hour ride, at the end of a month of six-hour rides, and I was extremely fatigued. We were coasting down a hill and talking. I wasn't in the ride mentally. We hit a bump and my hands went off the handlebars. I fell forward and went straight down, without any time to react. My fall broke a couple of fingers. This is a perfect example of losing concentration because I was too tired and almost home. You're never home until you're off the bicycle.

SECTION 3
TRAINING: BASIC PRINCIPLES (Connie)

SCIENCE, EXPERIENCE, INTUITION, AND LUCK

Training Is a Dynamic Process

Every athlete talks about training. Training is synonymous with sports. Think of *spring training* for baseball. *Training camp* for football. Gymnasts and basketball players "practice" instead of train, but it's all the same. In every sport, athletes must practice their craft to improve skills and conditioning. But what *is* training? Basically, it is a system of overload and response. Cycling imposes stress on the body, which responds by adapting. In cycling, this translates to increased endurance and greater strength. But these improvements are not static. Just as the body responds with greater capacity, several weeks of no training—detraining—will result in decreased capacity. Training is a dynamic process, as intricate as it is simple.

When carried out systematically, training leads to improved performance. As individuals, we have widely varied needs and responses. One athlete may thrive on training thirty hours per week, another may need just fifteen, yet on race day the two may be equal. If we weren't different, creating training prescriptions would be easy. We can't give you a specific program because we don't know enough about you. What we will provide is information from which you can plan your own training program.

Training Demands Specificity

To derive the most from any training plan, specificity is essential. If you want to improve your cycling, you must cycle more. Cycling can be viewed as a puzzle with many interrelated pieces—hill-climbing, time trialing, endurance, descending, and sprinting. Each of these pieces must be integrated to develop a total program. For example, if you want to improve your climbing, you must either climb or simulate climbing through interval training on your bicycle. If you want to improve your sprint, you must repeatedly speed down the road explosively.

He who trains the most does not necessarily improve the most or perform the best. Part of the success of the Soviet athletes throughout the last few decades has been attributed to their large athlete pool. They were able to take this large pool and funnel them all through exhaustive and intensive training that few can handle. Many of those who survive go on to be world-class athletes. Others, many with legitimate talent, end up going back to where they came from, having failed to survive the system.

I witnessed this when I was in Moscow where packs of young riders would train daily near the Olympic Park. They were in third- or fourth-generation clothing and rode ill-fitting ancient bikes, but they rode and rode. This was their meal ticket and their chance to ultimately get out of the Soviet Union as part of their national team. Now young Soviets dream of following in the footsteps of 1988 Olympic gold medalist Viatscheslav Ekimov, who is reportedly paid half a million dollars per year to race with the Dutch professional team, Panasonic.

We saw this among their gymnasts, too, who trained in the gym adjacent to the Olympic Velodrome. Many young girls below the age of ten were training daily in the gym. Their physiques were perfectly sculpted from hours of training. Which ones would make it?

The Outcome of Specificity for Cyclists: Suppleness

One thing all serious racing cyclists must do is to cycle—and only cycle during the season. A quality of muscle called suppleness develops from cycling. Suppleness can be characterized as firm yet soft muscles. It allows the muscle to relax during the rest phase of the pedal stroke. This quality also enables the cyclist to pedal at a high cadence for hours, working and recovering throughout each pedal stroke. But more than that, the supple muscle can respond to speed changes, enabling a cyclist to maintain a steady tempo during a race and then break away at a higher speed and finally sprint even faster. The cyclists' muscles are trained to accommodate these pace changes. The supple muscle allows the blood to easily deliver nutrients to the working muscle fibers, which helps to sustain activity at any speed. Massage helps develop this quality; a good masseuse can tell when a rider's legs are fit by feeling muscle suppleness.

Demands on the muscles are great during long-distance cycling. If your average cadence is 90 per minute, that means 5,400 strokes per leg per hour, and more than 20,000 strokes per leg during the course of a 100-mile ride. A 10,000-mile season represents more than two million pedal strokes *per leg*. Some might call it monotony or redundancy, but in training talk, it is *specificity*. The body adjusts, accommodates, and adapts. Improvement follows.

Cyclists become so specialized, and their muscles so used to the limited range of motion required in the pedal stroke, that when they are late for a flight and have to run to get to the gate, they tend to suffer from muscle stiffness for days. A cyclist's legs are not used to the jarring or the stress of carrying the body's full weight. The old axiom, "Don't stand when you can sit, don't sit when you can lie down," applies to the elite cyclist who, when not riding, can usually be found off his feet.

Take a Systematic Approach

Training must be approached as a process that takes time. Results do not come automatically, and every cyclist's body responds differently. Training must be systematic, which means it must be thorough, regular, and organized. You must build in frequency, in a series of repeated efforts over days, weeks, months, and even years.

Beyond Science

Ultimately, training programs are based on an eclectic mix of scientific and experiential fact, intuition, and just plain luck. It is a guessing game of sorts, but knowing more about the physiological basis for training might help you progress toward a more sound training program. Knowing why you are doing what you are doing and then doing it over time will lead you along the road to increased performance. Isn't that where you want to be?

Recipe for Success?

Think about the ingredients needed to be a good cyclist. They can be divided into four broad categories: physical, technical, mental, and mechanical. First you must develop the obvious physical qualities of stamina and speed. Second, you need to have technical skills to sprint and climb efficiently, and be able to corner and descend at speed. Third, you must possess mental qualities that encompass a wide range—tactics, toughness, perseverance, relaxation, and positive imagery. Finally, mechanics can be critical in your performance outcome—proper bike fit and equipment choices are all part of the game.

The recipe for a successful cyclist combines the ingredients above, but in what order? In what amounts? Is a pinch of stamina and a cup of speed enough? Does a pound of perseverance and toughness outweigh a pound of speed?

You will find that successful cyclists are made up of a combination of these ingredients, but the combinations vary among champions. There seems to be no formula that determines a champion. Champions are born, and then made. This applies to all of us. We all need to work to be our best. Good, thoughtful training rounds us out as individuals, by maximizing our strengths and minimizing our weaknesses. Training is what makes good cyclists great.

Different types of training concentrate on developing different capabilities and capacities. To be a good cyclist, you must blend the various types of training to gain specific improvements in each area. What you will find is that it seems there is not enough time in the week to train all these different areas, but with careful planning, you will manage to cover most, if not all, of the bases.

Heart Rate and Training Zones

A lot has been written about training programs designed around target heart-rate *zones*. This type of specificity is the result of increased scientific knowledge and the widespread use of heart-rate monitors, which enable you to easily check your pulse as you ride. Heart-rate training adds accuracy to training. Zones are divided into categories based on the physiological response that a particular heart rate elicits.

We are not fanatical advocates of strict heart-rate monitoring, but instead establish zones that combine your subjective response (how hard it feels) with your actual heart rate. This allows the athlete flexibility within a workout to evaluate how hard the effort is, an evaluation that the heart-rate monitor will substantiate or contradict. Once I was out for an easy ride with Scott Berryman, a national track team sprinter who had just returned from a difficult European racing trip. He was tired, and his heart rate was in the high 150s when he was riding easily. When we went up a hill, it went into the 180s. This kind of response is indicative of overtraining. Scott needed a break.

When heart rate–based training first became popular in the mid-1980s, many athletes were told that training below a heart rate of 120 to 140 beats per minute (BPM) was a waste of time. This is not the case in cycling, where your weight is being supported by the bike. It's easy to ride relatively fast while maintaining a heart rate below 120 BPM or roughly 60 to 70 percent of maximum heart rate. In other sports, like running and cross-country skiing—where you support your body weight—it's almost impossible to do the exercise with a pulse below 120 BPM. Cycling relies primarily on one large muscle group, the quadriceps. If you are constantly pushing on every ride, your quadriceps will never recover from training. If your *legs* are dead, *you* are dead.

This is one reason that cross-training is beneficial for the recreational cyclist. By complementing your cycling with running or roller-blading, for example, you can increase your fitness by using other muscle groups and let your quadriceps recover.

Roy Knickman is one racer who, as a young professional in Europe, followed the training methods of Paul Koechli, who was then La Vie Claire coach. Koechli advocated a demanding plan based on heart rate and building endurance. In the early winter, Roy was training hard on his bike for four to five hours a day. He was training so hard, no one would ride with him. After six weeks, he was fried. It took him several months just to recover.

That's why recovery training and very light endurance training (pulse 100–120 BPM) is the base of any good program. You have to learn to go slow before you can go fast. Going slow gives your body a chance to recover and adapt. You can improve because you are building, not always tearing down. A cyclist spends well over two-thirds of his time on the bike at this slower pace.

Maximum heart rate can be accurately determined during a graded exercise test in a laboratory, or you can run your own maximal test. Select a hill and do several hill sprints with little rest on a day when you are feeling good (don't try this when you are fatigued). Make each effort harder than the last, and use a heart-rate monitor or take your heart rate after each sprint. After several sprints, your pulse will peak at or near your maximal heart-rate value.

Maximum heart rate decreases as you get older. The formula for approximating maximum heart rate that is frequently used is 220 minus your age. This is based on averages, and if you are in training, you are not average.

The best method for taking your pulse is to lightly put one or two fingers on one side of your neck, just below your jaw. Feel your pulse through your carotid artery. Count for ten seconds and multiply by six to get your beats per minute. A watch or cycle-computer with a time function, mounted on your handlebars, will make this easier on the road. Unfortunately, bumpy road surfaces make pulse-taking more difficult, which is why a heart-rate monitor is so effective for cyclists.

Training Systems: What and Why

Endurance training. The bulk of your bicycle riding is training your body to pedal mile after mile at a level that is less than 65 percent of your maximum effort. More than half and up to two-thirds of your training miles will be at a relatively easy intensity. Endurance training—often referred to as LSD (long, slow distance) training—is the base of your fitness. It prepares your body by developing your cardiovascular system, muscles, and metabolism to handle the other training you throw in the system. Endurance training enlarges your capillary network and improves pulmonary function, which delivers more nutrients to working muscles and better carries the waste products away.

Endurance training also develops your slow-twitch muscle fibers, upon which cyclists rely heavily. These fibers are designed for distance, and they prefer to burn your body's almost limitless supply of fats. Your body stores a limited amount of carbohydrate, which is needed in small amounts to fuel the burning of fats. A well-fed athlete's body stores more than 350 grams, or almost 1,500 calories, as glycogen, enough energy for less than two hours of cycling. "Hitting the wall," or "bonking," is a condition brought about when your carbohydrate stores are exhausted and quite suddenly you cannot go on. Your body still has adequate fat supplies (in even the leanest athletes, there is enough fat to last several weeks), but the fuel line is shut off without some carbohydrate source available. Hence the axiom, "Fats burn in a carbohydrate fire." Carbohydrates are stored as glycogen in your liver and muscle, and are carried in your blood as glucose after ingesting drinks such as the sports drink Max, or a sugary soda like Coke, or foods such as Power Bar, or a cookie.

Simply stated, endurance training teaches your body to be more efficient, sparing the finite carbohydrates by using the more infinite energy stored in your body as fat. Training increases the size and number of a cellular structure called the mitochondria. Called the "powerhouse" of the cell, the mitochondria is the site of fat metabolism. Training increases the cellular enzymes responsible for liberating and using fat. These adaptations reverse quickly when training is stopped for several weeks.

By the way, that fats are the preferred fuel does not mean that you need to include more fat in your diet. Any excess food you eat is stored as fat whether you consume it as carbohydrate or protein or fat. (See Nutrition for Performance, page 210).

Endurance training is done year-round on and off the bike, and is generally done at a heart rate below 130 beats a minute, a pace that can be thought of as "guilt-producingly easy." Yet endurance training is effective and essential. It provides the base from which you can do other, more intensive, forms of training.

MUSCLE-FIBER TYPES

There are two primary muscle-fiber types: slow-twitch and fast-twitch. Slow-twitch fibers are also called red muscle fibers because they have more blood flowing through them than the fast-twitch or white-fiber type. Slow-twitch fibers are your endurance fibers. They are smaller and designed to last. They are also called oxidative fibers, which means they rely on using oxygen to burn fats for fuel, a capacity that is developed with endurance training.

Fast-twitch fibers are larger and white in color, because they have a smaller blood supply—and rely less on oxygen (which is carried by the blood). The main energy pathway is the non–oxygen dependent (*anaerobic*) or glycolytic pathway, which burns readily available glycogen, glucose, and creatine phosphate. Unlike fats, these energy stores are limited. Lactic acid is a by-product of this pathway. Fast-twitch fibers are built for speed, not distance.

There is an "in-between" fiber type, known as the "fast oxidative glycolytic" fiber. It is larger than a typical slow-twitch, but redder (more oxygenated) than a typical fast-twitch. The result is a fiber that has more strength characteristics, yet is fatigue-resistant. This is a highly favorable fiber type for a cyclist.

Physiologists believe that individual fiber makeup is fixed at birth, but training will develop the potential of the differing fibers. Not all muscles are composed of the same ratio of fiber types; for example, the so-called "postural" muscles that maintain body posture are naturally composed primarily of slow-twitch fibers: they are built for distance.

Fiber typing, an invasive procedure requiring a biopsy, is currently not a practical process for many athletes to undergo. A very thick needle punctures the muscle and extracts a sample—usually in a laboratory setting. Samples are thinly cut and stained to distinguish the fiber types, then individually counted or computer analyzed.

Anaerobic Threshold, or AT. This is a popular and controversial term in today's training vernacular: popular because every endurance athlete seems to be aware of the AT, controversial because scientists and coaches do not agree on the definitions, implications, and applications of the AT. Scientifically, AT is the point where blood lactate starts to accumulate nonlinearly (see graph 1). The point where the athlete can work for extended periods lies just below the point where lactate begins to build up. Above this point, scientists believe that lactate accumulation is the culprit leading to decreased performance. Fatigue is not a clearly understood phenomenon, but when lactate levels are high, your muscles burn—making you uncomfortable and eventually forcing you to back off and slow down. But the good news is that the AT is highly trainable (see graph 1), and a high AT is critical for cycling success.

In this case, *anaerobic,* which means "without oxygen," is technically a mis-nomer. Why? Because, theoretically, there is adequate oxygen available to the working muscle. In times of great energy demand, however, like climbing a hill or chasing after a breakaway, the body's metabolic demand is so great that the balance is upset. The energy pathway that yields lactic acid is quicker in supplying energy. The trade-off is that you continue the high-intensity cycling, but you pay a penalty—increased lactic acid. At high speeds, your muscles rely more on the fast-twitch glycolytic fibers (see muscle fiber typing inset), which prefer the anaerobic system. Performance is impaired when lactic acid accumulates. Raising the threshold where lactate starts to accumulate will increase your high-speed staying power.

Graph 1

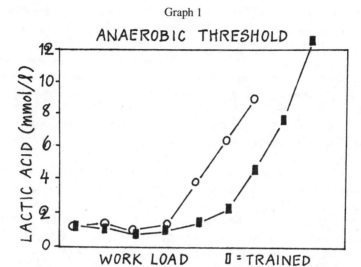

The point where lactate increases nonlinearly during progressively harder work is known as the anaerobic threshold. Notice how training delays the point where lactic acid starts to accumulate and extends the AT to a harder workload.

A NOTE ON LACTIC ACID

It gets a lot of bad press, but it is not as sinister as commonly believed. Lactic acid is actually recycled in the body while you exercise and is used as a fuel supply in prolonged exercise, such as longer bike rides. How this is accomplished is fairly simple. Your muscles have an enzyme that freely enables lactic acid to convert back to a product that can be fully oxidized or metabolized—in other words, it gets used up. Further, lactic acid can be carried in the blood back to the liver, where it is converted back to a readily usable intermediate through a process called *gluconeogenesis,* which is a big word for "making new glucose." By the end of exercise, most of the lactic acid already has been converted and used. The implication of this is that, contrary to popular myth, the stiffness and fatigue you feel after you train or race is not from lactic acid, because it's not there. It's been used up.

So what does the AT mean for you as a cyclist or triathlete? The AT represents the threshold level you can maintain in a time trial, a long climb, or a fast race. Think of your AT as your stamina—the speed you can maintain over prolonged time. Your anaerobic threshold is your *sustainable pace.* Greg LeMond maintains a pulse of

184 beats per minute in a time trial. This probably represents a sustainable pace that is almost 95 percent of his maximum. Davis's sustainable pace is more in the range of 175 beats per minute, about 90 percent of his maximum heart rate.

There are a few ways to determine AT. The laboratory method involves working at progressively increasing intensities. For example, the resistance on the bicycle ergometer is increased every three minutes. After each three-minute bout, your blood is sampled, usually by fingertip puncture, as you might have done in the doctor's office. Your blood is analyzed for lactic acid. As the workload increases, your blood lactate will remain relatively constant until it starts to spike upward (see graph 1). This is the AT.

Another test is the Conconi test, named after Professor Francesco Conconi of Italy's Ferrara University. Dr. Conconi designed this test to help Italian cycling superstar Francesco Moser train for his successful 1984 hour-record ride in Mexico City (51.151 kilometers, or 31.96 miles), which still stands. For the Conconi test, you need a heart-rate monitor, cycle computer, and a Turbo-trainer, on which to pedal your bicycle in a stationary setting (Conconi did most of his research on a velodrome, but a stationary bike will do). This is a graded exercise test in which you continuously increase the workload—on the home trainer you increase the speed and gearing—to reach your AT. Conconi found that at the point that breathing accelerates and lactic acid accumulates, your heart rate actually levels off. The leveling-off point is determined by graphing the heart rate against the workload or cycling speed. The problem with the Conconi test is that the leveling-off "point" is not always clearly identifiable (see graph 2). The advantages of the Conconi test are that it is noninvasive and that you can do it yourself at home.

Careful monitoring of your heart rate will help you to more accurately pinpoint your AT without scientific testing. For example, the pulse you can sustain in a long climb or in a race will indicate what your approximate AT is. Research has shown that the AT is generally the point at which you *feel* you are going "moderately hard." This subjective response is not completely reliable, because other factors come into play, such as whether you're having a good or bad day and how demanding your recent workouts have been. The AT point marks the beginning of when your riding starts to become uncomfortable, but not to an extreme. Usually when you are at your AT, you are breathing fairly hard and conversation is impossible without gulping for air every three or four words.

The AT is highly trainable, meaning you can increase it with work. Your AT will improve as the season progresses.

Training to raise your anaerobic threshold can take on many different forms. If you live in the mountains, you can climb for a sustained period of time (over twenty minutes) at slightly-above-comfortable-conversation pace (zone three: see chart) and you will be raising your AT. Without mountains, you can do interval training like the "extensive" intervals documented in the following training-exercise section; or, when training in a group, do twenty-minute echelon sections where you rotate the

Graph 2

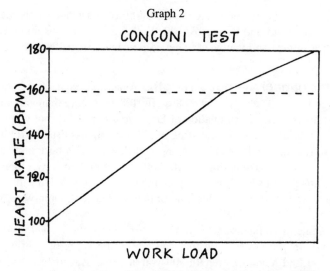

The Conconi test can be done with a heart-rate monitor on your own bike. As you increase the workload, your heart rate increases linearly. The anaerobic threshold is the point where heart-rate increase levels. In this case, the breakpoint is at a heart rate of 160 beats per minute.

lead and keep the pace high but manageable. Racing for more than twenty minutes or maintaining a high pace for that long also will increase your AT.

Systematic training will raise your threshold to a more desirable 80 percent and even in excess of 90 percent of your maximum heart rate. This means you can sustain a pace nearer and nearer to your maximum capacity. This is your goal. If you can race at twenty-eight miles per hour without building up lactic acid in your muscles, you will be ready to respond to the demands of racing below that speed, as well as above that speed. You have raised your sustainable pace, which will ulti-mately help you raise your maximal pace necessary for attacks and sprints.

Heart Rate Zones:

Training Zone	Target Heart Rate (% maximum)	Subjective Effort	Training System
ONE	< 65	Easy	Aerobic
TWO	65–80	Moderate	Sub-A.T. Endurance
THREE	75–90	Moderately Hard	A.T.
FOUR	90–95	Hard	VO^2
FIVE	95–100	Extremely Hard	Sprint

To calculate target heart rate percentages, multiply heart rate by the desired percentage of maximum and divide by 100. For example, if your max heart rate is 188 beats per minute and you want to get 65 percent of that: $188 \times 65/100 = 122$.

Anaerobic capacity—gut strength. Anaerobic capacity is your ability to tolerate high lactate levels. During a hard effort lasting more than a minute, lactate levels start to rise. The accumulation of lactic acid is painful, but you can build a tolerance to it which we call "gut strength." To racing cyclists or triathletes, this capacity is crucial. You know the feeling: your leg muscles burn and you want to quit, but you push yourself through it. Your anaerobic capacity represents your ability to withstand this local, intense pain in your legs; it is tied in with your ability to generate power. Fortunately, this kind of pain is transient. Otherwise, you would have to stop.

In the middle of an intense ride, you may experience the *second wind phenomenon*; one minute you are so tired that you are on the verge of quitting and then, suddenly, you find renewed strength and you are able to resume riding hard. Just why this happens is unclear, but it is widely believed to be an adaptation mechanism and may be related to your body's anaerobic capacity.

To give you an idea of the levels we are talking about, the measurable lactic acid levels at rest are less than 1 mmol/l (millimole per liter), which is scientific-speak for the standard way of measuring lactic acid and is expressed as a concentration, or how much lactic acid is in your blood. At your AT, it is less than 4 mmol/l, while the maximum levels attained on the bicycle under maximum exercise might jump to 12 to 15 mmol/l.

High-intensity cycling, whether intermittent or prolonged, will result in increased muscle-lactate levels. Hill sprints of sixty seconds are best for developing this capacity (zone five). Long intervals, done above the AT (zone four), also will build this capacity by training your body to quickly eliminate lactic acid from the system. By raising your lactic acid levels in training, you teach your body to respond and adapt, thereby effectively reducing the concentration more quickly.

Remember that your lactic acid levels are a function of how much lactic acid your body is *producing* and how much your body can quickly *remove*. The net is what is measurable—how much is actually in the blood. This is a dynamic process. With training, your body learns to produce less because of increased reliance on your oxygen-dependent pathways. Training also speeds up lactic acid removal, or reconversion back to an oxidizable product.

Aerobic capacity. Endurance and stamina are key ingredients in cycling performance. Aerobic capacity is a measure of your ability to take in and consume oxygen; the amount of oxygen you use is proportionate to the amount of work that you do. As you increase work, you increase your oxygen demands, or *uptake* of oxygen. Oxygen is used in the production of energy, which enables you to sustain muscular contraction, which enables you to turn over your pedals. A maximal oxygen uptake test, called VO_2 max, which stands for the *volume of oxygen* your body consumes at maximum effort, is a standard laboratory test.

VO_2 MAX

The equation for deriving VO_2 is as follows:

VO_2 = Cardiac Output × Arteriovenous oxygen difference.

Cardiac output is defined as the stroke volume, or amount of blood ejected from the heart multiplied by the number of times the heart beats. Cardiac output can exceed thirty-five liters (nine gallons) per minute at maximum. The arteriovenous oxygen difference is a measurement of how much oxygen is going to the muscle from the heart on the arterial side and how much is returning to the heart on the venous side. This means that the volume of oxygen consumed is a product of how much blood is pumped from the heart (delivery of oxygen) and how much oxygen is used (extraction of oxygen).

In a laboratory setting, VO_2 is determined by measuring the expired air during exercise. By knowing the percent of oxygen in the inspired air, which is fixed at 20.9 percent, we calculate how much oxygen is being used based on the percentage of oxygen in the expired air.

Through training, you can raise your VO_2 max by 10 to 30 percent, although this capacity is primarily genetically endowed. Training results in increasing the oxygen supply, primarily by increasing the blood volume and the amount of blood the heart ejects. More oxygen is used by the working muscles due to cellular changes, including enzymatic alterations, which speed up cellular metabolism. Top cyclists typically have high VO_2 max values, exceeding 70 ml/kg/min (which means the amount of oxygen consumed in milliliters per kilogram of your body weight per minute) for men and 60 ml/kg/min for women. Bob Cook, a U.S. national and world team rider and super climber in the 1970s, had a max value in excess of 80 ml/kg/min, which is in the superhuman range.

Marathon runners and cross-country skiers typically record the highest values for VO_2 max of any athletes, exceeding 80 to 85 ml/kg/min in world-class men. (Women rarely attain values higher than 75 ml/kg/min.) These high values are due to the highly aerobic demand of their sports.

Neither of us has exceptionally high VO_2 max values. We weren't tested at the peak of our careers either, which had more to do with issues of convenience and privacy than a lack of scientific interest. We did not have access to equipment and testing under conditions that we could supervise. In national team or other settings, it seemed that the information was more *comparative* in nature; thus, the results were part of the overall competitiveness of the team. In fact, one testing session I participated in early in my career was widely quoted and published, much to my dismay. I now know that chronological data would have been instructive, but the psychological component of the test wasn't worth the hassle at the time.

Many coaches believe that short-duration, high-intensity intervals (such as the pyramids detailed in the training exercises listed in this chapter) are optimal for developing VO_2 max because they allow your body to tax your oxygen-transport system repeatedly—without building up lactic acid, which enables you to keep the work level high. When you do these intervals your breathing rate is very high and your heart rate reaches near-maximal (zone five), but your legs do not—or should not—burn. You also feel this way in a criterium with several "primes," or lap sprints, where you make an effort and recover, make another effort and recover, and so on.

PHYSIOLOGICAL ENDURANCE TRAINING ADAPTATIONS

Increased cardiac output due primarily to increased stroke volume because of stronger cardiac muscle.

Increased capillarization of the muscles.

Increased blood volume. This will also increase the cardiac output and help increase the body's cooling rate.

Increased mitochondrial capacity, which means increased extraction and utilization of oxygen.

Increased VO_2 max due to increased cardiac output and increased utilization of oxygen.

Increased respiratory capacity of the oxidative or slow-twitch muscle fibers.

Increased anaerobic threshold. Less lactic acid is released and more is taken up at submaximal workloads. At higher workloads, lactic acid levels increase due to the recruitment of the fast-twitch (glycolytic) fibers. Tolerance of lactic acid is also increased.

Decreased resting heart rate and, possibly, decreased maximal heart rate.

Increased muscle glycogen storage.

Carbohydrate sparing, through increased reliance on fat for fuel.

Sprint Training

This is often the neglected part of a cyclist's training program. Why? Because most people either say they can sprint already or they lack the talent. Either reason

Sprinting ability can be improved dramatically in training, and the results will show when you race. Doug Shapiro, left, is nicknamed "The Bullet" for his speed. Here he demonstrates classic sprint form, with Jeff Pierce coming on strong on the right and Davis in the middle.
PHOTO CREDIT: MICHAEL CHRITTON

overlooks the fact that this capacity can be improved tremendously. We practice sprinting regularly, although even Davis has to be coaxed into a sprint workout at times because he gets tired of it and also knows he is expected to perform even in training. Don't let sprinting bother you. Your training results won't be published in *VeloNews*. But sprint training will help you build speed for other areas—like attacking to break away or bridging gaps when rivals attack to make a bid to go off the front. Sprint training also will help build power, which is a premium for a successful cyclist. Sprint training is done based on quality of effort. After a good sprint, your pulse will be near maximal and you should rest fully between sprints.

Sprinting is a key element in cycling. The overwhelming majority of races come down to the sprint—from a two-rider breakaway to a spectacular mass-pack sprint. But even if you are a recreational rider, or a triathlete, who may not need to give it all in the last 200 meters, sprinting is still good to practice because it jazzes up training rides. Does your training partner kill you on the hills? Here's your chance to get him back. Sprinting is a blast.

Basics. Standard sprint practice includes doing five to ten 200-meter sprints—about thirty pedal revolutions of a 53-15 gear. It's a good idea to do your sprint training at least once a week from March (or earlier if weather and your fitness permit) through October. Even in the off-season, sprints are a good way to keep your sprint-muscle fibers in shape. Sprinting is fun, so don't neglect it. Sprinting is also key to winning races, so just do it.

The best sprint sessions are with a group of two to six riders, taking turns simulating all kinds of situations: late jump, early jump, surprise jump, from behind, from the front, going long and incorporating a double jump, uphill and downhill, head wind and tail wind. You name it, you can try it. Give yourself the advantage of a tail wind or slight downhill so that you can really turn over a big gear—as you would in a pack finish.

It is always helpful to have a coach riding with you, or on a motorcycle, to point out your mistakes and see what you are doing right. But since coaches are few and far between, you may want to go out with a training partner, or group, and critique each other and review each sprint. Learn from your mistakes. Learn to accentuate your strengths so that when you are in a race, you will make a move that suits you.

Consider getting someone to drive a motorcycle so you can ride behind it and practice motorpacing. This imitates race speed, and forces you to jump around a fast-moving rival—as you would in a race. First get up to speed—but not so fast that you are doing the whole sprint behind the motorcycle. Tell the driver to signal with a beep when you should jump. The objective is to work on passing a rival at speed; the driver might have to slow down a bit so you can get by. Then take advantage of the slingshot effect and jump out of his draft to overtake the motorcycle.

If you don't have access to a motorcycle, there are many variations of sprint games to play, some of which I will share with you. As long as you do some sort of concentrated sprint workout at least once a week during the season, you will improve. Whatever you do, have fun with it.

Ins and Outs

I coach many riders, including Dede Demet, who is on the U.S. national team. I like to have my riders practice something called Ins and Outs. I adapted Ins and Outs from a running coach, who believed they helped fool the nervous system into working harder, despite fatigue. I don't know if that is true or not, but the game seems to enhance a sprint program. Start by jumping out of the saddle in a big gear, preferably with a tail wind or a slight downhill, for ten revolutions (counting one leg) and then sit back on the saddle, spinning for another ten. Repeat these intervals in and out of the saddle three times each. You will have spun a total of thirty strokes (a distance of about 200 meters) in the saddle and the same distance out of the saddle for a total set of sixty strokes, or about 400 meters.

We normally do three sets and break them up by varying the stroke count to eight-ten-twelve, or some other variation. When you try this, you will be surprised at how out of breath you can get in just one set. You might be fooling your nervous system, but you aren't fooling your lungs. Take a full and active (light pedaling) rest of three to five minutes between each set, and then do the next set. Do three sets as warm-up for your sprints. This helps to sharpen you up for the real meaty sprint training by overcoming those first awkward and sluggish sprints that are typical of sprint sessions.

Canadian Speed Play

Steve Bauer and Alex Steida played a game that developed from when they started out in Canada as track riders and trained specifically for speed in the saddle. They were known for accelerating rapidly from the sitting position and surprising everyone by opening a considerable gap without looking like they were doing anything differently. Suddenly, they were up the road in a clean breakaway. Nobody chased, because Steve and Alex didn't call attention to their effort the way they would if they got out of the saddle and thrashed their bike back and forth as they accelerated.

To help develop this speed, they played a game that involved one of them sitting on a twenty-dollar bill, with half of the bill exposed. The object is to stay firmly on the saddle and sprint away from other riders, who also remain on their saddles, and chase after the twenty-dollar bill, trying to grab it. The game is also fun and highly entertaining, combining speed training with bike handling. We tried it and laughed hysterically at the moves riders would make in an effort to keep from losing their money, or in trying to get it.

Downhill Sprints

Using the downhill is a good way to duplicate the effort of a race. Sprinting down hills emphasizes pedal action, because you're working at a speed that is closer to race speed and you can emphasize the quickness of acceleration. You also sit when you spin, again working on that in-the-saddle acceleration.

Do you live in Kansas and have no downhills? Try using a tail wind.

Uphill Sprints

Uphill sprints are a great form of training (as are head-wind sprints if you live in a flat area). Ron Kiefel was always the best hill sprinter. He could go faster at the top of a hill than anybody I have ever seen, but it did not come purely naturally to him—he worked on it, just as you should. Davis and Ron would go halfway up a medium-length hill and then sprint the last 200 meters. They would shift into their big front chainring and stay pretty evenly matched. When Davis would start to get gassed,

Ron would take off, but Davis improved with this type of work. They used to do the same hill over and over again, but in unfamiliar terrain, we often kept it more spontaneous. It is hard work, requiring maximum concentration, but it yields big dividends, not just specifically in uphill sprinting but in all sprinting situations. I attribute my increased sprint capability to this training in 1983 and 1984. Don't do this until you have a solid fitness base, usually in May or June.

Ron won two professional races in Italy by employing this sprint tactic. One was in the 1985 Giro d'Italia, on a stage that finished up a three-kilometer hill. Ron was in the pack when he took off at the base of the hill with Gerrie Knetemann of Holland. Francesco Moser of Italy took off in pursuit. Knetemann sat on Ron's rear wheel the whole way. Knetemann and Moser, both former world champions, were following Ron, who rode right away from them for the stage victory. In our Morgul-Bismark bike shop in Boulder, there's a great photo of Ron winning, Knetemann

Ron Kiefel's uphill sprint training has paid off for him in race wins around the world. Here Ron wins the final stage of the 1988 Coors International Bicycle Classic in Boulder.
PHOTO CREDIT: DAVID EPPERSON

hanging his head down right behind for second, and Moser some bike lengths back, with the whole field bearing down on them.

Davis theorizes Ron has an extraordinarily large heart. He and Davis have gone out on training rides together, both of them were wearing heart monitors. They would both be riding at the same speed, but Davis's heart rate would be 188 and Ron's 168. Ron must have a massive stroke volume, which is the amount of blood pumped out of the heart with each beat. Practicing uphill sprints with Ron helped Davis to improve his sprint finishes, because it develops power.

One specific power-building exercise is to go out and shift into a big gear so that you are pedaling slowly, 30 to 40 RPMs, while sitting rock-still in your saddle. Don't even use your arms, but rest your wrists on the handlebars. Ride like this for several minutes. In essence, this is a form of weight training, but it is cycling-specific. Andy Hampsten prefers this type of training. It was suggested to him by Massimo Testa, the Italian team doctor for Motorola.

In bicycle racing, specificity is key. Triathletes run one day or go swimming and ride a bicycle another day. A bicycle racer wants to train his muscles as specifically as he can for the given exercise. Instead of using weight training, use the bicycle as a vehicle for weight training.

It's important to have a lot of variety in your training, though it should still be specific to cycling. Incorporate short jumps of fifty to eighty meters, with sprints of 200 meters and longer sprints of up to 800 meters, into one session.

Don't sell yourself short when it comes to sprinting. If you practice, you have to improve. A good example is Alexi Grewal, who is not known as a great sprinter. In the 119-mile 1984 Los Angeles Olympic road race, Alexi was dueling for the gold medal with his breakaway partner, Steve Bauer. Steve is a terrific sprinter and was expected to win the sprint. But Alexi had worked and worked on his sprint, and both of the riders were exhausted from their breakaway effort. When they dashed for the line, Alexi just waxed Steve. It wasn't even close.

Alexi's performance shows that any skill can be improved. *Great players train their weaknesses, good players train their strengths, and poor players don't train at all.*

Recovery Training

Considerable emphasis is placed on what you might consider to be aggressive training, but recovery training, which is passive, is just as important. This training is done at or below zone 0. Recovery training is ideal one or two days a week, or as the day's second workout. When you feel run-down, recovery training can be exceptionally rejuvenating. Former national coach Eddie B. calls this a bicycle walk. No pressure on the pedals. Just good form and enjoying riding your bike.

The line between recovery training and endurance training is a fine one that has more to do with *intent* than with effort. Use your recovery training to refreshen you.

TRAINING EXERCISES

Interval Training

Adding order and interest to improve your performance. Most people want and need more order in their training. We have tried many training exercises over the years. Some we like more than others, and some are more effective than others. We listened to what other athletes do and studied other sports. Some of this training comes directly from our friend and colleague from Holland, Henk Zonneveld, who has been a great addition to our staff at the Carpenter/Phinney Camps. He has a flare for creative bike play, technique, and interval training, which the Dutch especially need in their training because Holland is so flat.

One advantage of interval training is that the work is easy to quantify—you know how much work you are doing and at what effort. Designing a program around interval training is of value for the coach and athlete, but at the same time, it can be psychologically demanding and require a high level of self-motivation. If you have other alternatives, like fast club rides or races, the opportunity to motorpace, do time trials, or otherwise meet some of the training objectives in a group situation where it might be easier for you, by all means do it. Try to find a balance in your training and don't overlook one area altogether (like climbing or sprinting). Becoming a balanced rider requires an organized program and balanced practice.

Rest right. Remember that the key to getting the most out of the interval is to follow not only the directions for the *work* interval, but all the directions, including the *rest* interval, the terrain, gearing, and number of sets.

What to do when? Different types of training can be mixed together; others are better off left for separate days. You can see how to put different types of work together in the speed-play section (page 158). Most of all, remember that quality work (any of these intervals or exercises can be described as quality rather than quantity) must be done with some minimal level of freshness or recovery from the previous day or previous workout. You cannot do quality work in every workout, every day. Adhere to the hard day/easy day theory of training, or mix moderate, intense, and easy days. Typically, we recommend going easier Monday and Friday, doing the bulk of the specialized training from Tuesday through Thursday, and then race or do long group training on the weekend. Whatever your weekly format, be sure you insert the quality work.

How to start? Everyone will have a different starting volume, depending on the level of experience and preparation. Do too little, rather than too much. If you are starting out, limit interval or quality work to twice a week. Plan to increase the volume in increments of 10 to 20 percent per week. If you do ten minutes of long intervals (ten minutes of intensity) in the first week, aim for twelve minutes the next week, fourteen minutes the third week and reduce to twelve minutes in the fourth week. This is in keeping with the weekly building and recovery block system of training. Short intervals could be increased by sets, starting with three sets and increasing by one set each week or at two-week intervals. Increased intensity can be done by adding new types of training. Remember that adequate recovery is essential.

TRAINING EXERCISES FOR CYCLISTS

Notations: $''$ =   seconds

$'$ =   minutes

RPM   =   cadence

(53–15) =   indicates gearing; in this example:
front chainring = 53-tooth cog,
rear gear = 15-tooth cog (use gearing as close to recommended as possible)

Remember Your Heart Rate Zones:

Training Zone	Target Heart Rate (% maximum)	Subjective Effort	Training System
ONE	< 65	Easy	Aerobic
TWO	65–80	Moderate	Sub-A.T. Endurance
THREE	75–90	Moderately Hard	A.T.
FOUR	90–95	Hard	VO^2
FIVE	95–100	Extremely Hard	Sprint

1. Short intensive intervals

Short intensive intervals should be done at a speed that is close to 90 percent of max, zone four. In the beginning of the year, use a small gear and a work:rest ratio of 1:2, where you work five seconds, rest ten seconds. As you get into the season, reduce the ratio to 1:1, where you work five seconds and rest for five seconds.

a. Pyramids:

5"-10"-15"-20"-25"-30"-25"-20"-15"-10"-5"
or
10"-20"-30"-20"-10".
High RPMs, greater than 110.
Repeat three to seven times.
Rest (easy cycling) five minutes between sets.

b. Fifteen/fifteens:

15″ work/15″ rest continuously for 5′.

Repeat 2 to 3 times.

Cadence high.

Recovery time between sets is five minutes.

Pulse will increase to near your maximum, always slightly above AT during work phase (race speed).

Benefits: increase aerobic capacity,

increase pedaling efficiency and leg speed, and

condition body for quick recovery.

2. Long intensive intervals:

Duration of work = 1′–5′

For example:

Pyramids: 1′-2′-3′-4′-3′-2′-1′

or

Repeats: 5 × 2′.

Intensity: Zone three.

Full recovery to pulse rate to 120 before new start but not less than one minute rest.

(In the early season, ride on the inside front chainring, and as the season progresses go to the big ring.)

Benefits: Increase lactic acid tolerance, and

increase pace and time-trial capabilities.

3. Short extensive

Extensive does *not* mean intensive; you are working your leg speed and driving your respiration up. Conversation will be difficult during the interval, but you are not working hard enough to feel local leg pain. These intervals mimic a long steady climb for flatlanders. The temptation is to do these too hard.

Work 1′/rest 1′, or work 2′/rest 1′.

Use the small front chainring, same gear for rest and work, but increase RPM from 100 at rest to 110 for work phase.

Legs should feel no pain.

One set is twenty to thirty minutes of the work/rest cycle; you can repeat the set twice.

Intensity: Zone two to three.

Benefits: Increase anaerobic threshold,
          simulates long climb,
          good recovery for next day (no training "hangover"), and
          helps improve pedaling action.

4. Attack training

Simulate attack of a race, make the effort near maximal.
Big-gear effort, preferably from good training speed to race speed.
Duration of roughly 500 meters (less than one minute).
Intensity: Zone four to five.
Repeat three to six times, depending on nature of the total training.
Benefits: Prepares you for racelike efforts and builds power.

5. Sprint Training

a. Ins and Outs 3 × 10 to 12 revolutions (each leg) with same length recovery (1 set = 10 strokes on/10 off; 12 on/12 off; 10 on/10 off).
Repeat this set three times as warm-up for sprints. See sprint training text for more detail. Big gear, fast acceleration out of the saddle.
Maximum speed.
Zones four to five.
b. Jumps of 80 to 100 meters for out-of-the-saddle acceleration repeat three to five times.
c. Sprints of 200 to 400 meters.
Do the longer sprints with a second jump, where you sit down, shift up and go again.
Intensity: Zones four to five.
Full recovery between each.
Repeat five to ten times.
Early season, downhill or tail-wind spin sprints.
Later season, flat big-gear sprints and uphill sprints (see following).
Ideal for groups of four to eight, take turns jumping and attacking.
Benefits: Improve your speed,
          build power, and
          win races!

6. Hill sprints:

Do uphill sprints after you have established a base, usually not until late spring.
Select a moderately steep hill.
Come into the hill at good speed, shift into a bigger gear and make the jump decisive.

Duration = 30″–60″.

Intensity: Zone five.

Repeat the sprints three to ten times, but stop if you become too ragged.

Full recovery between each effort.

Progression: After several weeks of this training, you will be able to make the jump in the big chainring. This will be good practice for races where you might attack from a climb where everyone is in the small ring and you need to shift up quickly and accelerate rapidly.

Note: Because hill sprinting takes its toll, do this training Tuesday or Wednesday if you plan to race on the weekend, because you will need extra recovery time.

Always finish the workout with some high-RPM spin-type sprints. You should be very tired.

Benefits: Increased power and
> increased anaerobic capacity (gut strength).

7. Speed Play

This type of training originated in Sweden. It should contain many changes of speed and be purposeful but free-form. Work in zones two to five.

Ingredients: Mix up some climbing, jumps, sprints, long intervals, faster echelon sections and attacks.

For example, during two-hour ride:

5 × 80 meter jumps,

3 × 500 meter attacks,

3 × 2′ long interval,

1 × 30′ fast echelon or 30′ climb, and

2 × 250 meter sprints to finish the day.

Ideal in a group of four to six riders.

Benefits: Simulate race variables,
> work on speed, and
> have fun.

8. Long climbs

Climbing steady for twenty to forty-five minutes.

Intensity: Zone three.

Benefits: Improve AT,
> develop your gut strength, and
> helps to build power.

9. Motorpace training

Ideal for elite riders and for peaking.

One to two hours, with varied tempo and terrain.

Intensity: Zone three, up to zone four.

Try sprinting around the motor at least three times, with a long windup sprint at the end.

You should also try two to five efforts of one to two minutes out in the wind, not behind the motor (like long intervals without the full recovery).

Motorpacing behind a car is not as ideal as a small motorcycle because it is too easy, but if a car is the only option, be sure to do some interval-type efforts out in the wind.

Benefits: Improve leg speed,
          AT training,
          train at race speed for less energy cost, and
          high-speed sprints.

10. Partner Pacing

No motorcycle? Have your ride partner pedal a gear of 53-17, and you draft behind, pedaling a gear of 39- (your small ring) 17 for five minutes, then trade places with your partner for five minutes.

Each set = 10′.

Repeat once.

Intensity: Zone three to four.

Benefits: Helps build leg speed and
          builds power.

11. Power Training

Weight training on the bike.

Do this in-season, when you have a good base.

Ride in large gear up a long climb (or into a stiff wind)—gear 53-17.

Let your RPMs be low, around 50–60.

Intensity: Zone four.

Work for three to five minutes, rest fully (spin until pulse down to 120), repeat three to five times.

Keep your upper body steady; drive with your legs.

Benefits: Develops cycling-specific power.

Note: Beware of developing bad habits. Concentrate on a steady upper body.

Home-Trainer Workouts
45–60′ workouts on your bike at home or at the gym.

1. AT training

Warm-up 15′.
20′ Buildup set continuously as follows:
5′ @ 53-15   (zone three)
5′ @ 53-14
5′ @ 53-13
5′ @ 53-12.
Recovery riding 5′.
5 × 20″ big-gear sprint.
Short rest 1′ between each sprint.
Warm-down 5–10′.

2. Speed work:

Warm-up 10-20′.
5 × 1′ big ring (53-17)/1′ small ring (40-17). Zones three to four.
Maintain same RPM in both minutes
    (don't bog down in the big ring—
choose sustainable RPM of 90–110).
Recover 5′-easy spin.
5 × 45″ big ring/15″ sprint;   Zone four.
1 minute recovery small ring between each.
Recover 5′ after.
Finish with 3 × 30 revolution sprints—
    near-maximal effort (zone five), with full recovery.
Warm-down for 10′.

3. Aerobic Capacity:

Warm-up 10′.
1 × 5′ set of 15″ work/15″ active rest ($^{15}/_{15}$'s).**
Recover 5′—between each set.
1 × Pyramids 5″-10″-15″-20″-25″-30″-25″-20″-15″-10″-5″**
1 × 5 minute set of $^{15}/_{15}$'s
10-minute warm-down.

**(see short intervals for clarification)

MAKING A PROGRAM

Designing a Training Program

The Calendar Year. The essence of a good training program is managing time. You cannot design your own training program without knowing how much time you have available to train; this includes the number of hours a day, week, and year. Even if you are a full-time athlete your time is limited, and you must manage it well. More is not better. What you do counts, not how much you do. Begin the process of designing a program with a general idea of how much time you have to manage. Get out the calendar and start counting weeks. How many to the start of the season? To the big races?

This is your first crucial step. It will give you a framework to develop a sound personal program. It is amazing how quickly time passes if you don't stay on top of the calendar. (See page 177 for program worksheet.)

The macrocycle: formulate your seasons. A cyclist has many seasons, which conjure up images of change. It might seem as if you have just the *off-season* and the *competitive season*. But when you dissect the year, there are actually many distinct seasons. These large blocks of time are referred to as *macrocycles*. A cyclist's year should be organized first by large blocks of time, with this demand for change in mind, in which the focus of training shifts from the general to the specific. Think about how you divide your year. A recreational cyclist might have only three seasons:

Off-the-bike season (fall/winter),
Base season (spring), and
Event season (summer).

A cyclist in California might have the following seasons:

Recovery or off-season (fall),
Base (winter),
Early (spring), and
Competition (summer).

How time is spent in each season depends on where you live, your goals, and your opportunities. Generally, the pattern that has worked for us in Colorado, based on the demands of the racing season and the climate, is the following:

Recovery	October 1 to November 15
Cross-training	November 15 to January 15
Base/specializing	January 15 to March 15
Early competition	March 15 to June 1
Main season	June 1 to late September or early October

Take time to decide how you would reasonably and logically define your seasons.

The Microcycle: building blocks. Over the years, we have worked with a training system that involves stacked building blocks (microcycles), based on Soviet training theory. Each block is defined by its volume and intensity, which increases over a period of weeks, followed by a reduction to let the body recover. A building period of three to four weeks is ideal, followed by a week in which the volume will be reduced by 10 to 20 percent, and the intensity reduced by 25 to 30 percent. When you begin the next building cycle, start where you left off—at the peak of the previous cycle (see graph 3.).

This way, you are not *constantly* building, but *consistently* building. By allowing this recovery time, you are giving your body a break, which should lead to adaptation. The lighter week lets you evaluate your recovery and gives you a good starting point for the next cycle.

Graph 3

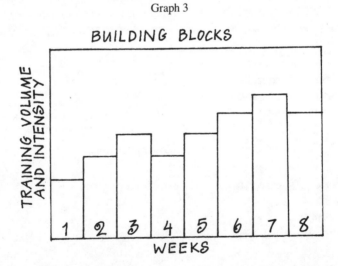

Organize your training around weeks that build in volume and intensity and then drop back to recover. The third week is the peak of the first cycle. The fourth week represents a recovery week, which is of equivalent volume and intensity as the second week. Resume the next cycle at the peak of the first cycle (week 5 equals week 3), and build from there.

Obviously you will want the recovery weeks to coincide with important events as the season progresses. Design your program to peak for the important races. To maintain a performance plateau, reduce your training and emphasize recovery.

If you have a ten-week block, consider looking at two five-week cycles (four weeks to build and one week to recover), or a four-week cycle, followed by a six-week cycle in which your recovery might be spread out more gradually for two weeks.

This type of planning works well for the recreational cyclist who wants to build up for a long one-day ride or multiday tour, like the Denver Post Ride the Rockies. For example, a ten-week buildup of 1,000 miles is something a novice or intermediate rider can manage. Use the first four weeks for the base adjustment period to get used to your bike, averaging less than 100 miles a week. Recover on the fifth week. Follow up with a four-week block, where you average 150 miles a week. After a week of recovery training, you are ready to go.

Days: Planning Your Week

Typically, a single week for most cyclists represents five or six training rides and one or two days off. Elite cyclists train every day, often twice, for seven to ten workouts a week.

Hard vs. easy days.   Balance hard training with easier recovery training. Cycling doesn't tear your body down like running, so the typical cyclist's week has blocks of hard days, which work different systems. For example, Tuesday: aerobic capacity; Wednesday: AT, endurance, and power; Thursday: sprint.

Two-a-days.   To achieve ten work periods in one week, you must train daily, with two-a-days on at least three of the days and no total-rest day. The double-workout days might be made up of an early-morning ride when you have a later afternoon race, or a late-day ride after a hard early-morning training. On some days it is appropriate to train hard twice, but you must already have sufficient base for your body to handle this. Twice-daily workouts are a luxury if you have the time, because you can accomplish much more, often in shorter periods of time. Moreover, you have the added effect of more recovery training, and your body learns to quickly recover between workouts.

How you design your week depends on how much time you have and what your opportunities are. Evaluate this based on your limitations. You may work a full-time job, or go to school, or devote yourself full-time to cycling. Whatever applies, make the best use of your time. One common mistake occurs when riders have less time to train and they try to train hard all the time. Make the best use of your time, and *recover*. You are investing your time, so invest wisely.

Hard stretches in earlier preparation phases will be offset by the easier stretches as you find your peak at the height of the season. After all, the training cycle is overload, recovery, and getting a response from your body. Once you hit your main competitive season, you will have to balance the right amount of rest with the right amount of training. Knowing what you can handle at this time in the year will take some experimenting.

Experimentation does not mean making drastic changes from week to week. Instead, try moving the various days of work and recovery within the week, or try juggling building weeks and recovery weeks to see where you gain your best advantage. Err on the side of doing too little, because too much can send you over the edge and may take weeks of recovery.

Understanding the Macrocycle: A Detailed Look at Your Seasons

Recovery season. Everybody needs time off, to rejuvenate and relax. Let this time of year be unstructured. Feel fresh and unburdened. Take at least two weeks completely off during this four-to-six-week period. The remaining time should be active rest, with four to five days a week of easy riding or other light aerobic training. Go out riding with friends, with no real purpose other than to feel good and unpressured. Start to adjust to other activities, like hiking, skiing, and running.

Cross-training. Cross-training is not new, although the shoe and apparel manufacturers might make you think otherwise. Cross-training is a multisport approach to training. Triathletes are a good example of cross-trainers. Running, swimming, and cycling complement each other. The lack of specificity compromises top performance, yet benefits greater overall body strength. One reason speed skaters have traditionally become good cyclists is that they ride during the off-season. The bike is good for skaters because they use the same muscle groups, but in a different range of motion. Speed skaters also run, do simulated skating exercises, and rollerblade. Figure skaters and gymnasts use dance as a complementary activity. Most athletes use some sort of weight training to build strength. The multidiscipline approach to training increases the challenge by necessitating the learning of new tasks, and makes the training more appealing over the course of a year or a career.

Cross-training is fun. When you look for appropriate cross-training alternatives, keep in mind that you need some carryover from one sport to the other. Minimize the risk of injury and be sure the sport is something you can do regularly.

Off-season training in general is critical to your next season's success, because it gives you a base to improve from. Further, you will have an advantage over your competitors who are not training, or who might be doing the same old riding. The off-season is the most creative time of year, when you can tailor your training to meet your interests as well as your needs. Davis loves to cross-country ski and

Cross-country skiing is ideal winter training for the cyclist who lives in snow country. Davis trains to compete in fifty kilometer (thirty-one-mile) ski marathons during the cross-training season.

PHOTO CREDIT: JOHN KELLY

relishes the time of year when he gets to strap on his skis. But before he does that, he is roller-skiing or roller-blading, hiking with ski poles, running, and doing upper-arm work to prepare him for the time when the snow falls. His enthusiasm for skiing helps him maintain a high level of fitness through the off-season and gives him something to look forward to.

When you live in a year-round warm-climate area like southern California or Florida, the temptation is to keep riding, but we think it is best to give yourself a mental and physical break. Cyclists should not rely on their road bikes for training in the winter—regardless of where they live. Why? The issue of staleness is applicable, but remember that cycling employs a limited range of activity. Your body will not maintain a muscular balance without incorporating some other activities at some time of the year.

There are many healthy options for a multisport approach to the off-season: cross-country skiing, hiking, running, swimming, and, of course, mountain biking. If you have the technical skill for ice-skating, roller-blading, or rowing, these are also great options. An indoor activity like weight training is excellent for building

Off-road riding on your mountain bike will help you avoid staleness by providing you with a change of scenery. Mountain biking will also increase bike-handling skills, cardiovascular fitness, and bike-specific strength. But Davis and his training partner Skip Hamilton find that the biggest benefit is that it's fun.

PHOTO CREDIT:
JOHN KELLY

all-over body fitness. Dance, yoga, or a good flexibility class will help increase your coordination and improve your posture and flexibility.

Some cyclists have begun cross-country ski training and racing in the off-season as an adjunct to their cycling. Tom Schuler has formed a cross-country ski club whose members include Davis, Greg LeMond, and former 7-Eleven rider Jeff Bradley. Cross-country skiing complements cycling because it is an-all body, aerobic sport that doesn't pound muscles and tendons. Cross-country ski races range generally from ten kilometers (6.2 miles) to marathon distance races of forty or fifty kilometers (twenty-four to thirty-two miles) that take more than two hours. Sally Zack, 1988 U.S. Olympic cyclist and fourth-place finisher in the fifty-mile 1991 world championship road race in Stuttgart, Germany, is a devoted cross-country ski racer.

To indoor bike or not. During the early off-season, too much time on a stationary bicycle (whether it be an ergometer or your bike on a home trainer) increases your chances for staleness. There will be plenty of time for stationary training later when the weather is bad and you want—or need—to ride. Limit the stationary bike to weight-training warm-up and/or warm-down.

Cycling is a gentle exercise, because you do not carry your own weight. As a result, give yourself time to adjust to off-season activities. Expect some muscle stiffness as you try other exercises or activities. Listen to the warning signals that your body sends out. Avoid the potential for injury by making the transition to other activities methodically. Running provides balance to a cyclist's legs, because while cycling primarily uses the front of the thigh (the quadriceps muscles), running uses primarily the hamstrings (the back of the thigh muscles). But running can lead to injuries, so use caution. Running will enable you to maintain your cardiovascular (heart and lungs) fitness, but will not maintain your cycling-specific muscle strength. One of the greatest advantages to running is that you can get a great workout in less than an hour, which is not possible on the bike. But running alone is not enough in the off-season, so run wisely and in balance with other activities.

The old saying, "Flying in January, dead in June" has been borne out many times. Off-season cross training is not only refreshing and rejuvenating but also enables you to expand your range as an athlete. At least consider mountain biking in the off-season to give you a change of scenery and improve your cycling skills while maintaining your fitness. Mountain biking maintains specificity while adding terrific variety.

The off-cycling season is also the best time to strengthen parts of your body that may be weak. Andy Hampsten, who is five feet nine inches and weighs 145 pounds, uses the winter to cross-country ski, mountain bike, and lift weights. Andy has made himself into a *sturdier* rider over the years because of this off-the-bike work. It enables him to go the distance.

Going to the gym. Joining a good health club is a good idea for the off-season. Not only will it provide you with a place to do your weight training, but many clubs also have pools, saunas, and steam rooms that are nice in the cold months. Health clubs usually have trained personnel to help you set up a good weight-training program. You have many choices—free weights, or systems like Nautilus and Universal. The type of machinery that you train on is not nearly as important as how you perform the exercises and how consistent you are. What you want to do is strengthen your whole body to minimize injury, which is the primary reason not to do free weights unsupervised. Ten to twelve weeks of weight training is optimal in the off-season.

Circuit training is a defined set of ten to twelve exercises done at high repetition with light weights. There is some criticism of this form of training, since it does not enhance your aerobic capacity. This training suits the cyclist who does not need to build maximum strength but instead looks to develop all-around body fitness through a more endurance-based weight program. Circuit training is very beneficial for groups; it takes the tedium out of the weight-room experience and adds an element of friendly competition and play.

Circuit training is done as follows: The work period is thirty to forty-five seconds, with a rest period of fifteen to thirty seconds. The set of ten to twelve exercises is repeated three times, with a two-to-five-minute rest between sets. One set takes ten to twelve minutes, and the full workout would take less than forty-five minutes, plus warm-up and warm-down. When designing a circuit-training program, incorporate dynamic jumping-type exercises with more standard strength-building exercises like the bench press and the squat. Target all muscle groups, with one-third of the exercises for the lower body, one-third for the upper body, and one-third to include all-body and stomach exercises.

You can easily set up the circuit training at home, using some of the following easy-to-obtain equipment: a pull-up bar; car tire filled with sand (twenty to forty pounds) to put across your shoulders for squats and lunges; dumbbells for a variety of arm exercises; a standard bar with weights for "cleans" and bench presses; a bench for step-ups, calf raises, and bench presses; medicine ball, jump rope, rowing machine, stationary bike, and so on.

Lifting incredible amounts of weight during the off-season will not necessarily mean increased cycling performance. What you are looking for is an increase in your body's general strength, with emphasis on muscle groups in the stomach, back, legs (hamstrings, quadriceps, and calves), and arms. That may not directly relate to going faster on your bike, but it will make you a better all-around rider, strengthen your sprinting and climbing technique, and help to delay the onset of fatigue when you are on the bike for a long time.

Poor cross-training choices include sports that are likely to cause injury. You might not think of running as dangerous, but if you have a tendency to knee injury, it might not be wise. Many ideal sports will not benefit you if you lack aptitude or skill; speed skating, for example, must have been learned at a young age to be of much benefit. Roller-blading is excellent training if you can do it with reasonably good, safe technique. Roller-blading up a mountain climb is great training, but coming down is risky business. Davis routinely roller-blades up Flagstaff Mountain in Boulder, then hitchhikes down.

GENERAL TRAINING-PROGRAM GUIDELINES

No training book would be complete without sample programs, although we include them with caution. Training is a personal process. The goal of this book is to give you the basic knowledge to go forth and develop a program that works for you. What follows is strictly a framework. The range of training time, miles, and intensity is great, and would accommodate beginners through elite levels. Please refer to the training exercises for the specific training cited and for a legend of the notations. We have also indicated the target training heart-rate zones, which are also listed in the section on training exercises (page 155). A training worksheet follows this section to help you begin the process of designing your own program.

GENERAL GUIDELINES: CROSS-TRAINING SEASON

Monday	Weight training (circuit or heavy weight)
Tuesday	Light endurance training 1–2 hours (zone 1)
Wednesday	Endurance training 2 hours with speed play or climbing (zones 1–3)
Thursday	Weight training followed by 30–60 minutes of endurance training (zone 1)
Friday	OFF (see notes)
Saturday	Weight training plus 1–3 hours endurance training, mixed tempo (zones 1–2)
Sunday	Endurance training 2–4 hours plus aerobic capacity intervals (zones 1–4)

Minimum hours: 6–8 (5–6 workouts per week)

Maximum hours: 20 (7–10 workouts per week)

Notes

—There is no such thing as a typical week at any time of year, especially in the cross-training season, because this is a time of variety and personal preference.

—If you have time during the week, consider taking a weekend day off since your season revolves around weekend efforts. Your family might appreciate it, and so might you.

—Be sure to have a minimum of one ultradistance day (in excess of three to four hours) per week if your races are longer than 100 miles.

—Consider training with heavy weights twice a week and circuit training once a week in the early weeks. Then switch to circuit training once a week and heavy weights bi-weekly.

—Hiking (hilly), running, cross-country skiing, roller-blading, and cycling are all forms of endurance training. Try to ride twice a week, road or off-road, during the cross-training season.

The Base Season: Specializing

Begin specializing. Ride the bike more and reduce your other activities. The weather is improving and your motivation to ride—and ride some more—is at its peak. You are ready!

Typically, you can maintain your circuit-training (or weight-lifting) program twice a week for the first four weeks of the base period, then once a week for four weeks before phasing it out altogether.

If you live in a northern area, like the Midwest or Northeast, where spring comes late, continue running, hiking, or skiing longer, but get a start on your bike even if it's indoors on the home trainer. (See home-trainer ideas in training exercise section on page 160.) When the weather is cold but rideable, consider two-a-day rides to get your mileage up without risking frostbite.

Now is the time for careful overload on the bike, without concern for structure as much as finding good technique and beginning the specificity period. Be smooth. Develop your pedal stroke by concentrating on a good spin, especially on the downhills. Take time to build up your mileage base. For example, avoid jumping from 100 miles to 400 miles a week. You might feel good for the first week or two, but then you will experience a period of excessive fatigue, so beware. It takes two weeks to adjust and two months to adapt. Give your body a chance. This is a building program, so give it time.

A general guide for the jump to the base season might be to limit the increase in hours to 25 percent from one week to the next. For example, if you have been training ten hours a week, don't suddenly leap to fifteen or twenty hours. Increase instead in increments of two to three hours per week. This sounds like a lot, but your body can take a lot on the bike, and you will not risk injury as you would as a runner. If you are in a training camp for one or two weeks and you anticipate that you will double your previous workload, remember to give your body a week or more to recover afterward. Your primary risk in increasing your workload too quickly is in overall fatigue and inability to digest and sustain the workload. If you use the building-block format, you will, it is hoped, accommodate this escalating training and, more important, adapt.

A general rule is to put in a minimum of 1,000 miles of good base riding before you are ready for speed work and races. However, if you are careful with your gearing (err on the side of smaller gears), you may race before you reach 1,000 miles. You probably will have some base-season races, but they must be viewed as secondary to training. Whatever you do, try not to be overly concerned with the results. Instead, let the races act as your early speed work, and get in additional miles on race day by taking a long warm-up and warm-down or even a second ride. Group rides provide you with some free-form speed work and help you to redevelop your pack-riding skill. Don't worry if you aren't among the leaders—it is early yet.

You can ride hilly and flat terrain in this phase. During early season it's difficult to discipline yourself to sit in the saddle on climbs, and the tendency will be to stand until you develop power in the saddle. Force yourself to sit as much as possible, coming out of the saddle only to rest your sitting muscles and to power over shorter steep sections.

GENERAL GUIDELINES: BASE SEASON

Monday	2–3 hour endurance ride (zone 1)
Tuesday	2 hours with long intervals (small gearing) (zone 4)
Wednesday	2–3 hours mixed terrain, speed play (zones 1–5)
	For example try: city-limit sprint signs, 2 × 15-minute fast echelon or 30–40 minute climb and 5 × 500-meter attack training
Thursday	2-hour ride with long climb or extensive intervals (zone 3)
Friday	Easy rest or recovery training
Saturday	Group ride—2–4 hours (zones 1–2)
Sunday	Group ride—2–3 hours (zones 1–5)
	5–10 × sprints

Minimum hours: 12
Maximum hours: 18–25
Mileage range: 200–500

Early competition season. This is a highly specialized time of year that requires the most care in planning. You can easily do too much and find yourself in a valley of fatigue. Or you may not do enough, which will prevent you from hitting your peak in the main season to come. Do your interval and speed training during the week and race or participate in fast training weekend rides. You've got your base—now add speed.

Typically, mileage is high during this phase of training. You should feel fairly tired daily. But after an easy day, you should feel refreshed. If not, cut back your training to ensure you are digesting what you are taking in. Monitor your morning pulse and weight (see training diary, pages 180–182); this will help you detect overtraining.

Undertraining usually results from putting too much emphasis on early-season races. Unless they are extremely important races, try to train through these early races without resting. This might compromise your early results, but will pay off later.

GENERAL GUIDELINES: EARLY COMPETITION SEASON

Monday	Endurance training 1–3 hours (zone 1)
Tuesday	Interval training (intensive) 2 hours (zones 1–4) 2nd training: Recovery 1–2 hours (zone 1)
Wednesday	Speed play/mixed terrain 2–4 hours Emphasis on AT training (zone 3)
Thursday	Sprint training 2 hours (up to zone 5) Optional 2nd workout to include: Recovery training (zone 1) or Motorpace/training race of 1 hour (zones 3–4)
Friday	Recovery training 1–2 hours (zone 1)
Saturday	RACE plus 1–2 hours additional (zones 1–5)
Sunday	RACE plus 1 hour additional (zones 1–5)

Minimum hours: 14
Maximum hours: 21–23
Mileage range: 225–500

A solid training program and the support of the crowd helps Davis over the Col de Colombiers during the 1990 Tour de France.   PHOTO CREDIT: BETH SCHNEIDER

Main Competition Season

You have been preparing for this. You have done the bulk of your training—now it's time to perform. Assuming a solid race schedule, you may now use the time between races to focus on recovery, base maintenance, speed work, and some limited intervals. If you are not recovering from the races, take additional time off from intensive work (intervals) and reduce your climbing miles, but keep up the sprints.

Stay sharp. Motorpacing is a good way to maintain your leg speed for the races and is especially effective in bringing out your race-pace attacks and sprints. Not everyone has the luxury of motorpacing, but fast group rides and training races offer alternatives that are excellent midweek and midseason sessions when you may be burned out on structured interval training. Your body still needs stimulus. Chances are that you just need less of it.

GENERAL GUIDELINES: MAIN COMPETITION SEASON

Monday   Recovery/endurance training 1–2 hours (zone 1)

Tuesday   2 hours with short interval training (zones 1–4)
             or
             Fast club ride/training race/motorpace (zones 2–4) and
                 optional second ride-easy for less than 2 hours (zone 1)

Wednesday   Endurance training: mixed terrain, mixed tempo 2–4 hours
                 (zones 1–3)

Thursday   2–3 hours with sprint training (zones 1–5)

Friday   Recovery training 1–2 hours (zone 1)

Saturday   Morning ride 1 hour easy (zone 1)
             Afternoon race (zones 2–5)

Sunday   Race (zones 3–5)
             Long warm down (zone 1)

Minimum hours: 12
Maximum hours: 25
Mileage range: 200–500

GENERAL GUIDELINES FOR TIME TRIAL TRAINING AND PERFORMANCE

- To be a good time trialist, you should ride the biggest gear at the most optimal cadence for the duration of the event, be it a one-mile prologue or a 100-mile triathlon leg.
- Time trialing requires you to have both a high anaerobic threshold to maintain a high pace and muscular power to push the gear at your desired pace.

- Your target pace is a function of *gearing* and *cadence*. For example, at a cadence of 90 RPMs in a 53-15 gear, your speed is 26 MPH. Increasing the RPM to 100 but keeping the same gear (53-15) gives you a speed of 28.5 MPH. At 90 RPMs, but a bigger gear of 53-14, your speed would be 28 MPH.
- For your training, you will need to establish your target pace and train that pace. Drive your pace up, so your intervals are slightly above what you are capable of doing in a prolonged time trial.
- The best intervals for time-trial training are longer intervals (two to five minutes), which are done with complete recovery (heart rate below 120) before a new start.
- Four to eight weeks of specific training is adequate for time-trial training, assuming a solid base.
- How many intervals you do depends on the nature of the event. A shorter-duration, high-speed event like the pursuit (3,000 meters or less than four minutes for elite women and juniors, 4,000 meters or less than five minutes for elite men) requires you to do two to three times the distance of the event in training. For example, a 4,000-meter pursuiter might ride a total of 12,000 meters in training in heart-rate zone 4.
- Longer time trials require you to do only a portion of the event in intervals. For example, if you are training for a relatively standard forty-kilometer (twenty-four mile) time trial, you need only do less than half the distance or time of the event. In this case, you would build up to doing ten to twelve kilometers or twenty-five to thirty minutes of intervals at race pace, which would be in a heart-rate zone of 3–4. Do time trial–specific intervals once each week. Start with no more than twenty minutes of intervals and build at the rate of two to four minutes per week. Remember to cycle your training, so that you decrease the volume and intensity every fourth week (see training, page 162). One day each week of motorpacing or climbing for forty to sixty minutes in target heart-rate zone 3 will also enhance your time-trial ability by increasing your AT.
- Time-trial performance can be greatly improved through training, appropriate gear selection, and aerodynamic equipment. Warm up well for the event. You should be warm and damp from perspiration before the start. If you use new equipment, be sure it is adjusted properly and working well. Once you start, give yourself several minutes to hit your race pace and cadence. Common mistakes include starting too fast and in too big a gear. This will lead to early fatigue. Remember, when it's over you will feel that you could have gone harder, so pull out all the stops as you near the finish and give it everything you've got.

GENERAL GUIDELINES FOR STAGE-RACE TRAINING

Training for stage or multiday racing requires you to have a solid fitness base, and the ability to go hard day after day. Some people seem to have an innate capacity to improve in a stage-race setting; others need to work on it. Basically, stage-race training is a systematic process of letting your body get accustomed to hard efforts with short recovery. It is essential to eat properly during stage racing, because early fatigue will result if you cannot replenish your glycogen stores on a daily basis. When training for a five- to seven-day event, try doing four consecutive days of hard training. Do your *simulated stage race* twice, once about one month before and once about ten to fourteen days before the stage race. Follow your normal weekend racing with two days of hard training that simulates racing, like motorpacing or fast group rides. In this case, train hard Saturday through Tuesday and recover on Wednesday. Sprint training follows on Thursday, a long easy-endurance ride on Friday, and a race again on the weekend. After this stretch, you may need to take more than one day to recover.

When training for longer stage races—fourteen or more days—try the four-day simulated race and recover one day, followed by another four-day (Thursday through Sunday) period. Be sure to do this when you can sacrifice your weekend performance to concentrate on the training. If the weekend racing is shorter than the stages you are preparing for, ride for an additional hour after the races. Ride twice if the race falls in the early morning or late afternoon. The goal is to ride a lot. Postrace recovery is important. Listen to your body to determine when you are ready to resume hard training.

GENERAL GUIDELINES FOR PEAKING

Peaking is an art in any sport, especially in cycling, where generally a peak plateau of weeks is desired, rather than a specific day. Reaching your peak involves many factors, including a solid base, a systematic building period of at least six months, good health, and some luck. If you have used the building-block system of training (see page 162), you know how effective recovery is and how your body responds to rest.

Everyone responds to rest differently. Some seasoned athletes experience a performance decline when they rest, but most respond to a system of increased rest and reduced work. After you have developed a solid base, you will lose little fitness by reducing your training by 20 to 30 percent over a period of two weeks. Two weeks should be adequate to bring your freshness level up to your fitness level, where you will achieve maximum performance. Aim to reduce your training initially by a lot and then pick it back up enough to sharpen but not fatigue you. This is a trial-and-error process. Err on the side of too much rest.

General Guidelines for Novices

Beginning racers must give themselves time to adjust to cycling. The duration of daily training is great, in excess of one to two hours each day. This raises the metabolism and puts great stress on the energy pathways. Be sure to eat enough to replace the calories burned up. A general feeling of malaise or tiredness is common for novice cyclists because of the great metabolic demand.

It is important for novices to train in groups. This will not only increase your bike-handling skills, but will also increase the speed at which you can train. In other words, you can ride faster than you would alone, and with less effort. Try training twice a day, once a week. This will help your body more quickly adapt to cycling and enhance your recuperative powers. If you plan to race, race as often as you can. Midweek club races are excellent if they are well-organized and relatively safe. A target of twelve hours a week is ideal for the novice, with a goal of two or three hard sessions (including races) each week.

GENERAL GUIDELINES: MAIN SEASON TRAINING— NOVICE CYCLISTS

Monday	Recovery training or rest day (zone 1)
Tuesday	2-hour speed play, (zones 2–5) including:
	3 × 2-minute long interval
	3 × attacks of 500 meters
	3 × sprints of 200 meters
	1 × 20-minute echelon or steady AT pace (zone 3)
Wednesday	Long ride 2–3 hours, mixed speed/terrain
	or
	Club ride/race (zone 3)
Thursday	2 hours with 3 × "Ins and Outs," 5 × flat fast sprints (zones 2–4)
Friday	Recovery training or rest day
Saturday	RACE or long group ride (zone 3)
Sunday	RACE or simulate race by riding with fast group, try attacking then dropping back several times (zone 3)

Do one double workout day during the week if possible.
Total hours: 12–15
Total miles: 200–250

Your Own Training Program

Write a daily schedule for your next week based on your time available, your level of fitness, and your goals. Guidelines and reminders:
- Don't forget to work on your weaknesses, as well as your strengths.
- Try to work on your AT two days, and allow one or two recovery training days.
- Train consistently, but vary the intensity so that you recover. In other words, try

the hard day/easy day format, or hard/moderate/easy days. Find out what works for you.
- Use the opportunities you have available to your advantage.
- Aim to train most of the physiological systems in a given week—or every other week.
- Most of all, be realistic.

DESIGN YOUR OWN PROGRAM
Put It All Together:

Training worksheet to help you coach yourself.

Evaluate how many hours you have each day to train.

Evaluate on daily basis if you will ride alone, with a training partner, or a group, taking into account other obligations (work, family, school).

	Hours/time of day available	Alone or group? Other opportunities (i.e., club race?)
Monday	_____	_____
Tuesday	_____	_____
Wednesday	_____	_____
Thursday	_____	_____
Friday	_____	_____
Saturday	_____	_____
Sunday	_____	_____

Now get out your calendar and evaluate the coming year.

How many weeks do you have to build up for your first race or tour? _____

How many weeks until the peak of your season? _____

How many miles/hours have you ridden to date this year?

_____ In the previous twelve months? _____

List your three primary weaknesses. 1. _____

2. _____   3. _____

List your three primary strengths. 1. _____

2. _____ 3. _____

What is your idea of the ideal work? _____

Your goal for *this* year is: _____

Your goal for *next* year is: _____

Write your training program. Be precise: include duration, intensity (intervals), terrain, and other related material.

SAMPLE WEEK

	Duration	Intensity	Terrain
Monday			
Tuesday			
Wednesday			
Thursday			
Friday			
Saturday			
Sunday			

Look at what you have written. Have you left anything out?

Make out a schedule for the next four weeks, building up for three weeks and dropping back to recover on the fourth week. Be sure to include all the ingredients. Keep a training diary. Evaluate and reevaluate. Plan, adjust, and readjust. Remember that coaching is an inexact science. Good luck.

WEEK ONE
DATES: _____.

	Duration	Intensity	Terrain
Monday			

Tuesday			
Wednesday			
Thursday			
Friday			
Saturday			
Sunday			

WEEK TWO
DATES: _____.

	Duration	Intensity	Terrain
Monday			
Tuesday			
Wednesday			
Thursday			
Friday			
Saturday			
Sunday			

WEEK THREE
DATES: _____.

	Duration	Intensity	Terrain
Monday			
Tuesday			
Wednesday			
Thursday			
Friday			
Saturday			
Sunday			

WEEK FOUR
DATES: _____.

	Duration	Intensity	Terrain
Monday			
Tuesday			
Wednesday			
Thursday			
Friday			
Saturday			
Sunday			

Now you have a start! Be consistent. Be realistic. And listen to yourself.

Keep a training diary so that you can mark your progress. A training diary is very helpful, particularly for finding out what works and what doesn't. Keeping track of your activities helps you to know yourself. Despite the technology our computers and heart monitors offer, you still have to listen to yourself.

Keep a detailed training diary to evaluate your performance. Be neat and precise. This way, you can review what you did and how you felt. My training diary was never complex, but provided basic information that was easy to review.

Start by recording your daily morning pulse and the number of hours you slept. Take your pulse while you're still lying in bed. Record how you felt upon waking, using the school grading scheme of A to F, where A is great—you feel ready to take on the world—and F is terrible—you feel horrible. Also record your morning weight, which will help determine if you have a rapid weight loss, a sign of overtraining.

Next, record the details of your training. Indicate the obvious—the miles, terrain, quality work (intervals, sprints, climbs). Indicate when you rode and whom you rode with. What was the weather like? How did you feel? Rate the perceived intensity of the workout as follows:

1–3	Easy
3–6	Moderate
6–8	Moderately hard
8–9	Hard
9–10	Extremely hard

Finally, briefly indicate the not-so-obvious factors that affect your performance, such as work or personal life issues. If you are moving, or have problems at work or at home, make a note of it.

All these factors affect your training. Generally, when you have a slump, you can look back to see what might have triggered it. Too much training? Too much family or work stress? Sleepless nights? Your training diary will provide the clues to help you solve the riddle of nonperformance, as well as improved performance. When you succeed, you must also look to evaluate and ask yourself, why? Was it the extra day of hard work or the extra day of rest? What works for *you*?

A word about morning pulse. Under stress, your resting heart rate may go up, resulting in a slightly restless sleep. If your morning pulse is high, then you know your body is still recovering from workouts. Or it could be because you are worrying about your personal life. In any case, it indicates a failure to recover and you have to adjust your training accordingly.

When I was a teenager living in Norway and training for speed skating, I worked out twice a day almost every day. I adapted to this training well, but became homesick after almost three months. The stress of my homesickness combined with the stress of training sent me over the edge. One morning, quite out of the blue, I woke up to a pulse of seventy-two beats per minute. My normal morning pulse was usually under forty beats; my morning heart rate almost doubled. I had missed all the little warning signs, but when my pulse shot up I knew I had to back way off. I went home early, resting a lot and recovering very slowly.

Your training diary is important. On a trip to San Francisco in January 1982, our car was broken into and all of our luggage was stolen. The only thing we really missed was Davis's training diary from the previous year, which he had brought to review as he made plans for the coming season. Everything else that was stolen was replaceable, but the training diary wasn't. It was if he had lost a whole year.

TRAINING DIARY ABCs

Answer the following questions:
   HOW? WHAT? WHERE? WHY? WHO?
   A. How far?
   B. What did you do specifically?
   C. Where did you go?
   D. Why did you do or not do what you planned?
   E. Whom did you ride with?
   F. How hard was it? (1–10 subjective rating system)
Be specific—including valuable information, such as:
   A. Sleep—number of hours
   B. Pulse upon waking

C. Weather
D. Distractions (obligations, stress, etc.)
E. Weight
F. Subjective Rating (A–F)
C. See what you have done: weekly review.
    A. Weekly hours spent training
    B. Cumulative hours ridden to date
    C. Weekly miles ridden
    D. Cumulative miles ridden to date
    E. Summary: Did you meet or exceed your weekly expectation?
    F. Race report: Tactics, missed opportunities, mistakes, gearing.

OTHER CATEGORIES

Women's Racing (Connie)

Women's racing has undergone dramatic changes since the mid-1970s, when I started in the sport. Few women raced then; only about 200 of the approximately 2,000 licensed racers in the country were women. In recent years, the number of women entering the sport has gone up considerably. They make up the fastest-growing segment of the U.S. Cycling Federation's growth rate, increasing by 327 percent in the 1980s, to about 3,500 of the governing body's 35,000 members.

While the number of women for many years has been low, the quality of performances in international competition has been high. In 1969, Audrey McElmury Levonas launched the modern era of American cycling when she captured the forty-three-mile world road-racing championship in Brno, Czechlosovakia. She became the first U.S. rider ever to win the world road title and wear the coveted rainbow jersey of world champion. Then came three sensational Michigan sprinters who also garnered world championships: Sheila Young, Sue Novara, and Connie Paraskevin. Miji Reoch won a silver medal in the 1975 world championship 3,000-meter (1.9 miles) pursuit event in Rocourt, Belgium.

Sheila and Miji inspired me. After I burst on the scene in 1976, two highly competitive teenagers, also speed skaters from Madison, followed—Beth Heiden and Sarah Docter. It was only natural that we became teammates. But the three of us together proved no match for Keetie Van Oosten-Hage of Holland, who won several world titles on the road and track, dominating the 1978 and 1979 Red Zinger Bicycle Classic. In 1980, Beth won a bronze medal competing in the Lake Placid Winter Olympics as a speed skater, and that summer she became the second U.S. woman to win the world road-cycling title. She beat the competition on one of the hilliest world championships courses ever, in the thirty-three-mile road race in

My success in the Coors Classic gave me a national reputation and put women's cycling on the map. Here, a huge crowd enjoys the medal ceremony after my win at Vail in 1984. Jeannie Longo of France is second, Genny Brunet of Canada is third.

Sallanches, France. Sarah was a fifteen-year-old sensation, both on the bike and on skates. She won stages in the Red Zinger Bicycle Classic, and became Junior World Speed Skating Champion. Her career ended when she fell victim to a case of severe athlete burnout, which sadly forced her to retire from competition.

For many years, promoters seldom included a separate women's event in the race program. Part of the reason was that only a handful of women riders showed up. So the women were almost always put together with another category. In Wisconsin, we raced with the masters (then called veterans) men riders, aged forty and up. Although we competed for separate prizes, the men had to chase every move we made because, after all, it was unseemly for the women to finish first. Indeed. On other occasions, we were put in with the Category 3–4 (beginner) men. Those races quickly taught me basic crash avoidance, how to find a safe wheel to follow, and the art of racing survival.

My cycling career began with a steady diet of racing: I raced on the track once or twice a week, raced Wednesday-night club races, and participated in weekend road races. I raced with men and women, both locally and nationally.

On Memorial Day weekend in 1977, I flew to the East Coast for some "big" races. I raced three days for *a total of thirty miles.* We raced five miles in Hartford, Connecticut, ten miles in Fitchburg, Massachusetts, and fifteen miles in nearby Walpole. (The men's main events in each city all were fifty miles.) I won all three races and promptly wrote to the race promoters to thank them and beg them to lengthen the distances for the women's races.

At the national championships, women's events were held early in the morning, before the spectators were awake. Even at the world-championship level, we generally competed at a disappointingly short thirty-mile distance, sometimes not even on the men's course, which race officials deigned to call "too difficult." At our own 1977 nationals in Seattle, the women raced on an "easier" course than the men. In the 1978 worlds in Cologne, Germany, we raced on the men's flat team time-trial course.

The event that changed the general perception of women's cycling was the Red Zinger Bicycle Classic, which became the Coors International Bicycle Classic in 1980. This event brought most of the strong women in the world together for a week to ten days every summer. We covered challenging courses, learned the value of team riding, and learned to race hard.

We also had the advantage of racing in America, which gave us a chance to build our confidence on our turf. Another advantage was the crowd support: the people of Colorado turned out to watch and cheer for the women as much as they did the men. This brought a great deal of respect to women's racing. We were treated as equals. That certainly was not the case later when women were introduced as a kind of side show to the men's Tour de France. Again women were forgotten during the Coors Classic once the big-name pros arrived, like Bernard Hinault and Greg LeMond.

The Red Zinger made me a local cult hero and the Coors Classic made me a nationally known Olympic contender. I owe my reputation to Mo Siegel, who founded the Red Zinger, and Peter Coors, who sponsored the Coors Classic. And I am forever in debt to Mike Aisner, who kept the women's racing lively by bringing in the best competitors he could find.

These were exciting and frustrating times and, without a doubt, times of tremendous growth. In retrospect, being part of those days made 1984 more special. So much had changed. All the riders who stood at the starting line in Los Angeles made history by competing in the first-ever Olympic cycling event for women. Credibility, excitement, interest, and—finally—respect. It was a long time coming.

Credibility, excitement, interest, and finally, respect. The 1984 Olympic Games featured women's cycling for the first time ever.   PHOTO CREDIT: PETER BROUILLET

Longo's Legacy

After I stopped competing in 1984, Jeannie Longo of France took off like a woman possessed. Longo had raced in my shadow here in the United States. It seemed as if she took more second-place finishes in the Coors Classic than any other rider. Her world-championship results were not outstanding, with the notable exception of a silver medal on the road in 1981. In the closing kilometer of the Los Angeles Olympics road race, she had a mechanical failure that kept her from contesting the sprint for the medals. Saddled (literally) with what must have been terrible frustration, Longo resolved to be the best in the world. Under the guidance of her husband, Patrice Ciprelli, she blossomed and became a prolific champion.

Jeannie Longo had raced in my shadow in the United States. She is pictured here behind me in the 1984 Coors Classic.   PHOTO CREDIT: BETH SCHNEIDER

A lean and uncompromising Jeannie Longo took off like a woman possessed and dominated women's cycling from 1985 through 1989. She left behind a legacy filled with records, titles, and lingering questions.

PHOTO CREDIT: BETH SCHNEIDER

Longo owns the record books for most of the 1980s. She gobbled up every record in sight, on indoor and outdoor tracks from Paris to Moscow to Mexico City. She set records from three kilometers to the hour record. (Her best was the hour record at altitude in Mexico City, where she went 46.35 kilometers, or 27.1 miles.) From 1985 to 1989, she won four world road titles.

Longo failed only in her bid to win the 1988 Seoul Olympics, due to a broken hip suffered from a fall in the world-championship team time trial the month before the Games. Monique Knol of Holland, a sprint specialist, soundly won the fifty-one-mile Seoul Olympics road race that ended in a bunch finish. Longo controlled the pace, ironically, from the back of the pack. Everyone was so concerned with what Longo was doing that few attacks were made.

She followed her Olympics disappointment by trouncing the competition in the 1989 worlds in Chambéry, France. On the road, she won the forty-six-mile championship. On the track, she triumphed in both the 3,000-meter track pursuit and the points race. After her remarkable triple at the worlds, she announced her retirement.

Longo's career has been controversial. Whenever a rider is so dominant, rumors are bound to fly. But in her case, a positive drug test (for ephedrine, a stimulant found in some herbal teas, over-the-counter cold medication, and asthma medication) in 1986 after her record attempts was enough to launch the rumors into orbit. In addition, Longo had experienced a substantial weight loss. In a year, she transformed from chunky to lean and sinewy. Was it the training? Diet? Or something else? Questions linger about Longo. They always will.

What remains are a string of victories and records that will stand for some time, and she is still riding. Longo snuck out of retirement after a year, showing up at the 1991 Ore-Ida race under the name of Jane Ciprelli. A feud with her federation over pedal sponsorship left her without a team in the 1991 World Championships. (But she has Barcelona and the 1992 Olympics on her mind and, as I write this, is looking for either another country—possibly Luxembourg—or a change of policy from France so that she can ride for her native country.)

In her brief retirement, another rising star from France, Catherine Marsal, emerged as cycling's new leading woman rider. Catherine won junior world titles in 1987 and 1988 and captured the 1990 women's forty-five-mile world road title in Utsunomiya, Japan. Longo was absent, but French domination continued.

Where does that leave women's cycling in the nineties?

In the United States, women who excel at cycling have come from other sports backgrounds. The fitness developed through other sports has helped women to make the transition to cycling easier, and their almost instant success in cycling is no doubt appealing to other women. Inga Thompson, who is currently the dominant American rider, is one example of an athlete who has made such a transition. Her background as a nationally ranked high-school cross-country runner helped her earn a spot on the 1984 Olympic team in her first year of competition, and she was a runaway winner of the 1991 national road race and silver medalist in the 1991 world championship road race. She has competed on two Olympic teams and is still chasing world and Olympic titles.

Ruthie Matthes, who came to cycling from downhill skiing, divides her time between road and off-road racing. In the 1990 world championships for both disciplines, she earned silver medals. She is the 1991 world mountain bike champion. Sally Zack, 1988 Olympian and fourth in the 1991 world championship, was a gymnast and cross-country runner before becoming a successful cyclist. Dede Demet, 1991 Pan-Am gold medalist in the team time trial, was a world-class speed skater before devoting herself full-time to cycling. Connie Paraskevin-Young and

Janie Eickhoff, both speed skaters, earned medals in the 1991 world championships on the track. As a whole, U.S. women have earned a worldwide reputation for excellence.

Currently, no rider dominates quite the way Longo did, although the Dutch riders won big in Stuttgart: Leontien Van Moorsel pedaled away with the 1991 world championship road race and Dutch newcomer Ingrid Haringa—formerly a speed skater—won both the women's sprint and points race world titles.

As cycling's international governing body, Union Cycliste Internationale, eases its distance restrictions on women and as the sport continues to attract top athletes, the races will become more competitive—much more so than when I first started racing. Cycling is not a sport that draws many women because it is, frankly, too demanding. There will never be a flock of women lining up to devote a big chunk of their lives to a sport that is so difficult and involves such risk-taking, especially with so little monetary gain.

Yet for those who do choose the sport, it is a wonderful road to travel, and one that extends around the globe. Women still have trouble pushing themselves to their limit. They tend to be timid about challenging the established power brokers. Winning is an art form in cycling, and I believe part of what Longo learned in 1985 was how to win. Once she got a taste for it, she was insatiable.

I hope the women who read this also will get a taste for winning. Remember that it's not necessarily the strongest who wins; often, it's the smartest. Part of being smart is training wisely, conserving your energy when you can, and when you go for it, go all the way. Don't be afraid.

I hope you will take some chances and be less intimidated by what you think others will do and more in control of what you can do, because you can do more. Try escaping in the closing laps of a race instead of waiting for the field sprint. Or try an early "suicide" breakaway. Race to win. You might get a taste for it. And take it from me—it tastes pretty good.

TRAINING ISSUES FOR WOMEN

Basics

Training for distances of thirty to ninety miles can be time-consuming, and, for the elite athlete, such training requires a full-time commitment. Most women have the same fundamental problems: lack of bike-handling skills, lack of self-confidence, and upper-body weakness.

Diet and body fat. Another problem has arisen only recently: a preoccupation, even an obsession, with diet. The extra-lean body types of Longo and Marsal have sent the message that thin is in. Leontien Van Moorsel, 1991 world road champion, reportedly dropped more than thirty pounds over a two-year period. There is a point of diminishing returns when evaluating weight loss. Cycling does not require you to be as thin as a runner. You can carry up to 13 or 14 percent body fat easily and healthfully; if you get lower than 10 percent, your performance may suffer.

Your ideal weight will be reached if you eat well (a low-fat, high-carbohydrate diet) and train right. Your body will "settle" at a weight that is easy to maintain and optimal for you. Of course, there are a few exceptions: some women have a weight problem that needs more management. Whatever you do, don't rely on the mirror to tell you if your weight is right, because some of us never appear to look thin enough in the mirror. Weigh yourself every day at the same time of day. Let the scale be your guide.

Further, you must learn to eat sensibly and not make your diet such an ordeal that you can't even eat out in a restaurant. Many elite cycling women travel to Europe with cookpots and a cache of food. It is a good idea to control and stabilize your diet, but flexibility is key to travel survival.

I was at a meeting once with Priscilla Welch, an extremely slight runner who won the New York City Marathon in 1987, and she said that she ate out at least once a week for "practice." Sounds silly, but it has merit. We get spoiled eating good foods at home, and when we eat out we may feel unwell because we eat the wrong foods, or eat too much. It is possible to eat well at restaurants. For the 150-plus days of traveling required at the elite level in cycling, you had better be able to adapt or you will let your body down—and you have done too much work for that.

Bike-handling skills are best developed in pack-riding situations and by studying the technical section of this book. Spend some time riding around pylons (see riding techniques, page 89). Practice your cornering and descending. Try to keep up with faster riders. Pack riding can be intimidating, so practice the bumping skills.

Even national and world team riders need refresher courses to help them relax when they touch elbows. I sent two riders on the 1991 U.S. world team to a grassy field for bumping, following a training session during which it was evident that they needed a little remedial work. Bike handling comes naturally to some. For example, Inga Thompson of Reno, Nevada, was a good downhill skier before she took up cycling. Those skills transferred to cycling and helped make her bike handling skills good right away. Others take years to learn. You can expedite the process, but you must work on it.

Mountain biking is an excellent way to improve your bike handling. You experience uncertain terrain, rear-wheel skids, and front-wheel instability, which will teach you how to respond. If you don't have a mountain bike, consider throwing some heavier tires on your road bike and head for the dirt. No excuses—find some dirt and start sliding.

Women crash more often and more quickly than men. Men see a crash and work to avoid it. I am always amazed at how many single-rider crashes occur in men's races compared with women's races, where one rider goes down and a whole flock go down around her. Crash avoidance begins with confidence. Believe you can get by the crash—don't let yourself be herded into it. Don't panic when you see a crash. Protect your front wheel because it is the most unstable part of the bike.

Self-confidence can be elevated by a system of goal setting and goal achievement. Self-talk will help you instill belief in yourself and dispel doubt. Believe in yourself like the little train in the classic children's story who says, "I think I can, I think I can." That carries a powerful message to children and adults. You must believe in yourself if you are to accomplish anything, whether it be in cycling, school, or business. "I think I can." Say it over, believe it, and then you can act on it.

You are doing all this training to improve. Are you improving? Visualize yourself against your competition. Are you winning? Or at least reasonably staying with the pace? Whatever the case, you must set goals and visualize yourself achieving them. Don't be intimidated on the starting line just because the local hotshots show up. They get nervous, too. When I was a young speed skater, my father reminded me, "The good skaters put their pants on one leg at a time, just like you." When you race, do your best. Try to stay with the best riders. Once you can stay with them, take the next step and leave them behind. Then you can go from "I think I can" to "I know I can." Finally, you will say, "I did it." And from there, the sky is the limit. Confidence doesn't just happen—you have to work at it.

Women need to learn crash avoidance. Improving your bike-handling skills will help you to increase your confidence and your ability to get around a crash.

PHOTO CREDIT: BETH SCHNEIDER

Upper-body weakness must be addressed in the off-season and can easily be corrected through training. The best approach is through systematic weight training, at least three times a week for a minimum of twelve weeks and optimally twenty weeks. You can do this anywhere—at a fitness center or even in the home with a few simple weights. The advantage of a gym is that there is usually some instruction, which for the novice is critical to getting started. There are many variations on weight training, but as long as you are working all parts of the upper body (lower body, too, of course), you will gain strength.

Other good alternatives for cyclists include aerobic activities like cross-country skiing, swimming, and rowing. In 1983 I broke my arm, and I found swimming in the off-season really helped get my arm strength back. If you hike or roller-blade, take ski poles with you. For hiking, cross-country ski poles of at least chin height are good; for roller-blading the poles need to be taller since the roller blades add several inches of height. The poles will really help your shoulder and upper-arm strength, as well as enhance your cardiovascular fitness since you are working more muscle groups and will need more oxygen.

Pull-ups are hard, but they are excellent for building shoulder strength. Most women find that doing even a single pull-up is difficult, so start by doing reverse pull-ups. Use a stool to get your chin over the bar and work on slowly (to the count of ten) letting yourself down. Soon you will gain the strength to do pull-ups, and can then build from doing one or two to ten or more. Push-ups can also help. Start by doing them on your knees and progress to the more standard off-the-toe variety.

Even more risky sports like rock-climbing, basketball, and volleyball will help your arm strength while sharpening your coordination.

The Three Common Training Errors and How to Avoid Them

I have observed that there are many women who put a lot of time into training and racing but neglect their weaknesses.

The most common training error is to ride too many miles at one speed. You lose leg speed and snap that are crucial to success in women's races. Don't be seduced into always riding with cyclists who are better than you either, unless you take your turn at the front. You can't always sit in their shelter, or you won't know what to do when you ride with those who are not as good as you but can stay with you. How will you shake them? First, you won't have the acceleration, and, second, you won't be used to riding out in the wind on your own.

The second most common error is lack of power, usually from undergearing on the hills. To build power, you must ride a good-size gear when climbing. A little power work on the hills will go a long way toward increasing your race fitness. Many women try to sit and spin a tiny gear uphill. (This can be seen even on the elite level: The top U.S. rider, Inga Thompson, could not match the power of the Dutch rider

Leontien Van Moorsel in the 1991 women's world championship road race in Stuttgart. Tiny Van Moorsel was powering a big gear smoothly and riding away. She beat Thompson for the gold medal by almost two minutes.) Try upping the gear, with a goal of 70 RPMs for your cadence. Rise out of the saddle on the steeper stretches. Start a longer climb in an easier gear and switch up one or two cogs to a harder gear midway. Stand up to keep the gear going, then sit and push. Use the descent to spin your legs in training, which will aid recovery and leg speed.

The third most common training error is a lack of sprint training. Starts are usually fast and then slow considerably. Try to be among the leaders during the race and *don't get dropped off the line.* Then, you must have the fastest finish. Women's races typically finish with some kind of a large group sprint. Working on your sprint is essential.

You hear people say, "I'm not a born sprinter." The answer to that is to train your sprinting—bring out your potential. If you do not have the snap to be a 200-meter specialist, work on going from 400 meters out, or farther. Or learn to be the best and fastest cornerer. If you shoot through the turn with a ten- or twenty-yard advantage, you might take at least part of that advantage to the finish. Work on your sprint and you will be happy you did (see sprinting, page 148).

Do sprint training at least once a week from March to September. If you hate sprint training, consider that this schedule works out to less than thirty sprint sessions for the whole season. You can do that. And when you start to enjoy success, you'll be encouraged to sprint more frequently.

Prescription for Success

To be among the leaders at the finish, you need many qualities. They include a high anaerobic threshold, high aerobic capacity, good anaerobic capacity and, of course, good tactics. When the going gets tough, you have to be among those who get going. So you need to build an endurance base and sharpen your speed, then read the races well.

Try to get a training group together. It is difficult to do everything alone. Women, masters, and juniors training is basically similar. Find riders you are comfortable and compatible with, not riders who are overly competitive. It helps to ride with better riders on occasion, but not all the time. Your training group should meet for long road rides, fast group rides, and sprint training. Interval training is best done alone.

Be careful not to train only with the best men, because you will invariably ride too much (too far) and not get in enough quality work or speed changes. Don't forget that men's racing (the higher categories) demands are different because their races are usually twice as long. It is wonderful to ride 100 miles in less than five hours, and you might be sensational at riding twenty miles per hour behind someone all day long. But what about a twenty-five-mile race at twenty-six miles per hour? Where will you be? Train for performance.

You need not ride more than two-thirds or three-quarters of your maximum race distance. Training seventy-five miles at one time is adequate training for an occasional ninety- or one-hundred-mile race. Train for time, not mileage, and remember that few women's races exceed three hours' duration. Keep in mind that the pros don't ride 180 miles daily just because their races are occasionally that long.

To get your mileage up, it is better to train twice a day, with a daily total of no more than eighty miles, at least twice each week if you have the luxury of time to do so. In this way, you can get your weekly hours up above twenty without having the long, leg-deadening rides.

Beginning riders also can benefit from twice-a-day training once every week. Try doing a good one-and-a-half to two-hour workout in the morning, followed by a light (one hour or less) afternoon ride. This type of double riding benefits all cyclists during the season; it helps speed recovery and reinforces the tactics for active recovery on the bike.

Novice riders can benefit from *a minimum of twelve* and a maximum of up to twenty hours a week of training, which equals about two to three hours daily. That might sound like a lot, but cycling is time-consuming, and little benefit for racing performance will derive from a training program of less than twelve hours a week. Also, remember that the less time you have available, the more concise your training must be, and the less time you will have for recovery training. So use your time wisely if you have less of it. If you have the luxury of more time, put it to good use by incorporating more active recovery training. Believe me, going slow will help you to go fast.

Make a plan of action based on what you need to work on and what your opportunities are. There is not enough time in the week to do everything, so try not to fritter your time away on the bike. Making a plan is discussed in the training section, but I'd like to offer some personal guidelines to give you an idea of how to structure your week.

Women and Masters Men—Elite or National Class

(Juniors: Note that these guidelines also might apply to you, but do a group training Tuesdays instead of intervals.)

GENERAL GUIDELINES: EARLY COMPETITION SEASON

Monday	Recovery training 1–3 hours (zone 1)
Tuesday	2-hour ride with intervals
	3–5 × pyramids or 3–5 × long intervals (zone 4)
	2nd session: 1-hour recovery (zone 1)

Wednesday	3-hour ride: mixed terrain, speed play (zones 3–4)
Thursday	2-hour ride with sprints (zone 5)
	2nd session: 1-hour recovery (zone 1)
Friday	1-hour recovery training (zone 1)
Saturday	Race plus 1-hour ride
	or
	1-hour motorpace plus long warm-down
	or
	3 hours training with partner pacing (zones 3–4)
Sunday	Race plus 1-hour ride
	or
	3–4-hour endurance ride including long climb (30–60 min)
	or
	2 × 30-minute fast echelon (3–6 riders ideally) plus 5 × attacks (zones 3–4)

Total hours: 18–20
Total miles: 300–350

GENERAL GUIDELINES: MAIN SEASON

Monday	Recovery training
Tuesday	1st session: 2 hours, preferably with long, steady climb of 20–40 minutes (zone 3)
	2nd session: 1-hour fast group training race/ride or 1-hour motorpace w/5 × hill jumps (zones 3–5) plus warm-up/-down time
Wednesday	3+ hours, mixed-terrain speed play include long climb and high-leg-speed descent (zones 3–5)
Thursday	1st session: 2 hours with 8–10 sprints, including 5 hill sprints (zones 4–5)
	2nd session: 1–2-hour recovery training (zone 1)
	or
	rest and do this 2nd session on a race day
Friday	1-hour recovery training (zone 1)
Saturday	RACE (zones 3–5)
	plus good warm-down
Sunday	RACE (zones 3–5)
	plus good warm-down

Total hours: less than 20
Total miles: 275–350

FOR WOMEN ONLY—SPECIAL AREAS OF CONCERN

Menstrual Irregularities

Compared with elite distance runners, few elite cyclists experience *amenorrhea,* which is the absence of a menstrual period. If you are amenorrheic, see your physician. The causes of exercise-induced amenorrhea are not clearly understood. Factors such as diet and particularly low meat intake; psychological stress; body weight, particularly low body fat; and high training volumes all have been linked to amenorrhea. Because only a relatively small group of female athletes are affected, few thorough studies have been conducted.

Amenorrhea has one primary negative side effect. Due to hormonal changes, the body's calcium needs increase. Studies show that the bone-density loss among chronically amenorrheic women is significant. This is an even more serious hazard in cycling; a crash can easily result in fractures of low-density, "brittle" bones. Fortunately, easily digested calcium is available at drugstores. One particularly effective source of calcium can be found in Tums, better known as an antacid.

You should also know that the absence of menstruation does not mean you are infertile. In other words, you can still get pregnant, because chances are you are still ovulating. Ingrid Kristiansen of Norway, the world record holder in the women's marathon, found this out the hard way. Her performances in running races started to inexplicably slip, so she went to the doctor and found out that she was five months pregnant with her first child.

Dysmenorreah, or painful menstruation, is a condition that can be more troublesome. The cause of painful menstrual cramps is not known, but theories range from a disease called endometriosis (the presence of endometrial tissue in places where it is not normally found) to high levels of prostaglandins, a hormone thought to stimulate uterine contraction.

There are two generally effective ways to deal with this problem: birth-control pills and/or anti-inflammatories (which are available over the counter or by prescription). Other measures that help reduce this cyclical pain include the old standbys—a heating pad and relaxation. However, you should always consult your doctor about health issues.

To control premenstrual water retention or bloating, try minimizing your salt intake. But don't limit your fluids—they are vital to your health as an athlete. Premenstrual anxiety may well be exaggerated during racing season, but you can work to control it and learn to recognize it for what it is, which may make its effects less dramatic.

Pregnancy and Cycling

Cycling and pregnancy mix. From experience, I know that pregnancy has a similar effect on your body as being at extremely high altitude; your performance is reduced, your heart rate and ventilation are elevated, you are easily dehydrated, and you urinate frequently. How much you exercise depends on how you feel. Every pregnancy is different, so don't compare yourself with other women and don't expect too much. Your body will let you know what you are capable of, and your doctor will help you set guidelines. Most of the guidelines found in the books on pregnancy are for sedentary women, so ask your doctor what someone with your level of fitness can expect to do.

Some women can cycle safely right up until the time of delivery. Miji Reoch stirred quite a controversy when she rode her bicycle alone almost ten miles to her downtown Philadelphia hospital to deliver her baby. She had read that exercise would stimulate the labor, thus reducing its length. Besides, she said, she had been riding regularly and felt comfortable with this means of getting herself to the hospital.

The ultimate question is not so much safety (if you are adept at cycling and choose less-traveled roads) as comfort. With the weight of the baby sitting squarely on top of your bladder, you will feel a persistent urge to urinate. This made me quite uncomfortable after the fifth month, and I curtailed my cycling.

The Masters: Life-style choices

A whole new breed of racer has dominated the late 1980s and early 1990s—the masters racer, or athletes over the age of thirty-five. Masters racers make up almost half of the 35,000 licensed racers in the United States.

Based on our observation, there are three main categories of master's racers: neophytes, racehorses, and born-agains.

Neophytes. The first-time, wish-I-did-this-as-a-kid cyclist who entered the sport late. In our Morgul-Bismark bicycle club, Art Allen is a good example of a rider who never raced until he was forty years old. After a year or two of racing, he won many events and acquired the riding grace and physique of a Tour de France veteran. Genetically, he was gifted, and it is too bad that he didn't start cycling twenty years earlier.

There are many Art Allens out there who are contributing to the health of the sport in this country. The steady proliferation of extremely competitive masters events is reason enough for this group to stick with it. They might not make the

Olympic team, but they will reap rewards in race victories, good health, and the kind of challenge that makes life worth living.

Racehorses. You know them. They started racing in their youth and never stopped. They are racehorses that have not been put out to pasture. One notable rider is former U.S. Olympian Wayne Stetina. Stetina dominated the 1970s, winning five senior national championships and more recently, three masters national championships on the road. Hugh Walton raced on the 1976 Canadian Olympic cycling team and raced professionally. In 1991, he won the national masters road racing championship and world cup criterium championship, both in San Diego. Wayne and Hugh are examples of top racers who have families and work full-time. Both work in the cycling industry: Wayne works in Irvine, California, for Shimano American Corporation, and Hugh is general manager and vice-president of DashAmerica, Inc, the parent company of Pearl Izumi Technical Wear in Boulder, Colorado. You know what they do on their lunch hour—they ride their bikes.

One of the country's top masters duathletes (cycling and running) is Frank Shorter, popularly credited with helping spark the running boom when he won the 26.2-mile marathon in the 1972 Munich Olympics. Four years later, he won the silver medal in the Montreal Olympics. Shorter began cycling primarily as a means of injury prevention and rehabilitation. Now he trains extensively on his bike, as well as maintaining his running fitness. Frank has made a career off his athletic prowess and desire to maintain his fitness; he now routinely wins his age group in the Coors Light national biathlon series, and finishes in the top twenty in the open (all ages) division.

Born-agains. This category includes those who rode during an earlier part of their life and are back in it for the second time. George Mount, sixth in the 113-mile 1976 Montreal Olympics road race, is an example of a rider who fell off the cycling planet, disappeared into the workplace, and came back in 1991, after losing forty pounds, to win masters races.

Training Issues for Masters Racers

What all three categories of masters have in common is a love of the sport, but very few masters have enough time to train. It is important to understand that the needs of this group can be widely different based on varying levels of experience and fitness, and the greatest constraint—time to train.

Technical skills. Many top masters who have great fitness lack bike-handling skills. "It's hard to teach an old dog new tricks" applies. When you are young, being daring comes naturally. You have less fear and better reactions and motor-skill development. As you try new skills, you learn quickly. Younger riders act before they think; older riders think and then decide. Thinking makes the process more stilted, less natural.

Lack of bike-handling skills is dangerous in training and in racing, especially since many masters riders have the strength to keep up yet are hazards to be with in the pack or through turns—especially as they get tired. We get many masters-age riders at our bike camps, and they thrive on cycling's technical aspects: improving their cornering, working an echelon smoothly, sprinting faster. These are earned skills. They simply don't come as naturally as they once did. Take the time to learn them if you want to get the most out of your sport—safely. Or you might take the route that Jack Heiden, Eric's dad, took.

Jack proved that Eric's genes were no fluke when he took up cycling as a master in the late 1970s. He was good, and he won the 1981 National Masters Road Championship in the forty-five-plus category, but a few crashes got him thinking that it was not worth it. As an orthopedic surgeon, he could not afford to break his collarbone or injure his hands. So Jack got into sculling (single rowing) and has become one of the best masters scullers in the nation. These are the choices masters athletes with a family and job must make.

You can make your racing safer. All it requires is some practice. Many masters would not sacrifice an hour—twenty miles—of riding for an hour of technical-skill work. Remember that the technical skills might send you through the turns faster and safer, giving you greater benefit than that twenty miles you missed. Number one for you masters is to relax on the bike. Don't take all the tension from work and family onto your bike. Let it go. Concentrate on the task at hand. You will see great improvements.

Do or die? Mark Allen, the 1990 Ironman Triathlete winner and one of the top all-time triathletes, said that when he is racing, he is willing to put everything on the line—as if his life depended on it. Most elite athletes must take this kind of do-or-die approach.

Mark is a professional who will earn millions of dollars during his career. But for the older athlete who views his sport as a hobby, what should the approach be? You have found something you are good at, and you want to excel. Moreover, you enjoy racing's fraternity. Yet you must find a balance between your family, job, and the rewards that your sport offers. Don't give up. But remember that you need not race as if your life or livelihood depends on it, because even the most rewarding masters races are not going to make you rich.

Is this mellow approach reasonable? For many of you it is, and it will help to put cycling in perspective. For others who feel this may compromise them, then our advice is to race with abandon. These are individual choices. But you can race safely. Practice.

Allocation of time. Once your technical skills have been raised to a highly competent level, make the best use of your training time. Assuming a forty-hour workweek with commuting time and varying degrees of flexibility, you probably have ten to fifteen hours a week available for training. During the preseason, that means you have maybe six to eight hours to train on weekends and maybe six hours during the week.

We suggest you take no more than one day totally off the bike each week, and that you take one easy day of no more than an hour. That leaves you with two hours each day, ideally, for Tuesday through Thursday. This is plenty of time to build your fitness and maintain good form. When you look through the weekly training outlines on pages 194–195, you can see where you can adjust your schedule to make use of your time.

During competition season, your hours may be cut back due to weekend races, but you can keep your hours consistent by riding after short criteriums (less than an hour, which is typical for masters events) for at least an hour. If you have more time to train, great! If not, it will take more skill to put a training program together that yields results.

A word of warning: You need not train every minute at full speed. Training at one speed makes your legs dead and leaves you with no snap. You will not race well if you cannot adjust to speed changes. It takes more discipline and intelligence to train at the right speed than does constant hammering. Let your competitiveness come out on race day, not every training day. Use your time wisely. But maybe we don't have to tell you that, since you *are* reading this book.

Getting the most out of race days

Pay attention to the warm-up. Masters athletes need to warm up carefully, not only to get the body up to speed but also because the races are typically short and fast. Arrive at the race ready to go, with enough time to get dressed, register, and get your bike off the car. You need an hour to warm up, so that means getting to the race two hours in advance, if possible. Many masters events are either early-morning, making warm-up a chilling (literally) experience, or late-day. In the case of the late-day race, you will have the opportunity to ride in the morning before you go to the race, which will make your afternoon warm-up easier and shorter. If your races are usually late, get used to double workouts during the week by riding twice at least once midweek.

Warm-down. Devote thirty minutes to an hour to warm-down immediately after your race. This, combined with the warm-up and the race, gives you three hours for the day. That is plenty of time on the bike.

Training

Masters racers are confronted with the notion that the aging body is losing its ability to perform. Don't believe it. You can forestall performance decline through solid training. Your speed might be compromised as you get older, but you can compensate by increasing your aerobic capacity and your anaerobic threshold. A systematic training program will keep the effects of Father Time at bay. So what should you do with the chunk of time during the week? Think about the demands of your races. They are typically short, fast, and end up in a frenzied sprint. Your training should prepare you for the speed, the speed changes, and the sprint finishes.

Sprint training. This is the one area that is most commonly neglected. Try to fit in one sprint training one day a week. Do it! If you can arrange to do sprints with two or three others, that's great. Otherwise, do it alone. We suggest you do sprint training on Thursday, but you can experiment to see what works best for you. Try doing five to ten sprints in one or two hours. For more details, see the sprint training section (pages 148 and 157).

Hill sprints are a great way to build power after you establish a base—in the late spring or early summer. Do hill sprints earlier in the week, since you may not recover from Thursday hill sprints if you are racing Saturday. Find out what works for you through trial and error.

Full speed ahead. To prepare for masters races, try doing sets of the pyramid-style short-intensity intervals, which take almost six minutes per set (review the training exercises, page 155). By doing up to five sets you will raise your aerobic capacity, enhance your overall speed, and help your body adjust to speed changes. Choose your gearing to keep you sharp, not bogged down. We suggest you try these alone (you do not need a partner for intervals) on Tuesdays during the season. If your time is limited to the lunch hour, you can warm up and do three sets within an hour, with a short warm-down. Do these on Tuesday if you are sprinting on Thursday.

This program leaves Wednesday to fill. Try some medium-paced long-distance training. If you have access to hills, devote Wednesday to climbing and mixed speedwork. If you train with a group, two bouts of twenty to thirty minutes of fast echelon training will help your bike handling while building your anaerobic threshold. Either option is good and enhances your overall cycling fitness.

Masters riders don't have to train like a Tour de France rider, though most of you would like to. What you are looking for as a masters rider is quality training to meet the demands of quality racing. You can basically do these workouts over a long lunch break, in the early morning before work, or in the evening after work. No excuses!

If you don't race on the weekends, use the time for a long ride—lasting more than three hours on one day. If you race neither day, try simulating a race on the second day by using some speed-play training in a group. Try some attack training, group sprints, and faster echelon sections. Make the training fun; the competition among your riding partners should be spirited.

The Off-Season: a Time to Get Ahead

Not all masters racers maintain a consistent year-round training program, so if *you* train year-round, you can make up ground on them. Don't be too intense. Work on maintaining your aerobic base either on your bike (road or preferably some off-road), running, hiking, cross-country skiing, or roller-blading. Incorporate a weight-training program two or three times a week to help build strength. Weight training takes comparatively little time—less than an hour. Train a minimum of six hours a week in the off-season. If you have time for longer-duration aerobic training, then do it; otherwise, do what you can. Whatever you choose for your winter training, be consistent and enjoy it.

Work on your weaknesses in the off-season. If bike handling is your nemesis, consider mountain biking on loose surfaces, like gravel and snow. Andy Hampsten credits his off-season dirt and snow riding with enabling him to handle the treacherous icy descent on the Gavia Pass in the 1988 Tour of Italy, where he took the lead and kept it all the way to his historic victory. If pack riding scares you, find out about good, safe club rides where you can get valuable pack-riding experience. Riding with reliable riders will greatly increase your comfort and ease in a pack.

If your weakness is endurance, consider spending your weekend training time doing long-distance mountain biking, cross-country skiing, road riding, or hiking. Need to work on your sprint? Try doing some explosive weight-lifting or jumping exercises (called *plyometrics*), try the on-the-bike resistance training (see sprinting, pages 148 and 157), and do sprints in various mediums—running, mountain biking, or road riding. Work on different ways to be fast and, it is hoped, you can transfer that speed to your road bike when you need it.

Note to Juniors

Rule #1. My number-one rule for all but proven world-class juniors is to diversify during your teenage years, not specialize. There are many reasons for this, primarily to help keep cycling fresh and to avoid early burnout. The dropout rate is high among young cyclists, which is disheartening when you consider that cyclists peak in their twenties, or even later. Cyclists who have gone from being junior world champions to top professionals include Greg LeMond, the Belgian Eric Van-

Juniors and masters take note: At thirty-three, Mike Engleman was virtually unbeatable in 1991. He began his athletic career as a marathon runner and didn't start racing until he was twenty-five years old. The moral: It's never too late to start and it doesn't always pay to start too young. PHOTO CREDIT: KAREN SCHULENBURG

deraerden, and the Dutchman Michael Zanoli. But many more have left cycling because they failed to make the difficult transition to the senior ranks.

Davis was not a top junior cyclist, yet over time he worked up to being a world-class amateur and professional racer. Michael Engleman, Coors Light's winningest racer in 1991, did not even begin racing until he was in his late twenties. There are many variations on the theme of success, but avoiding burnout and having the patience to make the transition to the senior ranks are crucial to developing your potential as a cyclist.

Another reason to diversify your sporting interests when you are young is that you cannot know if cycling is the most suitable sport for you if you don't try other sports. Involvement in other sports will help you round out your general athletic abilities, which will make you a better cyclist in the long run. One thing we feel sure of, especially with junior women, is that you must be an athlete first, a cyclist second.

Because you are growing fast in your teenage years, your body is not as predictable in its training response as it will be when you get older. Growth spurts also contribute to non-training-related fatigue, making coaching a difficult job. Most teenagers also experience mood swings, which can have an effect on daily training and performance. Juniors waste a lot of energy being anxious, or enthusiastic, or mischievous. No junior was more hyper than Greg LeMond, but you still should work toward controlling your energy output. Juniors race with high energy, too, not always mindful of the task at hand. Chasing typifies a junior race. Control is difficult to learn at this age, but those who direct their energy into training and racing have an advantage.

As a junior, you also have many other things on your mind. School is a requirement. It is imperative that you finish high school. You can get the time you need for training without skipping classes; work with your school and your parents to achieve this. Don't go the route of the high-school equivalency test to get your diploma. Alexi Grewal, 1984 Olympic gold medalist, gambled with his future when he went this route, but it is far from ideal.

When Roy Knickman, a junior phenom who won three medals at the 1983 Junior World Championships in Wanganui, New Zealand, and then took the bronze medal in the 1984 Olympics, was asked what his primary concern as a junior was, his answer was simple: "Girls." You might laugh, but you know, too, that this is a complex and often overwhelming age for many young athletes.

Our best advice to juniors is to put cycling in perspective. Most teenagers feel that every day is do-or-die. But in reality you have many years to reach your potential. So enjoy the shelter of your parents and your high-school years—before you get turned out.

Junior Guidelines

Avoid intensive interval training. Interval training is hard mentally and physically. It is unnecessary when you are fifteen or sixteen; instead, put your time into fast club rides or races and concentrate on sprint training, climbing, and bike handling. If you do intervals, don't do them in a big gear, but aim for a cadence of 110 to 120 RPMs to build leg speed and pedaling style.

Avoid mega-miles. Many juniors ride too far, probably because they want to emulate their professional heroes, but this often leads to injury. You are doubtless still growing, so give yourself a break. You don't need to train more than twelve to fifteen hours a week if you plan to compete on a local level, twenty hours a week to compete on a national level, and more than that only if you are on the national team and plan to do international stage races. Work on your speed; your endurance will follow.

Invest in reliable equipment. Davis struggled as a junior, but most of his bad luck in races came because he wasn't prepared. You don't need the lightest state-of-the-art equipment, but you do need reliable, functional equipment. Learn to work on your own equipment.

Don't compare yourself. When you ride well, everyone tells you that you are the next Greg LeMond or Inga Thompson. Well, you are not—you are the next *you*. If you make a name for yourself, it will be because of you and what you can accomplish. Don't get caught in someone's shadow, which will only set you up to fail. Set your own expectations; don't let others dictate them.

Don't burn out and fade away. Give yourself time to mature. This is especially true of juniors trying to make the transition to the senior ranks. It's hard— give yourself one or two years to develop. Davis feels he got much stronger after he turned twenty. It takes time.

Brian Smith, a name you have probably never heard, is a classic example of a rider who was incredibly talented at age fourteen. He rode 500-mile training weeks and raced with the older juniors or senior men. He had a blind passion. He lived, breathed, and dreamed cycling. He was certain that he would be a great pro—and this was in the 1970s, when almost no American was a great pro. As you might expect, Brian couldn't sustain the pace—he was totally burned out at age eighteen.

PERFORMANCE ON A TIME BUDGET OF TEN HOURS PER WEEK

This is a general guideline and is geared to the cyclist who is training for up to fifty-mile races. This schedule assumes a forty-hour workweek, with weekends free. Make adjustments according to your work schedule. We have broken the year into three basic seasons—you may have more. Remember, you can do a lot on a little time if you plan carefully.

Off-season:

Monday	OFF
Tuesday	Weight training: 3 × circuits or 3 sets of 10 reps of 8–10 exercises. plus twenty minutes total time on the bike (including warm-up and warm-down) Total time = 90 minutes
Wednesday	60–90 minutes aerobic exercise, including: 25–40-minute steady work (zone 3) or if on stationary bike: AT workout from training exercises (page 157).
Thursday	Weights as Tuesday.
Friday	OFF
Saturday	1st workout: Weights as Tuesday (90 minutes) 2nd workout: 90–120 minutes aerobic exercise, including: 10–15 minutes total of long intervals (zone 4) For example: 5 × 2 minutes
Sunday	2–3 hours aerobic exercise, including 3–5 sets of short intensive intervals (pyramids) (zones 4–5) (with a work:rest ratio of 1:2)

Total hours: 9–11

Use the weekend to get your longer workouts in. If you are inclined to train Monday or Friday, do short recovery-type training.

Base season:

Monday	OFF
Tuesday	90 minutes: including 3 × pyramids (zones 4–5) (Work:Rest ratio 1:1) *and* 2 × 10 minutes partner pacing (zone 3) *OR* 20-minute AT work (zone 3)
Wednesday	75–90 minutes: including 30-minute climb or 2 × 20-minute echelon sections (zone 3)
Thursday	90 minutes: including 10 × sprints High RPM, downhill with tail wind
Friday	OFF or 1-hour recovery training
Saturday	1st workout: 2 hours fast group ride, including 3 × 500-meter attacks, 3–5 sprints or RACE 2nd workout: 1–2-hour recovery ride
Sunday	1st workout: 3-hour endurance ride or group ride or RACE (total riding time 3 hours) 2nd workout (optional): 1-hour recovery

Total: 10.5–13.5 hours

Note: In this season you really have to use your weekends to get a solid base. Six to eight hours total training time on the weekends; use the weekdays for shorter workouts and recovery.

Main season:

Monday	OFF
Tuesday	90 minutes: including 3 × pyramids or 10 minutes of long intervals
Wednesday	90 minutes: including 2 × 30-minute fast echelon *or* group training race *or* 30-minute climb
Thursday	90 minutes: 3 × fast downhill sprints 3 × uphill sprints 3 × flat tail-wind sprints
Friday	OFF or 1-hour recovery
Saturday	RACE plus ride 1 hour
Sunday	RACE plus ride 1 hour

Total hours: 9–12

(*Note:* If you aren't recovering well, use Wednesday to do a long endurance ride (up to two hours) and do no hill sprints Thursday.

THE TEN-WEEK ENDURANCE TRAINING PROGRAM FOR ALMOST ANYBODY

This general guideline is to help you prepare for a century ride (100 miles) or a recreational tour. Your goal is a modest 1,000 miles in ten weeks.

Week 1: Building: 3 × 25 miles
       Goal 75 miles
Week 2: Building: 3 × 25–30 miles
       Goal 80 miles
Week 3: Building: 3 × 20 miles, 1 × 30 miles
       Goal 90 miles
Week 4: Peak 1: 3 × 20 mile, 1 × 40 miles
       Goal 100 miles
Week 5: Recovery: 1 × 20 miles, 1 × 30 miles, 1 × 40 miles
       Goal 90 miles

Week 6: Building: 2 × 30 miles, 1 × 40 miles
         Goal 100 miles
Week 7: Building: 1 × 20 miles, 1 × 40 miles, 1 × 50 miles
         Goal 110 miles
Week 8: Building: 2 × 35 miles, 1 × 55 miles
         Goal 125 miles
Week 9: Peak 2: 2 × 20 miles, 1 × 40 miles, 1 × 60 miles
         Goal 140 miles
Week 10: Recovery: 2 × 25 miles, 1 × 40 miles
         Goal 90 miles

TOTAL MILES = 1,000

Mix It up: Ten-Week Endurance with Intervals

If you want to include some quality work in the second building phase, do long intervals (see training exercises, page 154) one day each week as follows:

Week 6: 4 × 2'
Week 7: 5 × 2'
Week 8: 2 × 3', 3 × 2'
Week 9: 3 × 3', 1 × 5'

Be sure to do some hill-climbing on another day. If you have limited hill access, try the short extensive intervals (see training exercises page 154) as follows:

Week 6: 10 × 1 minute work/1 minute recover
Week 7: 12 × 1'/1'
Week 8: 10 × 1'/1'
          3 × 2'/2'
Week 9: 2 × {10 × 1'/1'

Let the other days be purely endurance days, with mixed terrain and speed as you feel, rather than on a set schedule. The above intervals give you some anaerobic threshold work and some lactic acid tolerance work—which will improve your performance and add spice to your workouts.

SECTION 4

PERFORMANCE
(Davis)

BASIC NUTRITION FOR DAILY PERFORMANCE:
EAT TO RIDE OR RIDE TO EAT?

Cyclists love to eat. Ask why they ride and many answer, "To eat." Part of the appeal of bike tours to the recreational cyclist is the ability to eat a lot and still lose weight. Racers eat to perform. Cycling is a high-energy sport. It doesn't matter whether you ride to eat or eat to ride, but it does matter *what* you eat.

An active cyclist's nutritional needs are different from those of more sedentary people. You must make a conscious effort to make the right food choices. You can't train without being properly fueled—that's like trying to drive your car without gas. Daily training depletes your body's stores of glycogen, which is stored primarily in muscle and liver. An overnight fast—from after dinner to before breakfast—is enough to deplete your liver of its glycogen stores. It is essential to keep your tanks full—or replenished—daily. Low glycogen stores will make you feel tired and irritable.

Carbohydrates are basic to any athlete's diet. They provide an easily digested and delicious source of energy. Carbohydrates, which are made up of simple and complex sugars, should comprise 60 to 70 percent of your diet. Each gram of carbohydrate contains four calories. So a bagel containing thirty grams of carbohydrate will provide you with 120 calories of energy. In a 3,000-calorie-a-day diet, you would need to consume 500 grams of carbohydrate. Good sources of carbohydrates include breads, rice, corn, pasta, potatoes, pancakes, beans, fruits, and vegetables.

Protein need only account for about 10 percent of the calories in your diet, but growing teenagers require more. Each gram of protein contains four calories.

209

Protein is needed to keep your body in good working order. Once you stop growing, you need protein only for basic maintenance. Some protein is metabolized during exercise, but in small quantities. There is no need to overdo your protein intake. The best sources of protein are those lowest in fat, like white chicken meat and most types of fish. Red meat is an excellent source of protein and iron, but it can be high in fat. Cholesterol intake should also be monitored, especially if you have a family history of heart disease or high cholesterol. Your daily cholesterol limit is 300 milligrams; chicken and beef both have twenty to twenty-five milligrams of cholesterol per ounce.

Also note that the thigh or dark meat of chicken, even without the skin, still derives almost half its calories from fat, while many cuts of beef and pork derive less than 30 percent of their calories from fat. So shop and choose wisely, and eat meat in moderation. Other sources of protein include tofu, which is a soybean product that has only about 30 percent of its calories from fat. Nut-butters, cheese (both also high in fat), and beans are also nonmeat sources of protein.

What about fat?

The average American diet is loaded with it. As much as 45 percent of the total calories in the typical American diet are from fat. Fat is also highly caloric. Each gram of fat contains nine calories—more than twice as much as that found in carbohydrates or protein. Some fats also contribute to raising your risk of heart disease and should be avoided. "Good fats" are nonhydrogenated: for example, olive oil, canola oil, safflower oil. "Bad fats" are hydrogenated: butter, palm kernel oil, coconut oil. The nomenclature is confusing for the consumer. We used to hear about saturated fats; now they are referred to as hydrogenated. *Partially* hydrogenated fats are still bad—it's only a gimmick to make you think they are better for you. Cholesterol is a type of fat found only in meat products, but food manufacturers love to tell you that their product is "cholesterol free," even when it is obviously not a meat product.

Aim to reduce your fat to below 30 percent of the total calories you eat, and preferably closer to 20 percent. In a 3,000-calorie-a-day diet, that means that less than 900 calories should come from fat. You should eat no more and preferably less than 100 grams per day of fat. Fat lurks everywhere, especially in processed foods, so read labels carefully and use good common sense.

NUTRITION-FOR-PERFORMANCE DIET
60 to 70 percent calories from Carbohydrate
15 to 25 percent calories from Fat
10 to 15 percent calories from Protein

Choosing the right food is never easy.

Understanding Food Labels on Packaged Food

A key to reducing your fat intake is the ability to read and understand the labels of packaged foods. A decade ago, it was difficult to know what was in food because labels were nonexistent. Now most foods contain nutritional information, but this information is often misleading. Labels are confusing. Remember, one gram of fat is not calorically equal to one gram of carbohydrate, since fat has more than twice as many calories by weight. Calculate the percentages based on calories, not on weight. To do this, first *multiply* the grams of fat by nine and the grams of carbohydrate or protein by four. Then, to find out the carbohydrate percentage, *divide* the calories of carbohydrate per serving by the total amount of calories per serving and *multiply* by 100 to get the percentage.

For example: One Quaker Chewy Granola Bar contains 130 calories. Each one-ounce bar contains two grams of protein, twenty grams of carbohydrates, and four grams of fat. To find out what percentage of calories comes from carbohydrates:

20 grams carbohydrates × 4 calories per gram = 80 calories from carbohydrate.
80 carbohydrate calories ÷ 130 total calories × 100 = 61 percent of calories from carbohydrate.

To determine the fat contribution:

4 grams fat × 9 calories per gram = 36 calories from fat
36 fat calories ÷ by 130 total calories × 100 = 27 percent of calories from fat.

Your assessment: the calorie breakdown from the granola bar is in line with your daily dietary objectives. The biggest drawback in this product is that they use partially hydrogenated oils, which are not considered heart-healthy.

A national ice-cream maker, Dreyer's, makes a light version (Dreyer's Grand Light, Light Dairy Dessert) and advertises it to be "93 percent fat free." From the label you would guess that the product is seven percent fat. But a little math illustrates why you need to read labels carefully. The label says that a four-ounce serving contains 100 calories, with each serving containing four grams of fat, fourteen grams of carbohydrate, and three grams of protein. If you do your math:

4 grams of fat × 9 calories per gram = 36 calories from fat.
36 calories of fat ÷ 100 total calories × 100 = 36 percent calories from fat.

Your assessment: clearly, this frozen yogurt is not 93 percent fat free.

A good diet is easy to adopt, and over time your taste buds will adapt and you'll wonder how you ever survived your old ways. Choosing low-fat or nonfat alternatives to full-fat products greatly decreases your fat intake. Some easy-to-follow suggestions: drink skim milk, eat nonfat yogurt, take the skin off the chicken you eat, reduce the salad dressing you use, try baking muffins using nonfat buttermilk and fruit juices instead of butter or oil, eat fish or lean beef or chicken. Cook with less butter—steam your vegetables and learn to enjoy your toast with jam—no butter. To minimize your sugar intake, substitute fruits and honey. Lower your salt intake and drink plenty of fluids.

You can enjoy pizza and ice cream on occasion, but everything in moderation. If one meal exceeds the goal of 20 percent fat, make up for it later in the day.

Vitamins

Everybody has different ideas about what works for them. Taking handfuls of vitamins does contribute to producing very expensive urine; most of what you take in is excreted, because your body does not use it. We recommend that most hardworking athletes—especially those who travel regularly—take a daily multivitamin for insurance.

Women should take an additional iron source, at least part of the time, to avoid becoming anemic. Performance will be greatly compromised if an athlete develops anemia, which interferes with the oxygen-transport system by reducing the hemoglobin, or oxygen-carrying protein, in the blood. Iron is lost daily in urine and sweat. Iron loss is greatly increased in menstruating women. Most athletes' diets provide an inadequate iron intake. Compounding the problem is the fact that iron is not easily absorbed. Food sources of iron include beans, red meats, raisins, and dark leafy vegetables like spinach. Absorption of iron can be enhanced with vitamin C. Combine vitamin C–rich meals with iron sources or take your iron vitamin with orange juice. Iron absorption is inhibited by caffeine, so you should avoid colas or coffee.

Basic Food Groups

We grew up hearing about the basic four food groups: dairy; meat; vegetable and fruit; and breads and cereals. In grade school, we learned to eat two or more servings a day from the dairy group, which included cheese, ice cream, and other milk-derived foods; two or more servings from the meat group, which included eggs, meat, fish, poultry, cheese (again) and legumes; four or more servings from the vegetable and fruit group; and four or more servings from the breads and cereals group. These guidelines were established thirty-five years ago, in 1956. Isn't it time we changed?

New thinking, brought forth by the Physicians Committee for Responsible Medicine, a Washington-based nonprofit group, has stirred controversy because of its emphasis on carbohydrates and deemphasis on the meat and dairy groups. Instead of a square divided into four blocks of food, the PCRM has established a pyramid structure. At the base of the pyramid is the breads, cereal, rice and pastas group, with six to eleven recommended daily servings. Fruits and vegetables have been separated into the second tier. Three to five servings of fruits and vegetables and two to four servings of fruits are recommended. The top of the pyramid comprises milk, yogurt, and cheese (two to three servings) and meat, poultry, fish, dry beans, eggs, and nuts (two to three servings). At the peak of the pyramid are sweets, oils, and fats, which are recommended only sparingly.

This is clearly a nutrition-for-performance diet: high in carbohydrates and fresh fruits and vegetables, and lower in fat. This concept—hardly novel with endurance athletes—was met with great resistance and all but shot down. Why? Heavy lobbying by the meat and dairy groups.

Eating to lose

Weight reduction is a hot topic. It sells books. While weight *loss* isn't that difficult, *keeping weight off* is. You have to take a sensible approach to weight loss—change your life-style, your eating habits, and your exercise patterns. The bottom line of weight reduction is this: you have to take in less and burn more. If you are in heavy training, dieting will interfere with your training response and undermine your performance. If you train over twelve hours per week and still have a problem, analyze what you eat, but don't try a starvation diet. You will lose your fitness along with the weight. Losing one pound requires you to burn 3,600 calories of fat. Fad diets tend to stimulate water loss, which gives you a false sense of losing weight. It's not worth it to deplete your energy stores to the point where you can barely function, much less ride your bike. Be sensible.

Everyone's diet usually has a weak spot, like late-night munching or early-morning doughnuts. If you eliminate that weak spot and increase your energy output by cycling or even walking more—you will lose weight. For example: cut out desserts—this might total 500 calories per day out of your diet, or 3,500 calories a week. That's one pound right there. Now, add five hours of additional aerobic exercise per week to your schedule. That's another pound—or about two pounds per week, considered to be safe weight loss and, more important, weight you can keep off if you don't revert to your old ways. Whenever you diet, take a multivitamin to be sure you are getting what your body needs.

NUTRITION FOR RACE PERFORMANCE

Cyclists burn fields of food for calories. Events like the Tour de France, in which riders race daily for six to seven hours over twenty-one days, place an incredible demand on the body for fuel. A recent Dutch study showed that the Tour diet consists, predictably, primarily of carbohydrates. What was a surprise was that the majority of the calories were derived from refined sugars. Why? When a body has to consume as much as Tour riders do, it is difficult to stick to bulky whole-grain sources of carbohydrate. There simply is not room in the stomach and intestines, and not enough time or energy to eat it all. Instead, the athletes must go for the quick fix—high-calorie cakes and sweets.

This is borne out by the transcontinental Race Across America winners, who have admitted to feasting on McDonald's milkshakes and Chef Boyardee Spaghettios—right out of the can. Why? Both those foods are high in carbohydrates—exactly what the body craves.

High-performance foods are a boon to ultra-endurance athletes whose bodies are struggling to stay fueled with the right stuff. Even the standard Euro-fare of meat and rice for breakfast and dinner is not suitable to the changing palate. The 7-Eleven team brought a cook and a motor home along just to fill the need for better-quality food for the riders. 7-Eleven riders were treated to pancakes in the morning (unusual in Europe) and perfectly cooked pasta at night, an exotic plate in France. Further, increased sports-food technology has turned out a number of taste-pleasing high-energy drinks and bars, which have made the job of eating less work.

A DAY IN THE LIFE OF THE TOUR DE FRANCE RIDER

Eating is work during the Tour de France. By the end of the three-week, 2,500-mile event I am tired of eating. But eating is part of surviving. If you don't eat enough, you cannot perform.

Breakfast: Muesli (yogurt, oats, fruit cereal). Bread with jam. Pasta and an omelet mixed together (no sauce, no cheese). Water, juice, and coffee to drink.

During the race: Fruit. Power Bars. Muesli bars. In hot weather, Carboplex or Extran—highly concentrated carbohydrate solution. In colder weather: *paninis* (small sandwiches filled with fruit and cheese, ham and pineapple), maybe a candy bar or fruit tart. These are wrapped in foil, picked up in the feed zone in a special feed-bag called a musette. Lots of water and either a Max-type energy drink or diluted Coke.

After the race: Fluids to rehydrate. Sandwich and yogurt waiting in the room. More fluids on hot days. We rest and get a massage before dinner.

Dinner: Small salad made of crudités (French-cut vegetables, including corn, beets, carrots). Pasta with light sauce. Chicken or beef. Bread. Vegetables. Fruit tart or yogurt and fresh fruit for dessert.

Calories: over 7,000 a day.
         70 to 75 percent carbohydrates
         10 percent protein
         15 to 20 percent fat

Prerace meal. The prerace meal starts the night before you compete. Be sure to eat well, loading up with your favorite carbohydrate source. There is no secret to the prerace meal. It takes common sense to eat right. You should eat what you are used to, eat what sits well in your stomach, and eat early enough that you feel light but not hungry at the start of the race or ride. Most racers should eat three hours before competition. The training-table meal should be very high in carbohydrates, and, not surprisingly, low in fat. A small amount of protein will help the food "stick to your ribs." Ideal prerace foods include oatmeal, fruit, bagels, or pancakes (easy on the syrup) in the morning. Pasta and sandwiches are good for late-day races. If you have a food that you absolutely have to have, bring it with you when you travel; this will minimize the risk of ruining the event before it starts.

Carbohydrate loading came into vogue with the running marathon in the late 1970s. Carbohydrate loading is a proven technique of fooling your body into storing exceptionally high amounts of glycogen. The method involves training under a carbohydrate-restricted diet for several days and then, just prior to the race day,

Eat to perform. You can't get to the finish line in the Tour de France if you don't eat well and eat a lot. Here I finish fourth (on the far right) in a close finish in Mont St. Michel.
                                                    PHOTO CREDIT: BETH SCHNEIDER

eating a very-high-carbohydrate diet. Your body supercompensates after the deple-tion phase and you are able to carry more glycogen into the race. The primary drawback for runners is that glycogen is stored with water, causing a runner to gain several pounds during the process, which might leave him feeling heavy and full. Second, the depletion phase is taxing, because you are effectively starving yourself while you train, which might put the runner at a psychological disadvantage.

Carbohydrate loading does not work for cyclists—primarily because cyclists race often. A runner might compete in two marathons a year; a cyclist races twice every weekend during the season. It's not practical and it isn't necessary. A well-trained cyclist who takes care to go into a race well-fed will have adequate glycogen stores that can be enhanced through systematic en route feeding. Part of the problem for runners is eating on the go, which is much easier to do on a bike.

Find out what works. Skip Hamilton, a five-time winner of the Leadville 100, a 100-mile run on mountain trails, and performance consultant to the elite Special-ized mountain bike team, cautions athletes not to experiment in their racing with food and drink, but to carefully find out what works in training. Many highly potent energy sources are often fructose-sweetened, which cause gastric distress and stomach upset in many individuals. Fructose is used because it is five times sweeter than sugar—making the products more palatable. Hamilton also recommends drinking in the first few miles of a training ride to get the body hydrated, and drinking often during the ride. Drink before you are thirsty, because the body's thirst indicator lags behind your body's needs. Hamilton also suggests that athletes eat a high-carbohydrate meal within an hour or two of training to take advantage of a stimulated metabolism. This will help speed recovery for the next training ride.

Hamilton is a cofounder of Max Sportsdrink, a palatable and tasty drink that provides energy in the form of easily digested glucose polymers, and does not give you cotton mouth. There is a plethora of sports drinks on the market, from the old standby, Gatorade, to the newer kids on the block like Exceed and Max. Cyclists need an energy drink, not an electrolyte replacement. Most drinks should be watered down. Coca-Cola is also a popular drink, because it provides energy from sucrose and a metabolic kick from the caffeine; it is usually de-fizzed and diluted with water.

Power Bar, made by Power Foods of Berkeley, California, has been on the market since 1987 and is an integral part of the cyclists' diet. Power Bars are low in fat (8 percent), high in carbohydrate (70 percent) and easily digestible—almost a perfect food. The beauty of the Power Bar for us is that we can eat several bars each day for weeks and never tire of the taste (our favorite is malt-nut). Be sure to drink extra fluids along with the bar to enhance digestion and prevent dehydration. On a recent bike tour in France that covered many infamous Tour courses, my father categorized rides by Power Bar consumption—a three-Power Bar climb being the hardest.

Find out what works for you and be consistent with your diet. What you eat matters, so eat to ride and eat to perform.

TACTICS: DECISION-MAKING ON THE FLY

"A champion is afraid of losing. Everyone else is afraid of winning."
—BILLIE JEAN KING

Bicycle racing is a very tactical game. The sport is a great equalizer, because no matter how strong you are, you have to make the right move to win a race. Tactics are what separate winners and losers in bike races. Understanding tactics will greatly improve your odds of winning the race. Tactics begin with how you train and prepare for a race, and end with everything you do during the race.

Race-winning tactics must be dynamic, because you can never count on what the other riders will do on race day—you can only guess. Ride the race with a plan of action, but be prepared to react and respond. Intuition is an important element when reading a race: what do you think *might* happen? Concentration helps you to understand the race and your role in it. On any given race day, you might find yourself as aggressor, chaser, controller, or pack-filler. What role you assume will be based on how you feel, how strong your competition is, and what the course is like. No bike race is ever the same. Racing requires that you react to the challenges, act instinctively, and take calculated risks.

Don't think too much. Learn to trust your instincts and accept the consequences of your actions. It doesn't take an Albert Einstein to understand tactics, but they are complicated and you do have to think. More important, you have to move. Don't become a member of the "I should have . . ." team. It's better to die trying than to wait for the ideal race move and suddenly find the race is over before you made your big play. The good racer uses his opponents; he learns from his mistakes as much as he does from his victories. Think about your plan of action and don't be afraid to *just do it.*

Tactics involve a constant flux of decisions. Should I or shouldn't I? Will he or won't he? What is going on inside your opponent's head? Study your competition. Track sprinters take detailed notes on their competitors during a sprint match, taking note of tactics and gearing. Some riders are very predictable. Study your opponents' faces, maintain a poker face, and listen to yourself. Then devise the best strategy for you. Tactics make racing exciting and frustrating. Cycling is a thinking athlete's sport. Clearly, the strongest rider does not always win.

Race dynamics. Dissect a race to understand it better. Bike races typically start out fast and then settle. When it settles depends on many factors, but at some point, the action slows down and you get a chance to catch your breath. At the midpoint, the tactics become more focused—riders start laying their cards on the table. In the last several kilometers, the sprinters start to move into position and the speed accelerates until the final dash.

Many riders are dropped in the first few miles of a race because of the high speed. Therefore, the first tactic is to be warmed up and ready. Being too nervous wastes energy. If you're shaking, it's hard to get your foot in the pedal after the start. A good warm-up and advance preparation should help you be more calm. If you get jittery, cut the prerace caffeine—no Coke, coffee, or tea. Go to the line in a small gear so you can get going quickly; get to the line early so you can start up front. Don't be dismayed if you start in the rear, but be prepared to weave through the slower-starting riders so you don't lose the race before it starts.

Move up. Once the race is underway, *stay up front.* Riders who sit in the back half of the field are more likely to be involved in crashes or get dropped because gaps open more frequently. It's harder to sit in the back third of the pack than it is to sit in the front third, where the pace is more consistent. In the back there is an accordionlike effect through sharp turns, resulting in stop-and-go action.

Blocking is done to control the pace, and teams use this tactic to slow down a chase. When a teammate is in a breakaway, the team is obliged to move to the front of the pack—the more teammates the better. As the pace picks up, the team interrupts and disrupts the flow, making a consistent chase effort difficult, if not impossible. This often has the effect of demoralizing the pack, which ultimately might give up the chase. But if the pace slows considerably, riders will be fresher and will attack more. Blockers ride tempo at the front, maintaining a pace that thwarts attacks but does not threaten to catch the leaders. Blocking can also be more active: a team swarms to the front on a tight turn and slows the pack by cornering slowly. However, this does not give you license to be dangerous. Sprinting up to a turn and slamming on your brakes in front of other riders is never acceptable.

Blocking doesn't have to be obvious. Here's an example: several team members are at the front, riding a narrow section of road, and the lead rider accelerates. The second rider, a teammate of the lead rider, lets the gap open. His body language—he maintains the same posture—says he is working hard, but he is *soft-pedaling*. Before the riders behind know what hit them, the lead rider is out of sight. Play a good game when you block; you don't have to sit up as if to say, "Look at me, I'm blocking."

A common mistake made by American teams is to practically stop racing once a teammate is in the lead break. If your teammate is up the road with a group of riders, try to get another team rider up there to improve your team's chances. Instead of playing a negative tactical game, keep the race lively and aggressive. Your primary obligation is to keep dangerous riders at bay. Evaluate your chances of pulling even with the leaders. If it looks good, give it a shot.

The professionals and amateurs race differently. Pros stay in the game right until the end, but might let a breakaway get a five- or ten-minute lead in the early part of the race. They let that happen because they have confidence that they can reel in a breakaway, if need be, late in the race by riding *tempo* at the front.

In the pro peloton, team directors dictate the tactics to the team leader in the same way that a head football coach sets the strategy with the quarterback. But like the quarterback, the leader must learn to improvise and use his best judgment. Radio communication between the team car and the riders has improved the exchange of information during races.

WINNING BIG—A TIP FROM CONNIE

In 1989, Dede Demet won the Junior World Championships in Moscow under my coaching direction. Her race was based on one tactic: no matter what size group she was in, she would attack five kilometers (3.1 miles) from the finish on a steep hill, which was followed by a long false-flat section, before a fast descent and long finishing stretch. We trained on the course, practicing the attack several times in training. Dede had it wired to perfection. On race day, she only had to worry about one tactic. When the time came, she did exactly as planned and made a decisive attack—it was all or nothing. If she was caught, she would be dead. But that was her gamble. Her attack was helped by her American teammate, Jessica Grieco, who thwarted the chase. The pack closed in at the finish, but Dede held them off to win the race by several bike lengths.

Confidence, teamwork, and surprise. The tactic worked primarily because Dede had the strength to pull it off and the conviction that it would work. She attacked with 100 percent effort—no hedging. She had tried a similar race-winning move in the Washington Trust Classic in Spokane a few weeks earlier, which gave her confidence a boost. Second, she had a teammate who helped her. If the chase had gone unchallenged or unimpeded, she might have been caught before the finish. And finally, she surprised the field. The field was thinking about the sprint finish and no one wanted to kill themselves in the chase. Late-race attacks are ideal for non-sprinters.

Another surprise. I needed help on the final day of the 1981 *Self* magazine–sponsored series. This series included the Allentown Gotham Cup road race, Tour of Nutley, Tour of Somerville, and New York City's Central Park Race. The overall winner would be determined based on points accumulated over the four days; a Datsun was on the line. The contest shaped up into a duel: my Puch team against the AMF team. The matchup pitted two-time World Sprint Champion Sue Novar-Reber and me against Karen Strong of Canada and Sarah Docter of Madison, Wisconsin. I had to beat Sarah on the final day to win the car.

Our tactic was to let Sue lead me out for the sprint. Everyone would be expecting Sue to wait for the last two hundred meters in an attempt to try to win the sprint. Instead, Sue was to start sprinting at the 500-meters mark, taking me with her in her draft and setting me up for the win. It worked like a dream: I won the overall series title—and the Datsun.

This tactic worked for two reasons. First, the element of surprise—no one expected Sue to start sprinting so early. And second, I trusted her. Trust is essential to teamwork.

No team? One of the most common complaints comes from riders who do not have a team. But this complaint overlooks a crucial fact. Often what lies behind the perfectly uniformed riders of a well-sponsored team is disorganization, disharmony,

Teamwork helps. I have been fortunate to have teammates who have helped me to many of my 300 career victories. When I win, they win, as evidenced here in the 1989 Tour de Trump where I edge Greg LeMond (left) and Michael Zanoli (right)—and my teammates have their arms up back in the pack.   PHOTO CREDIT: KAREN SCHULENBURG

and a lack of tactical savvy. Even the biggest and best teams make mistakes. Sometimes there are two or three big teams feuding with each other. Often it's the lone rider who has the advantage. You may have more help than you thought. Suddenly your "team" numbers a hundred riders. Study the situation carefully and let your free-agent status work for you, not against you.

> "Winning isn't everything, making the effort to win is."
> —VINCE LOMBARDI

You have to put everything on the line and you never give up. When I came back to the United States and raced domestically, I got into some good battles with Michael Zanoli, former junior world road racing champion from Holland who competed in America for several seasons on the Coors Light team.

In the 1990 Tour of the Redlands in northern California, I kept attacking on the final stage, trying to get away. Finally, on the last lap, Zanoli, two Russians, and I broke free. Going up a hill, one of the Russians attacked from our breakaway. He had five bike lengths on Zanoli, who was five lengths ahead of me. We turned a corner and went across the top of the course. I was at a point where I felt that I would quit, because I was completely blown. But there was one little ember burning in me not to give up, because I really wanted to beat my rival, Zanoli.

We were all going as fast as we could and the Russian was still ahead, but I held even with the young Russian and Zanoli. When the pack turned another corner to make a descent leading to the final stretch, I saw the lead Russian look back and spot Zanoli. The Russian eased up. I had regained my strength, and at that moment, I absolutely knew I had both of them. Zanoli eased up as he joined the Russian. I quickly caught them and perched behind Zanoli's rear wheel. He jumped early for the last corner. But I knew that whoever was first through the last corner would lead down the final straight to the finish.

It was raining and the streets were slick, but I wasn't going to be denied. I sprinted hard and pulled up next to Zanoli. It was just the two of us. Now the question was, who would back off through the turn? Not me. Zanoli braked, and I shot through the corner to win the race.

WINNING SPRINTS

I have built my reputation and my career on winning sprints. No sprint is ever the same, although some general rules apply.

#1 Rule of Sprinting: Positioning

American road races tend to be shorter than those in Europe, so sprinting becomes a matter of being in the right position. Everyone wants to be near the front on the last turn, but nobody wants to lead. Don't be afraid to lead—you should still be able to finish in the top ten if you have anything left, and by being at the front you will avoid 90 percent of the crashes. Many riders wait too long to move up in the peloton or are unwilling to make the effort or take the chance.

I have a long sustainable sprint which I like to take advantage of on tight courses, by making my move two or three corners before the finish. I get to the front and take full advantage of my two best assets, my quickness and cornering skills. I sprint the straight stretches and hang it out through the turns. By the time I get to the final turn, no one is near me. This tactic works, and I like it because it maximizes my strengths, leaves less to chance, and greatly minimizes the danger of bunch finishes. It takes fitness, quickness, and good cornering technique to win this way.

Pick the Right Wheel

Try to stay on the wheel of the best sprinter. If he has a good leadout from a teammate or a friend, take advantage of it. I took advantage of the Motorola team leadout to win the first stage of the 1991 Tour Du Pont, which put me in a two-up battle with their best sprinter, Phil Anderson. The Motorola team lined up at the front for the final kilometer of the race, which was notable because there were several tight turns before the final 400-meter uphill finishing stretch. I rode partially in Anderson's draft, conserving my energy for the sprint even though the pace was in excess of thirty miles per hour. Coming into the final corner, Anderson went wide and opened a gap for me. I shot in behind Steve Bauer, who then pulled off the front as Anderson and I drag-raced to the finish line.

Pick the right wheel—in this case, I took advantage of the Motorola leadout to win the opening stage of the 1991 Tour Du Pont in Wilmington. PHOTO CREDIT: BETH SCHNEIDER

There was one factor that was not readily apparent that helped me to win the race—my ability to shift gears midsprint. Shifting technology took a giant leap with the accurate and reliable Shimano STI handlebar shifting system. Located in the brake caliper, the system enables the rider to shift under full pedal pressure out of the saddle or in the saddle. This enabled me to jump in a relatively small gear (the fifty-three-tooth front chainring and the fifteen-tooth cog in the rear) and shift down to the twelve, one tooth at a time. I made three shifts in the 400-meter span, but that enabled me to accelerate all the way to the finish and win the race.

The Motorola team evened things up, however, in the next-to-last stage of the Tour Du Pont when my Coors Light team provided me with a leadout that looked like a race winner. Before the final turn, teammate Steven Swart pulled off the front to let teammate Greg Oravetz lead. I was lined up right behind Oravetz, who unexpectedly overshot the turn, forcing me to go inside and take the lead too early—with 300 meters to go. Still, I thought I had it until Steve Bauer—who had taken full advantage of our Coors Light leadout—shot by me to steal the win in the final fifty meters.

Time Your Sprint

When you are ready to make your move to pass a rider or a group of riders, time your sprint to take advantage of the *slingshot effect*. When you enter the draft of another rider, you are literally sucked into it. You can feel this when a large truck passes you on the road and you have to fight not to be pulled into it. Take advantage of this phenomenon by accelerating into the draft so that you slingshot out of it. The biggest mistake is in timing your acceleration to get by someone as you leave the draft—instead of as you go into it. This tactic is very noticeable among track sprinters who sit several bike lengths behind their opponent and time their sprint to take maximum advantage of the slingshot principle.

Play Your Strengths

From experience you should know where your sprint strengths lie and take advantage of them. Is it your acceleration? Can you keep your peak speed up for longer than 200 meters? Whatever your strengths are, use them. You're effectively cashing in your chips.

At the 156-mile CoreStates US PRO Championship in 1988, Roberto Gaggioli of Italy and Dag-Otto Lauritzen of Norway were on a two-rider breakaway toward the end for a duel in the sun. Roberto's strength is his acceleration. In the last half-mile, he deliberately slowed the pace down. Dag-Otto watched Roberto like a hawk on the flat Ben Franklin Parkaway in Philadelphia, but he let the pace get too slow, just as Roberto wanted. First prize was $25,000; second was $15,000. They were almost at a walking pace with less than 300 meters left. Then Roberto got out of the saddle and abruptly opened up four bike lengths, which he kept all the way to the finish to win the event. He used his strength, which was his acceleration, and played that against what he knew was Dag-Otto's weakness (he couldn't possibly match Gaggioli's jump). It paid off with a big victory.

My strength is my top end. I am an out-of-the-saddle, big-gear sprinter. I try to use my arms and upper body to their fullest advantage for peak speed. But I also have superior conditioning and confidence, and I know I can respond to almost any challenge in the closing kilometers. My experience enables me to concentrate and narrow my focus so that time seems to slow down and I am aware of everything. Winning bike races is exciting and great fun, but it doesn't happen by magic—you make it happen by using your strengths to maximum advantage.

If you are not explosive but have good staying power, try to go early and as fast as you would if you were in the last 200 meters. In a criterium, that usually means going from the third-to-last or second-to-last turn—or, in a road race, going before the final kilometer—well before the sprinters start to smell the finish. Dutchman Joop Zoetelmelk did just that in the 1985 world professional championship in Montello, Italy. With one kilometer to go in the 165-mile race, Zoetelmelk—who was thirty-nine, the last year a professional rider can hold a license—knew the other leaders were planning their sprint. He took off. Everyone else hesitated to see who would start the chase. Zoetelmelk widened his gap until the sprinters finally reacted, but too late. Greg LeMond was forced to sprint for second, but he learned a lesson that paid off in the 1989 World Championship road race in Chambéry, France. LeMond chased every attack in the final five kilometers and then won the sprint for his second career professional World Championship title.

Sleigh riders

What if you go for it as Zoetelmelk did and someone just sits on your wheel? You have a dilemma that you must deal with quickly. Evaluate your chances based on who is drafting behind you. It doesn't take a genius to know if you are in a no-win situation. Is that rider just tired and can't take a turn at the front? Or will he (or she) beat you easily to the line? Is second place better than going back to the pack and risking finishing fifteenth? Or fiftieth? Do you have the time or the opportunity to attack the sleigh rider again? Don't overevaluate; make your decision and stay with it.

Promises, Promises

Riders try all kinds of verbal encouragement and make all kinds of promises in races. One top racer in our Morgul-Bismark Bicycles–sponsored racing club found that out the hard way when he broke away from the field in the final laps of a big criterium. One other racer was able to go with him, but was just sitting on and not working. Our intrepid racer was sure he would be beaten, which prompted him to yell to his breakaway partner, "Okay, we're splitting the prizes." The other rider *never* took a pull and *never* contested the sprint. Our rider thought that he would get killed in the sprint because he was working so hard. Instead, he won easily. The other rider was hanging on and very happy to finish second and have the promise of split prizes. What a deal.

Don't believe what you hear in a race. Lots of riders try in-race deals, or make verbal commitments "not to sprint." Don't believe it, even if you know the rider. Long before we were teammates, Ron Kiefel and I were in a breakaway together and I told him I wouldn't sprint because Ron was about to drop me on a hill before the finish. He slowed so that I could recover and stay with him. When I saw the finish-line banner up the road I lost my head and uncorked the winning sprint. I couldn't help myself. Needless to say, Ron was angry and I was very apologetic, but that didn't give him the race win. I felt terrible. It's always a good idea to keep your promises, but in the heat of the moment you never know what might happen.

Do It Alone

Much has been said about the glory of winning alone. It's not as exciting as a massive field sprint (what do you expect me to say?), but it is a lot more safe and a lot more sure. Winning alone leaves very little to chance. To increase your odds of winning, a solo breakaway is ideal, but making it work depends on timing, teamwork, and your own fitness. Don't underestimate the value of surprise. No one ever expects me to break away alone, but I did just that to win a hilly stage in the 1991 Tour of Fitchburg. If your competitors slot you into a category, surprise them and try something new.

An early-race attack may look suicidal to the pack, but it might pay off. Julie Furtado won the 1989 women's national road race with an early-race suicide move that went unchallenged. Furtado was an unknown then, but now is one of the top women on the off-road racing circuit and the 1990 world mountain bike champion.

In the 1991 U.S. senior men's national road race, national team riders Lance Armstrong and Steve Larsen were in a two-man break on a very hilly race in Park City, Utah. It was obvious that Armstrong was just playing with Larsen—who was strong, but no match for Armstrong. Armstrong had the tactical savvy to wait until the final climb in the closing kilometers of the race to leave his breakaway companion and ride in alone for the win.

Pick your strength and go for it. If you feel you are the strongest climber—attack on the climb. If you are the best descender—attack on the descent. If you are the best cornerer—pick a tricky turn. If you've got the fitness, go early.

Whatever you do in a race, *don't be afraid of winning*.

RACE ETIQUETTE: RIDE LIKE A PRO

Ride as if your livelihood depended on it. As a pro, I have learned to take chances at extremely high speeds—but I have also learned to depend on the other riders in the peloton. Gonzo moves are simply not acceptable.

The pro peloton is a fraternity. We are extremely competitive on the bike and friendly off the bike. I have always been able to pull out all the stops when I race against my rivals Steve Bauer or Eric Vanderaerden. But I leave it on the racecourse; after the race we congratulate each other and are friendly. Don't make the mistake of taking rivalry *off the bike*. You don't have to be best friends with your competitors, but show them respect, no matter what the outcome.

Rule #1. There are a few things you can do to keep the races safe. Keep your hands on the bars. For some reason, Americans think it's acceptable to take a hand off the bars to tap another rider, indicating that you want to move into his space. I think Americans think this is what is done in Europe.

Leave your rivalry on the racecourse. Here I chat with Eric Vanderaerden as we await photo-finish results in the 1989 Tour de Trump—where I narrowly beat him in Baltimore.

PHOTO CREDIT: BETH SCHNEIDER

It's not. Taking your hands off the bars is unstable and dangerous. Don't do it. If you want to move around in the pack, look for gaps or move to the outside. Be patient, and don't push people around.

Rule #2. In long races requiring a feed, be more relaxed as you enter the feed zone. Everyone gets anxious in the feed, and if every rider respected the others, everyone would get their food. Don't behave as if you are the only rider that matters. Attempting to improve your position in the feed zone is thoroughly unacceptable. Think of the feed zone as a neutral zone and relax.

Rule #3. Finally, if you have a mechanical problem—don't panic. I know that I have not stayed calm during every crash or puncture, but I also know that by remaining relaxed in such situations, you increase your chances of

Rule #3: don't panic if you have a mechanical problem.   PHOTO CREDIT: BETH SCHNEIDER

getting going again quickly and with more energy to put into the chase. I hate to see riders become so argumentative after a crash that a fight erupts. Stick to the task at hand. Think clearly. If you are in a criterium, do you have a free lap? Where is the support pit? Many races have been won by riders who persevered after a fall. You may not be out of it yet, so don't act as if you are. Take responsibility for your bike and help to get the handlebars aligned if they have moved. Let the mechanics know what you need—don't scream at them, or they might help the next guy and not you.

THE ENVIRONMENT

Whenever you ride, you face challenges from the riding terrain, your riding partners, and the environment. Being a competitive cyclist is like being a mailman; you have to be prepared for all conditions—wind and rain, snow and sleet, heat and cold. Racing and riding at high altitude present a whole different set of challenges. With a little knowledge, you can perform better.

Altitude

There isn't less oxygen at altitude, relatively speaking, but the air is thinner. The absolute percentage of oxygen in the air is the same as at sea level (about 21 percent), but barometric pressure decreases with higher elevation. As a result, the oxygen molecules are spaced farther apart. With each gulp of air, you take in less oxygen, and you have to increase your breathing frequency to compensate. The feeling of having to gasp for more air is disconcerting and uncomfortable when you are not used to it.

As elevation increases, performance decreases in endurance sports like cycling. In a laboratory, performance is measured by VO_2 max, which decreases 3 percent for every 1,000-foot elevation gain (even more at extremely high altitudes). Thinner air, however, provides less resistance and increases performance in jumping and some throwing events, as well as in events not compromised by the diminished aerobic capacity, like sprints under 200 meters. Bob Beamon's 1968 Olympic long jump world record of 29 feet 2½ inches lasted twenty-three years and remains the longest-standing Olympic record. He set it in the 7,350-foot altitude of Mexico City.

Cyclists seem to benefit from the reduced density of the air. Times at the 7-Eleven Velodrome in Colorado Springs (elevation under 7,000 feet) have been extremely fast due to both a fast track surface and reduced air density. The coveted "hour record" is held by Italy's Francesco Moser, who rode 51 kilometers (31.875 miles) in one hour at the Mexico Centre Velodrome in Mexico City.

Altitude Tips

Prevention of altitude sickness. 1) Drink plenty of liquids. Dehydration occurs rapidly at high altitude. Water is the beverage of choice; drink a lot and drink often. Caffeinated drinks like coffee and colas should be avoided, because they contribute to dehydration. Alcohol also leads to dehydration because of its diuretic effect. Your metabolism speeds up at altitude as your body tries to deliver adequate oxygen and maintain its acid-base balance, which is disturbed at altitude. Consequently, you lose fluids by frequent urination and increased breathing. Symptoms of altitude sickness include headache and nausea. If the problem becomes severe, see a physician. The remedy for severe cases of high-altitude sickness is to administer oxygen or to descend quickly.

2) Give yourself time to adapt. Although total acclimatization will take many weeks, you should plan to arrive seven to ten days before your competition if you have time. Take it easy for the first few days at altitude. Some riders come to altitude and push it for two or three days, then need a week to recover because the effects of the altitude are not always felt on the first day or two. Because of this lag effect, another strategy is to come up to high altitude the day before a race (especially a single-day event like a national championship) and then leave right after the event. The full effect of the altitude will not be felt on the first day.

3) Ascend slowly. If your destination is Vail, Colorado, where the altitude is almost 8,000 feet, plan to stop for a day or two in the lower environs of Denver or Boulder (elevation 5,400 feet).

Why Boulder? It is no secret that many of the country's top endurance athletes live much of the year at high altitude in Boulder. Endurance athletes may derive some benefit from living at altitude, because one of the long-term adaptations is the increase of oxygen-carrying red blood cells, but this is also an adaptation of endurance training anywhere. Most of the benefit of living in high altitude is in *competing* in high altitude. The U.S. riders who lived at altitude always performed well in the Coors Classic, which took place mostly at high altitude. One exception to this was Bernard Hinault, a five-time winner of the Tour de France, who won the 1986 Coors Classic. With no time to acclimatize, the Frenchman gained strength from start to finish and won the race in a dominant fashion.

IS BOULDER BETTER?

Many athletes choose to live in Boulder not because of the potential benefits of altitude training, but because of the endurance training–friendly environment. Boulder boasts an abundance of good running trails, roads to

Here, Mike Engleman and Scott Moninger display superior form and conditioning while soaring to victory at the top of the 14,000-foot Mount Evans Hill Climb. Training at altitude definitely helps your performance at altitude.

PHOTO CREDIT: KAREN SCHULENBURG

ride, and training partners. The terrain offers athletes a choice: flat to the east and mountainous to the west.

Boulder is a health-conscious town of 80,000 inhabitants. There are more than a dozen specialty bike shops and a handful of specialty running shops. In addition, there are specialty rock-climbing and mountaineering shops, ski shops, and general sporting-goods stores. Boulder's most popular health-food store, Alfalfa's, features a sit-down restaurant and everything from organic produce to range-fed beef. Famous athletes find the community to be supportive, not intrusive.

The town itself is young and active—the median age is 25.9—primarily because the University of Colorado is located in Boulder, with an enrollment of 20,000 students. Located thirty miles from the Denver Stapleton airport, Boulder is convenient for the athletic jet-set. Boulder's climate is ideal for training, with over 300 days of sunshine and surprisingly mild winters— typical afternoon temperatures in January reach sixty degrees. The arid climate and sunshine dry the streets after a snowfall, usually within a day.

Is Boulder better? The super-athletes who live there think so. Boulder residents make up a Who's Who of endurance athletes. Almost the entire Coors Light team live in or around Boulder (Phinney, Oravetz, Farmer, Knickman, Swart, Sheehan, Moninger, Engleman, and Grewal) and part of the Motorola team (Kiefel, Hampsten, Carter). Most of the women's national team live in Boulder, including Ruthie Matthes, Sally Zack, Maureen Manley, and Eve Stevenson. Triathletes include: Dave Scott, Mark Allen,

Is Boulder better? Many riders move to Boulder for the training-friendly environment, high-altitude benefits, mild climate, and good riding terrain—and never look back.

PHOTO CREDIT: ED KOSMICKI

Colleen Cannon, Erin Baker, Paula Newby-Fraser, and Scott Molina. World-champion duathlete Kenny Souza lives in Boulder. World-class runners Arturo Barrios, Ingrid Kristiansen, Rob DeCastella, Rosa Mota, and Frank Shorter have all called Boulder home.

Taking the Heat: According to Davis

Riding and racing in the heat is always a challenge. As machines, we are at best only 30 percent efficient. That means 70 percent of the energy we burn is released as heat. We produce heat like a car produces exhaust. To vent the heat, the blood vessels dilate (called vasodilation), which enables the blood to flow to the skin, where heat can be released by sweating.

The human body is remarkably adaptable; cyclists race in temperatures near freezing and in excess of 100 degrees. The body responds to heat in much the same way it responds to endurance training—with an increased blood volume and increased sweat rate. Being fit will help you to adjust to the heat more easily. The increased blood volume and accelerated sweat rate increase the cooling capacity of the body. Increasing the volume of blood enables more blood to circulate the heat from your core to the skin. Sweat is important because as it evaporates, it cools you. It is difficult for the body to cool itself in high temperature and high humidity, because the sweat doesn't evaporate quickly. The moisture sits on the skin, slowing the cooling process. Take it easy when you are first exposed to the heat; give yourself three or four days to adjust. And always drink plenty of fluids to compensate for fluid loss and to maintain blood volume.

The innovator. My early mentor, Stan Szozda, had no outstanding physical attribute but was a great racer in his time because he was a tough competitor and he studied the sport. He is five feet nine inches tall and has a wiry build. Wherever he had a weakness, he would find a way to adapt his body and skills so he could improve. He was self-taught and innovative. And he was good.

One of his weaknesses was that he would die in the heat. To improve his heat tolerance, he rode 100 miles in the heat and limited himself to two bottles of water to force his body to learn how to adapt. That isn't something I would recommend, but it worked for him.

I adapted some of this approach when I was preparing for the Los Angeles Olympics, since I also had trouble riding in the heat. I used to wilt in the same way that I wilted in a sauna; the heat was suffocating. I had trouble sweating to cool my body, so in the winter I forced myself to take more saunas. Soon, I became more comfortable in the heat. I started to love saunas.

In the spring of 1983 and 1984, I went to the Tour of Texas and rode in eighty-degree temperatures wearing a long-sleeve jersey. It was uncomfortable, but I learned to cope with the discomfort. My body adapted. I would ride hard during the day, then show up for a late-day race and compete. This forced me to adapt. Over time, it worked. Heat became much less of a factor in races for me—it was an element that I could deal with.

The 1984 Olympics road race was hot, with a tail wind up the long climb on La Paz Road. It felt as though we were inside a furnace. The temperature that day was nearly 100 degrees. I started with water bottles in both cages and another strapped under my seat. I was constantly drinking and pouring water on myself. My skin suit was unzipped down to the navel. I was trying to stay as cool as I could for the whole 119-mile race. But the heat must have been easier on me—because I was used to it—than for the Europeans, who live in a less severe summer climate.

Yet there are certain people who ride well in the heat. They emerge when everyone else is melting. Former 7-Eleven teammate Tom Schuler always comes alive in hot weather. One of Tom's nicknames is "Snail," because he does everything at his own pace. He could also be likened to a reptile, because he moves very slowly in the cold. But as the temperature rises, so does Tom.

At the 156-mile CoreStates US PRO Championship in Philadelphia on a torrid day in June 1987, Tom was a support rider on the 7-Eleven team, but not considered a contender. However, he rode incredibly well on a day when nearly everyone else, including myself, was wilting. Tom won and lowered the course record by a remarkable seventeen minutes.

Heat Acclimatization Tips

Increase your fluid volume. In order to increase your blood volume, stay hydrated. Drink plenty of liquids, especially water.

Cut the caffeine. When preparing for the heat, it's best to cut back or eliminate beverages that have caffeine, like coffee and colas. Caffeine exaggerates the effect of the heat by acting as a diuretic. Caffeine is a vasoconstrictor, which means your veins get smaller, increasing your blood pressure. In the heat, you need your veins to dilate, so they get larger. Vasoconstriction will hold the heat in, not release it. Another beverage that dehydrates you is alcohol, since it also acts as a diuretic. Of course you wouldn't consider drinking a beer before a race, but even afterward a beer can inhibit your body's ability to rehydrate. In the event that you do have a beer, make sure to drink additional water to compensate.

Wear a jersey. Wearing a jersey or even a T-shirt will make you cooler than wearing nothing. Without a jersey, you dry out quickly, especially in the arid West.

Before going out for a ride or a race, drink fluids until your urine is clear. Most of us don't drink enough fluids. One simple test is whether you have to get up to urinate at least once in the night; it's a good sign that you are hydrated. Another test is whether your urine is clear. After a long ride on a hot day, you might notice that your urine is very dark. That's a sign of dehydration.

Once on the ride, or in the race, drink early and drink a lot. It's difficult to prescribe how much you should drink during a ride. Factors like humidity, your size, how acclimatized you are, and how hydrated you are all come into play. Your thirst response usually comes too late—once you start to feel thirsty, you are probably already dehydrated, which will work against your performance. The key is to drink before you feel thirsty. Drink small amounts often, and keep drinking.

I've had a lot of problems with heat. In the 1990 Tour de France, on the stage to Bordeaux, which I had won three years earlier, I fell victim to heat illness—what I call a *core meltdown*. That day we raced nearly six hours in temperatures above 100 degrees. The heat hit me suddenly; one minute I was sitting in the pack and the next minute I could hardly pedal. I was so delirious, I don't even remember the last ten kilometers. My body had no sweat left. My core temperature hit 104 degrees Fahrenheit. My teammate, Bob Roll, stayed with me at the back of the pack and kept pushing me. Somehow I managed to stay with the pack. Once across the line, I collapsed. All night I had intravenous fluid replacements. I was packed in ice, which brought my temperature down, but I wasn't able to eat any solid food.

For the next couple of days, I struggled to regain strength. But on the third day, the Tour concluded with a 118-mile stage that ended in Paris, on the Champs-Elysées. Miraculously, I was sufficiently recovered—or at least inspired that the Tour was finally over—to get fifth in the mass-pack sprint to the finish. But I certainly suffered for it.

Wearing a white cycling cap, or a white helmet, is better than wearing nothing at all in the heat. Our team doctor, Max Testa of Italy, told me that one of the body's heat sensors is located in the back of the brain, which means that you should try to shield the back of your head from the sun. Before we were required to wear hardshell helmets, Max recommended that on hot days we always wear a bike cap turned around backwards, so the bill covers the neck. Wearing white is preferred because it reflects heat.

Now that hardshells are required, it's a good idea to always train in your helmet—not only for safety but also because it helps you to adapt to the weight and feel of the helmet. Those of us who complain about the heat of hardshells should know that in a recent laboratory study there was no difference in heat retention between those cycling with or without a helmet. In other words, no excuses.

Beating the Cold

Acclimatizing to the cold is just as important as acclimatizing to the heat. Many California cyclists suffer when they go to Europe, because the weather conditions are so much harsher there. It is harder to keep warm in cold-weather cycling than it is running, because of the speed factor. The cold air is colder when combined with wind—some of which you make on your bike. Hence, the wind-chill factor is lower on the bike. Proper clothing is essential for survival in the cold.

Winterize your bike. When you ride in the snow and ice, let some air out of your tires for better traction. I train in the winter on my mountain bike a lot, and have a pair of mountain-bike tires that have nail studs in them for extreme icy conditions.

It rains a lot in the winter in Vancouver, where former 7-Eleven riders Ron Hayman and Alex Stieda are from. They adapt their bikes by putting fenders on, and they protect their bodies with adequate clothing. Riding in the rain becomes a way of life, not an excuse for sitting indoors.

Australian Jeff Leslie told me about an early-season training camp that he went to in southern France in the 1970s as an amateur. It was pouring rain, making miserable conditions for cycling. So the cyclists sat around and played cards all day. That night, Eddy Merckx showed up with his team for their training camp. The next day it was still raining, so Jeff's team once again sat around playing cards. Eddy, five-time winner of the Tour de France, went out riding at ten in the morning and didn't come home until four in the afternoon—soaking wet. On the third day, it was still raining. But, inspired by Eddy's example, *everyone* went for a six-hour ride.

Protect your body. Moisture builds up as you sweat and chills you quickly. Effective layering of synthetic fibers can help. Avoid cotton, which gets wet and stays wet, making you cold. An overjacket that is breathable and does not trap the moisture is essential. A good Entrant or Gore-tex jacket is a great investment, because it will keep you warm when you get wet. When stretch Gore-tex came on the market, I had a special cycling jacket made. It was bulkier, but also warmer, than most jackets available at the time.

I was racing in Italy as a neo-pro in 1985, and the conditions were miserable. Six inches of snow lay on the ground at the start of one stage, and the riders wanted the race canceled. Instead, the start was moved twenty kilometers, where snow had not fallen. It was still cold at the start, and we rode into the snow and freezing rain all day. I used to dream about being a pro in Europe, but when I became one, the reality was certainly different from the romance. At least I had my red Gore-tex jacket—that saved me.

The next day I ended up finishing second in the final stage, which once again was held in freezing rain. I watched the replay of the finish on television, and it was close; maybe I could have won. Later, a reporter asked why I had worn such a bulky jacket for such a close finish. The answer was simple: I wouldn't have dreamed of risking losing the jacket by throwing it off before the finish. Maybe it wasn't aerodynamic, but at least it got me to the finish.

During the winter, I ride my bike—especially my mountain bike—in the extreme cold. Sometimes it's pure product-testing for Pearl Izumi, one of the few manufacturers of all-season high-performance cycling wear. There has been a quiet revolution in fabric technology that has enabled us to ride comfortably in more and more extreme weather. Hands and feet get especially cold, requiring warm but not bulky coverings for hands and feet.

Once during a severely cold winter day, when the temperature in Boulder was ten degrees below zero in the sun, we had the option of indoor training at the gym or some sort of outside adventure. Andy Hampsten called me up to go for a mountain bike ride. Not given to letting a challenge go unanswered, I agreed to go with him.

It was cold outside, but even colder when we were moving, because we created our own wind. The wind-chill factor when we were at speed was well below zero. But we were as prepared as possible. We put on layers of high-tech clothing designed to take the moisture away from the body to prevent chilling, and to keep the wind and cold out. We headed out for what would end up being a five-hour ride in the mountains' deep snow and slick ice.

How cold was it? Within the first hour, our water bottles were frozen solid. We tossed them, because they were unnecessary weight. Coming down the canyon on the return to Boulder, we had to stop every mile and run 100 or 200 yards just to warm up. But we were prepared; not one speck of skin was exposed on the descent; any exposed skin would have been frostbitten instantly. We had neck gaiters that covered the expanse from the neck to over the ears. We had hats that could be pulled low over our eyebrows and held in place with downhill ski goggles. We wore thick winter cycling gloves.

We survived. That was the sort of gonzo experience that we just love to do. It adds a certain dimension of adventure. Call it insanity. A lot of it, however, has a practical application and comes from experiences we had in Europe. So many times in Italy, Belgium, France, and Holland we raced in freezing rain. Andy's legendary ride in the 1988 Tour of Italy, during which he took the race lead while riding through a blizzard on the Gavia Pass, stems from the *toughness* training he has done at home.

I rode the semi-Classic from Milan to Turin in the spring of 1985. The race started in—what else?—freezing rain. All I could think about was quitting. But when I got to 150 kilometers (almost 100 miles), where I planned to quit and jump into a nice warm, dry team car, I saw that only thirty or forty of the 175-man field was left. Sensing an opportunity, I took my feed and put my head down. It was "only" 100 kilometers (62.5 miles) to the finish. I started to feel really strong. I finished fifth—a solid placing for me and a good lesson in staying with it.

Riding in extreme conditions is a process of knowing what to wear, not getting psyched out, and acclimatization. Six years of racing as a professional in Europe taught me that survival skills are a premium commodity that are best learned at home.

PERFORMANCE OBSTACLES

Find a Good Coach: the Objective Voice of Reason

Sadly, good cycling coaches are few and far between, but the benefit of having some help is immeasurable if you can find the right person. Some areas of the country have excellent resources, like Miji Reoch's Performance Training Group in Dallas, Texas. For a fee, Miji provides one-on-one coaching, group riding, and physiological testing and monitoring. Her approach is businesslike, informative, and, most of all, based on her decades of elite-level experience. (More information is available by writing to this address: Performance Training, 5111 Victor St., Dallas, Texas 75214. Tel.: 214/826-5445.)

Camps and clinics are held periodically and sporadically throughout the country. In a few short days, or an all-too-short week, you can learn what might take you years to figure out on your own. The United States Cycling Federation also offers camps that you can qualify to attend at the Olympic Training Center in Colorado Springs, Colorado and regional clinics. (More information is available from the USCF, 1750 East Boulder St., Colorado Springs, Colorado 80909. Tel.: 719/578-4581.) There is a proliferation of bike camps around the U.S., Canada, and Europe that you might research. The format for this book is from the Carpenter/Phinney Cycling Camps at Beaver Creek Resort. (More information is available from The Adventure Company, PO Box 915, Avon, CO 81620. Tel.: 303/949-9090.)

To find a coach, start locally. Visit your local specialty bike shop and inquire about local clubs. If you have a choice, attend club meetings and meet their top riders. Look for a club or group that is well organized, not only competitive. You won't get much out of getting dropped after a few miles—except a bruised ego. Often an experienced racer can give you many tips and good insight into what you are doing. However, many top cyclists have no idea why they are good, much less what it would take for you to improve. The best advice is to listen and be observant. You may not find someone that can watch over your every pedal stroke or delve deeply into your training diary, but you can glean information from a variety of sources and find out what works for you.

Training Pace vs. Racing Pace

Many people race very well in training. Then they get in a race and don't understand why they don't perform better. Why is that? Most of the time, the problem is that they perform in training. If you always ride a steady twenty or twenty-five miles an hour, you will have trouble in a race at twenty-eight or thirty miles an hour. Always pushing in training gives you dead legs. To develop suppleness, vary your training paces.

There is a curious paradox: if you want to race fast, you have to learn to ride slow. You will find this to be less of a paradox when you incorporate both hard and easy days (intensive work and easy recovery) in your training. Riding slow is part of the recovery process that enables you to ride fast. Active recovery is a process that occurs with each pedal stroke, at any speed. Cycling is not a static endeavor, but one that forces you to accommodate to changes in tempo and terrain.

To say that you can't increase your performance without being properly rested is true, but how much rest do you reasonably need? Most athletes are highly motivated to train, but not to rest. We are our own worst enemies. How much you need depends on you, your athletic or cycling history, your training program, and the other demands or stresses of your life. A training diary will help you to monitor your training response and help you evaluate your needs.

Consistency Pays Off

One of my heroes at age eighteen was the World Cup cross-country skier Thomas Magnuson of Sweden. As I understood it, his philosophy was that he was going to train more than anybody else in the world. When he reached a certain number of training hours—say, forty a week, which was as much as his body could absorb— he would train much harder in the time he had. He thought that if he trained harder than anyone else, he would be better than the rest of the competition. I thought this was a great approach, though I now know this extreme works for very few people.

But I did learn a valuable lesson from this great athlete, and that was consistency. It used to be that cyclists pretty much took the winter off from their training, or at least took off several months. Many did this for practical reasons, like the need to earn an income. I worked hard in the winter, setting aside three hours a day every day. I believe this helped me make up ground every winter on my competitors. While others who started out better than me were off their bikes, occasionally riding the rollers indoors or maybe running a little, I was outside at least three hours a day, putting Magnuson's philosophy to work. For a minimum of twenty-one hours a week, winter after winter, I was running up mountains, cross-country skiing, and going for long hikes. That helped me build up a foundation of hardness and consistency of effort that my body could take. There isn't a shortcut to becoming a great cyclist. You have to have a passion for it, because it's hard and demands a lot of sacrifice. You've got to really want to do it. And I really wanted to do it.

Despite talent and motivation, many riders progress to a certain level but then get stuck on a plateau. There are several ways of dealing with these plateaus. Doug Shapiro is a good example.

When I was a junior rider in the late 1970s, Doug had been a leading junior. He was so fast that he was nicknamed "Bullet." In 1980 he made the Olympic cycling team, but two years later he had leveled out and I overtook him. He was attending the University of Florida in Gainesville, where he would earn a bachelor's degree in biology, when I went down there as a member of the 7-Eleven team for a race in 1982. Doug got in a breakaway with me and another rider, and I won the sprint to take the race.

I expected to win, and I did. Doug was really mad that he lost, but his anger impressed me—it was a manifestation of his passion. I thought he had something. We were friends, and competitors. Since he was finished with school, I suggested that he move to Boulder to train with me. I knew that he could go further in the sport.

Doug moved to Boulder, and we wound up training together, especially that first winter. We were running in the snow, competing in footraces up the steep Green Mountain trail, cross-country skiing, and riding mountain bikes. Because of school, Doug had not focused on his off-season training. I had always used that time to make up ground on my competitors, and it worked for Doug, too. In 1983, he was second in the Coors International Bicycle Classic, then the biggest stage race in the country, and the following year he won it. In 1985, he turned professional and rode for the Dutch Kwantum team. That year, Doug became one of the first U.S. riders to compete in the Tour de France.

He had that spark of ability all along to make it all the way to major-league cycling. But he had reached a plateau and needed a change. I don't take credit for his success, because Doug did the work. But I know for sure that the extra work made the difference between being good and being great. It would have been easy for him to just blow it all off and get a job outside cycling, never having realized his potential. All he needed was somebody to tell him it wasn't the end of the line: "Let's go. You can make the next step."

Know When to Say When: Avoiding Overtraining

Whether you have a coach or you are self-coached, you have to know yourself. The first step in a sound training program is flexibility. Knowing how to adjust your training comes over time, from listening to yourself. Flexibility doesn't mean that every time you feel tired, or want to go to the beach, you skip a training session. Flexibility means that you maintain your discipline while remaining sensitive to your body's needs. Many athletes set a program for themselves and stick to it no matter what, but that's not smart. It's easier to blindly follow a program, but it makes no sense in the scheme of things.

Understand why you are training and what to train. When you understand what and why, you can understand how to build a program. If you have a coach, you can ask better questions. If you have a good one, consider yourself lucky. Even if you have developed an understanding about training from watching and studying the sport, you still need to have someone to look objectively at you and say, "You're beat! What do you mean you're going for a four-hour ride? Forget it." Or tell you, "You need to work more on your sprints."

One classic symptom of overtraining is when you lose your sense of humor. This applies to overdoing it anywhere—in business, in school, or in training. I know, because I lost my sense of humor in 1984 before the Olympics; I was so serious that nothing seemed fun anymore. Training is stress; performance under pressure is stratospheric stress. I thrive on the fine tension that a challenging life gives me, but the pressure to excel on one day and one day only was overwhelming. That kind of pressure can take the fun out of the process, and just as when you take the bubbles out of the soda, the whole thing goes flat.

Overtraining symptoms. Another symptom of overtraining is elevated morning heart rate. Some athletes actually experience a decrease in morning heart rate as a result of overtraining, but this appears to be rare and may be due to adrenal exhaustion (which decreases hormone output that stimulates the heart). Rest—or at the most, extremely light cycling—is the only antidote for overtraining, especially at this level.

Other signs of overtraining are linked. A rapid, sustained, and unexpected weight loss, not just a normal daily or monthly (for women) fluctuation, is a sign that you are unable to cope with the demands of training. This will erode your health and increase your chances of getting sick due to increased fatigue.

Increased irritability, which goes with losing your sense of humor, is a sure sign that something is out of balance in your life. Stress on the home front or in the workplace, combined with daily training, can be a deadly combination. Insomnia, which will wear you down faster than anything, is often due to the inability to shut out the stress of competition or training. Insomnia is heightened by elevated pulse, which leads to irritability. Other overtraining symptoms include general staleness and malaise—the feeling that you just don't care about riding your bike. Listen to yourself. You may need a few days, or even weeks, off.

The sooner you deal with overtraining, the more quickly you can resolve it. It has been documented that, if you continue pushing, you can cross over into what has been called the "valley of fatigue." It can take as long as six weeks to climb back out of this valley and resume your normal training to reach your previous performance level. Six weeks is a long time in the middle of the season. Your cycling season is long, but not long enough to lose a block of time like that. Listen to yourself. Close scrutiny of your body's response to training will get those warning lights illuminated sooner, when you can actively deal with the situation, rather than later, when you have no option but to lay off.

Add spice to your training: a solution to staleness. Like the old saying goes, "Variety is the spice of life." I used to have a friend who did the same ride every day—the same fifty miles. It was as though his bike were on rails. He got sick of the sport. I can see why.

Andy Hampsten and Ron Kiefel and I will go out and ride on dirt roads with our road bikes, just to do something different and make it fun. If riding is not fun, you're not going to feel good about what you do. One time we had set up a team ride and we all met at Ron's house on the north end of Boulder, in the middle of a fall Saturday morning. Decked out in our 7-Eleven duds, we were the Pied Piper of Boulder for the hundreds of weekend bikers. Suddenly our group size swelled from eight to eighty. We decided our best defense was a good offense, so we turned off onto a dirt road. That move shook off only a few from the pack. So we started going faster over some pretty rough, twisting country roads. On each turn, we lost riders. Twenty miles later, we were back to our core group. So much for our easy out-of-season weekend ride. I wonder if those riders who followed ever took those roads again on the assumption that that was the way we professionals regularly trained.

We headed for the dirt one day just because we were so stale. Ron Kiefel and I were training in Colorado Springs, Colorado, for the 1986 world championships and we were riding the same roads every day. To do something completely different, we looked at a map that showed a road we hadn't tried, leading to Cripple Creek, way up in the Rocky Mountains, around 9,000 feet altitude. We found the road and started going up. It wasn't long before we discovered the pavement ended, but we continued on the dirt road, which led to a high, arid plateau and sputtered out to a single track. We weren't ready to turn around—not yet.

We kept riding, on our regular road bikes, up the most horrendously steep slopes. We were reduced to pedaling about ten revolutions a minute. Finally, I couldn't even turn my pedals over enough to keep from falling right over.

Ron just laughed at me and miraculously kept going. I had to hike with my bike and I was sliding along in my bike cleats, until the slope eased off enough so that I could get back on and resume riding. We went an hour and a half up this dirt track. It was totally different and a lot of fun. We felt like a modern-day Lewis and Clark out on an expedition. That was adventure.

Illness: Coping with Colds and the Flu

We have all trained, raced, and overdone it when suffering from a cold. Generally, you should not race when you are sick, or train when you have a fever. My Italian team doctor once said that when you get a cold you can take all the cold medications and it will take six days to recover, or you can take care of yourself and it will take six days to recover. A cold is a cold. Once you feel it coming on, it's pretty hard to stop it, so minimize the lost training time and maximize the recovery. A recent study has shown that more people contract colds after they have been under stress.

Once we have a cold or feel like we're getting one, we like to rely on increased doses of vitamin C, a herbal remedy called Echenacea (found in health-food stores), and lots of fluids to cleanse the system. All over-the-counter cold medications must be taken with great care, since many of them contain ephedrine, which is on the banned-substance list because of its effect on the lungs. If you take this medication and get called up for a drug test at a race, you will test positive and face a six-month suspension. Be careful. Personally, we find these medications to be of limited value.

For the cyclist, the worst complication of a cold is bronchial inflammation (bronchitis), which takes longer to recover from and impairs your performance for two weeks or longer. Try to minimize your risk of contracting bronchitis by getting plenty of rest and flushing your system with fluids. Steam baths, steamy showers, and even sitting over a large bowl of steamy water will help keep you breathing more freely and at least help you feel better for a short time. Mom's steamy chicken noodle soup isn't a bad idea, either.

The common reaction after being ill is to try to make up for lost time. Don't try it. Be patient. Even a twenty-four-hour flu will knock you off balance for several days. When you try to do too much, you will push yourself back over the edge and require many more weeks to return to your previous level.

Cold prevention revolves around maintaining basic good health and staying hydrated after training and during travel. *Never* share your water bottle with anyone, and keep it clean. Always try to get adequate sleep. Another good method of cold prevention is to wash your hands frequently, since the germs seem to be transmitted not only in the air but also on surfaces. Colds are a fact of life, but if you are getting a lot of them (more than two a year), you should evaluate your life-style and make some changes.

Injury—it could happen to you.

I have had many injuries in my career, most of them the result of a spectacular crash. But those kinds of injuries usually heal quickly. It's the sneaky ones that you have to watch for. I know I was caught with my eyes closed. In May of 1989, during the Tour of Italy I felt a twinge in my left knee. I thought nothing of it until the next day, when it was so painful that I couldn't walk after the stage. I was forced to quit the race and did not race again for ten months. At first I thought it was an injury that had come on quickly, but later saw that I had failed to listen to the warning signs. In fact, it had been coming on for some time. It was diagnosed as iliotibial band syndrome. Your IT band is a dense band of fascia extending from your hip down below your knee. It is what gives your quadriceps their nice shape. An inflammation of the IT band was once thought to be a career-ending injury. I tried aggressive stretching, massage, and rest. Nothing worked. Finally, I had surgery in November. Part of my iliotibial band was removed by Dr. Jim Holmes and Dr. Andy Pruitt of Western Orthopedic Sports Medicine.

The surgery fixed the problem immediately; I was riding within a few days. But the hematoma from the surgery left me with a large, ugly bulge on my knee for several weeks. Within a month I was in California riding 500 miles a week. My rehabilitation involved constant care and attention by me, my massage therapist, John Hendershot, and my trainer, Andy Pruitt. Hendershot worked with the adhesions that had built up over time between the muscles and connective tissue. This reduced my muscular capacity, which obviously had a negative effect on my racing. Suddenly I understood how critical it was for me to be more active in my own care.

This was drilled home after a crash I had in Waco, Texas, in the spring of 1991. I was holding on to the support van, adjusting a broken strap on my shoe, when I lost my balance and fell on the wet pavement. To avoid going under the van—which was traveling at more than thirty miles per hour—I twisted sharply, like a cat trying to land on its feet. My bike went under the van and bounced back out, nailing me in the shin, but I stayed clear of the van. I was in agony because of the blow to my shin, which felt as though someone hit me with a sledgehammer. But I walked away feeling lucky that it wasn't worse.

I felt literally "bent out of shape" after the crash, and subsequent massage therapy was not enough. A few weeks after the crash, my back spasmed so badly that I was writhing on the floor in pain. Ron Kiefel recommended a massage therapist in Boulder, Raymond King, who had helped him through a serious back problem. King worked on me for one or two hours at a time for several days. I had actually lost an inch or two in height as a result of the crash, which twisted my musculature severely. The massage therapy enabled me to regain my full height and to relax the spasm.

But then my knee started to twinge again in June—also a result of the twisting from the crash. I called Andy Pruitt, who looked at my knee and said that the spot where it was injured was not the IT band. If it wasn't the IT band, what was it? I knew it hurt. I visited Dr. Michael Leahy, a top chiropractor who works with our team as part of the Chiropractic sponsorship. Dr. Leahy found excess scar tissue in the knee and worked it out aggressively. My knee problem melted away.

I now realize the value of taking full responsibility for my body—which has survived some sixteen years of racing and training. I am fortunate to have access to the best medical and health care possible. Injuries can slow you down like nothing else, but taking an active role in preventing them through proper bike fit and routine massage and chiropractic care will go a long way toward keeping you out of your doctor's office.

EPILOGUE

Now that you have gotten to know us, have fiddled with your bikes and your body language, re-evaluated your diet, designed and refined your training, and narrowed your focus—you have *no doubt* improved in some small and, hopefully, major ways. Remember that most of what you have read must be applied consistently—not just today, but tomorrow and the next day as well—to gain improvement. Once you find out what works for you, give yourself a little time to adapt. Who knows how far or how fast you will go!

For our part, we have spent all our adult lives refining our perspective and knowledge of cycling—considered by so many to be child's play. Perhaps we have resisted growing up, but it's more likely that we have taken cycling seriously not only because it is our vocation but our *avocation*. Cycling isn't just a job—it is a passion.

One marvelous aspect of cycling is that you are forced into the *here and now*. You may make mental notes about things you have to do or places you have to be, but your attention is mainly on the moment and you are forced into being part of the moment. Children are fully engrossed in the moment when they play—so perhaps cycling *is* child's play. And for a few hours each day we become children—eager, energetic, and very much alive. This puts you in touch with yourself and is part of the appeal of simply "going for a ride."

We hope you take this information, digest it, and use it to make your *here and now* safer, faster and, of course, more fun. Happy trails.

CONNIE AND DAVIS 1992

SUGGESTED READING LIST: REFERENCES

Bicycle Road Racing: Complete Program for Training and Competition, Edward Borysewicz with Ed Pavelka. Velonews: 1985. Eddie's book is a useful addition to your cycling library.

The Cyclist's Sourcebook, Peter Nye. Perigee: New York, 1991. An invaluable resource book for all levels.

Exercise Physiology: Human Bioenergetics and Its Applications, George A. Brooks and Thomas D. Fahey. John Wiley and Sons: New York, 1984. If you are interested in the science of your body, this basic textbook is an excellent source.

Greg LeMond's Complete Book of Bicycling, Greg LeMond and Kent Gordis. G. P. Putnam's Sons: New York, 1987. This book covers many of the basics and has some interesting anecdotes, but is short on training and tactics.

Hearts of Lions: *The Story of American Bicycle Racing,* Peter Nye. W.W. Norton: New York, 1989. Today's men and women cycling champions are standing on the shoulders of heroes going back twelve colorful decades.

Lore of Running, Timothy Noakes. Leisure Press: Champaign, 1991. This very readable book centers on distance running and particularly on the South African ultra-distance event, the Comrades Marathon. Many of the training principles and philosophy of training have direct application to cyclists.

Red Gold: Peak Performance Techniques of the Russian and East German Olympic Victors, Grigori Raiport. Jeremy P. Tarcher, Inc.: Los Angeles, 1988. A must-read for anyone interested in gaining a psychological edge through better mind control. A slim volume, but very interesting and easy-to-follow techniques. Like any training, you won't gain anything if you don't develop a systematic approach.

Serious Training for Serious Athletes, Rob Sleamaker. Leisure Press: Champaign, 1989. Sleamaker, trained in exercise physiology, is a noted coach of cross-country skiers and triathletes. His straightforward approach is useful, though the training program system he has developed may be too rigid for most cyclists. The framework and philosophy is good.

Training Distance Runners: The Art and Science of Optimal Training by Two of the World's Leading Experts, David E. Martin and Peter N. Coe. Leisure Press: Champaign, 1991. This thorough textbook combines an in-depth physiology section with a solid training philosophy. It spends a lot of time on Sebastion Coe's personal training, but even that is instructional for coaches and students of all sports.

Women, Sport and Performance: A Physiological Perspective, Christine Wells. Leisure Press: Champaign, 1991. A wealth of knowledge presented a comprehensive textbook. Very useful reference for all women's issues relating to health, fitness, and performance.

Recommended audiocassettes

Breaking the Mental Barrier, by Mannie Edelstein, featuring Davis Phinney, Scott Tinley, Joan Benoit, Frank Shorter, Mark Allen. La Jolla: 1991. (Available by calling 1-800 765-UWIN or writing P.O. Box 12176 La Jolla, California 92039.) It always helps to hear how successful athletes motivate themselves. This six-cassette series takes a systematic approach to improving performance through positive thinking.

INDEX

249

Books for the cyclist from Perigee

Greg LeMond's Complete Book of Bicycling
by Greg LeMond and Kent Gordis
illustrated with over 100 black-and-white photographs
A three-time winner of the Tour de France, Greg LeMond explains everything you need to know about buying, riding, and maintaining a bike, whether you are a recreational rider or a serious racer.

Greg LeMond's Pocket Guide to Bicycle Maintenance and Repair
by Greg LeMond
illustrated with 50 photographs and 20 line drawings
The perfect pocket guide for on-the-road bicycle care and repair—in a convenient format for seat pack or handlebar bag.

The Cyclist's Sourcebook
by Peter Nye
introduction by Davis Phinney
illustrated with over 100 black-and-white photographs
Inside this, the most comprehensive reference for cycling, you'll find listings of major recreational rides, an illustrated history of the sport, information on major cycling organizations, tips on how to a watch a race, and conversations with some of cycling's prominent men and women.

Training for Cycling
The Ultimate Guide to Improved Performance
by Davis Phinney and Connie Carpenter with Peter Nye
illustrated with 50 black-and-white photographs
From the world-renowned team of Davis Phinney and Connie Carpenter, this comprehensive reference teaches cyclists everything they need to know to improve handling skills, raise confidence, and increase competitiveness.

These books are available at your local bookstore or wherever books are sold. Ordering is also easy and convenient. Just call 1-800-631-8571 or send your order to:

The Putnam Publishing Group
390 Murray Hill Parkway, Dept. B
East Rutherford, NJ 07073

Subtotal $_____

Postage and handling* $_____

Sales tax (CA, NJ, NY, PA) $_____

Total Amount Due $_____

Payable in U.S. funds (no cash orders accepted). $10.00 minimum for credit card orders.
*Postage and handling: $2.00 for 1 book, 50¢ for each additional book up to a maximum of $4.50.

Enclosed is my   ☐ check   ☐ money order
Please charge my   ☐ Visa   ☐ MasterCard   ☐ American Express

Card # _____ Expiration date _____

Signature as on charge card _____

Name _____

Address _____

City _____ State _____ Zip _____

Please allow six weeks for delivery. Prices subject to change without notice.